THE CHASM COMPANION

THE CHASM COMPANION

COMPANION

A Fieldbook to *Crossing the Chasm* and *Inside the Tornado*

PAUL WIEFELS

With a Foreword by GEOFFREY A. MOORE

HarperBusiness

An Imprint of HarperCollinsPublishers

HarperCollins books may be purchased for educational, business, or sales promotional use. For information, please write: Special Markets Department, HarperCollins Publishers Inc., 10 East 53rd Street, New York, NY 10022.

FIRST EDITION

Designed by Nancy Singer Olaguera

Library of Congress Cataloging-in-Publication Data has been applied for.

ISBN 0-06-662055-4

02 03 04 05 06 ❖/RRD 10 9 8 7 6 5 4 3 2 1

In memory of my father, Frank L. Wiefels, M.D.

1925–2001

► Contents

Foreword

There are few distinctions in business life that have held up as well over time as that between *strategy* and *execution*. Like all polarities, however, there is a curious codependence and coevolution between these opposites. Strategy marches firmly out of the castle to take on the foe, only to find there are no horses today—now what? Execution out fighting with sword and spear finds itself no match for this new thing called a longbow—back to the drawing boards. Strategy provokes execution; execution provokes strategy—siblings squabbling back and forth to create that miracle of miracles, a family.

Thus it has been at The Chasm Group. Our strategy practice was launched in 1992 on the basis of a book, *Crossing the Chasm*, which was about coping with a difficult phase in the development of high-tech markets. Clients saw the problem and were active in engaging us to help them build strategies to solve it. Not a year into the fray, however, and already principles that once seemed engraved in stone now revealed themselves to be far more mercurial. In actual execution, it transpired, events played out one way in product companies, another in services companies. Outcomes evolved differently in capital- and asset-intensive businesses such as computers and semiconductors than they did in systems software or business applications. The PC industry played out very differently from enterprise computing. In short, far from being as simple and elegant as specified, things were in actual fact a mess.

That led to a second book, as messes are wont to do. This one was called *Inside the Tornado,* and it offered a much more comprehensive view of the strategy landscape, so that, now properly armed, we would not get caught out again. Nice try. All it did was move the boundary line for where ambiguity and complexity would make its next series of inroads. Once again, the reality and exigencies of execution began to teach and inform the idealized forms of strategy, leading to more messes and a couple of more books, and eventually to the realization that this is all a dance, and that the job of the strategy consultant, at the end of the day, is simply to keep dancing.

The book you have in hand records, if you will, the lessons from that dance. It is the first book from our group that is genuinely and explicitly focused on theories of strategy development *combined* with execution. It draws on a legacy of hundreds of Chasm Group projects, each focused on aligning a specific market development effort with the dynamics of the Technology Adoption Life Cycle. With those kinds of odds, as my family likes to say, even a blind squirrel can be expected to find an acorn or two. This book is an attempt to share these with you now.

Your host and guide for this journey is Paul Wiefels, a friend and colleague who, as the first person to join in this parade, can be said to have truly founded The Chasm Group, since it is hard to have a group until you have more than one person. Paul brings a wonderful array of operating experience to the task at hand, having cut his teeth in the advertising industry in the late 1970s; he then went on to a great run at Apple during the 1980s; then a stint at Ingres Corporation, then one of the large, independent relational database companies, where we met in the role of client and consultant; then on to Landor Associates, a leading branding consultancy; and finally to The Chasm Group, where he has spent the last decade working with clients to translate strategic ideas into programs that can make them come to pass.

What Paul has brought to all these efforts is wit (bordering on irreverence), critical intelligence—a discipline too often abandoned in marketing—and one of the best intuitive marketing minds I have ever met. In short, he knows whereof he speaks, and I am confident you will enjoy the ride he takes you on.

That ride—across chasms, through bowling alleys, up into tornadoes, and onto Main Street—is one that more and more of our economy is taking these days. In virtually every sector managers and executives are turning to technology-enabled innovations to create the next wave of competitive advantage to drive the next wave of financial returns. In so doing they subject their programs to the properties of the Technology Adoption Life Cycle, the granddaddy of market development models in our practice, the one from which all other models derive.

In this model arrays of market forces come to prominence and recede at various times in the cycle, causing companies to make various accommodations, each change seeming to repudiate the principles that drove success in the previous phase. It is an intellectual challenge just to grasp what is going on and why these changes are mandated. But it is even more a management challenge to lead a group of human beings through the program changes needed to accommodate the evolving market. Again and again, you will be asking the people you lead to turn their backs on behaviors that a year or two previous were the keys to their success. This is not a natural human behavior.

This book can help. It sets forth not only the vocabulary for understanding these changes, but also the program changes needed to bring them about. And it does so in a text that is peppered with real-world examples you and your team can use to test the applicability of a given principle or tactic to your own situation. In this it is a true "field guide" to the challenges of translating strategy into execution, something we at The Chasm Group have long wished to make available to our clients and colleagues—and now, thanks to Paul, we have.

GEOFFREY A. MOORE

Acknowledgments

This book is born of a diverse parentage. First, it is the genetic offspring of *Crossing the Chasm* and *Inside the Tornado,* authored by my colleague, Geoffrey Moore, to whom I am immensely grateful not only for his inspiration and encouragement, but for his friendship over the past ten years. Though I may have mangled Geoffrey's ideas (not to mention his prose) here and there, our partnership and collaboration is one I truly treasure.

Just as important, this book also reflects the wisdom of numerous individuals: my partners in The Chasm Group; the contributors to the actual manuscript whom I cajoled and pestered into writing something for me; my friends and colleagues who toil in the world of high tech; our clients, who have placed their trust in our counsel; and numerous others who have somehow captured my attention by their insights, wisdom, or well-meaning gaffes.

The idea of a field book is hardly novel. Yet, the ideas for *this* field book probably could not have been realized earlier either in my life as a high-tech practitioner or in our evolution as a firm. There is far too much to cover. This is not an excuse for procrastination but rather a tacit acknowledgment that to document and contribute meaningfully to the world of high-tech marketing and market development, one has to do a lot of "walking around"; that is to say, one needs both a lot of opportunities for working on problems endemic to the business, and a lot of people who are willing to share their experiences with how they have used our theories and practices. Happily, our clients, and my fellow travelers in this most intriguing of business categories, have provided both. Quite simply, this book germinated from two requests by clients, best summarized as: "What should we do next week, when you're not here?" Lest we give ourselves too much credit, clients knew exactly what to do: continue to run their businesses! What they were really saying was that the very nature of pursuing the myriad things necessary to compete in high-tech markets (not to mention mustering the personal energy to do them on a sustainable basis) usually had the effect of gradually causing one to lose a longer-term perspective on what could be expected in the future, until expectations came to be based on hope rather than informed intuition and experience. Many also asked: "We love chasm theory and all its metaphors, but can you net all this out for me, for crying out loud? Put it all together for me like you guys talk about it in person?" Gulp.

Two years and some months later, I thus commend to you this third book in a *trilogy* of sorts—written and collated with a lot of help from my friends. Special thanks go to my contributing authors, who include Nancy Schoendorf of Mohr Davidow Ventures, Peter Angelos of DMB&B Worldwide, Kevin Maney of *USA Today*, Stan DeVaughn, and Philip Lay of The Chasm Group.

The Chasm Group family and extended family weighed in as well. In addition to Geoffrey and to Philip Lay, I am indebted to my partners Tom Kippola, Mike Tanner, Mark Cavender, and Todd Hewlin for their ideas and suggestions, and to our Chasm Group affiliates, Greg Ruff, Michael Eckhardt, and Brian Nejmeh, who also provided valuable counsel. While we're here, things don't happen around the office without the invaluable assistance of Trina Cooley and Pat Granger, our business managers; and our technical adviser, Jonathan Dippert. Ginger Polk and Anna Moore contributed greatly to version control, graphics editing, organizing my calendar, and nagging me about "backing the damn thing up on the server!" Many thanks!

I have also been blessed with the support of numerous clients who variously contributed ideas, encouragement, and a sense of accountability as I went about this task. Special thanks go to Bruno Castejon at Hewlett-Packard, Gordon Stitt of Extreme Networks, Kate Hutchison at BEA Systems, and the team at Applied Biosystems, including Martha Trela, Julia Horak, and Carolyn Martin (who, like the sales VP that she is, kept asking, "When's it going to be finished?"). I also seconded a number of colleagues into a kind of personal focus group to solicit feedback and criticism that was enthusiastically provided by all. My thanks to Mary Doan, Teri Dahlbeck, Bronwyn Fryer, Steve Lombardi, Gary Elliott, Marty Brandt, Carolyn Andre, Mike Goefft, Melissa Eisenstat, Donna Novitsky, Paul DeZan, Mike Lucero, Carol Realini, Claire Sherwood, and Tom Kosnik at Stanford. Finally, my sincere thanks go to my literary agent, Jim Levine, who endured my "rookie mistakes" and knew exactly when to prod me; and my editor at HarperCollins, Dave Conti.

Closer to home, my children, Lauren and Jack, provide ample proof that a fascination with words and writing may be genetic. There is not a day that goes by that I do not take delight in their being.

▶ *Introduction*

During the last decade of the last century right through the millennium celebration, we in high technology were feeling our oats, down to the last kernel. For a while, it appeared as if the celebration would be never-ending. Technology-based companies flourished, and the high-tech start-ups, fledglings created as a result of the unprecedented amount of investment capital that had been generated by almost ten years of global business expansion, seemed to have their initial public offerings scheduled by the dozen. Each IPO redeemed the equity that had been lavished on virtually anyone savvy enough—or lucky enough—to be associated with each new company's birth. The center of this modern-day gold rush was California's Silicon Valley—not only a place but also a *state of mind,* as was noted by one of its longtime residents. People who cashed out of their options put their newfound wealth into Northern California's housing market, bidding up the price of virtually any house by offering hundreds of thousands of dollars over a seller's asking price. Style and good taste, often only a minor distraction to the acquisitiveness of many Valley residents, might command still higher prices but was certainly no guarantee of either. It seemed that wealth attainment could and should be a scheduled event, duly noted in one's handheld electronic organizer along with the weekly massage and the "play dates" organized for the kids.

A sense of profound, deep-rooted optimism and entitlement also seemed to flourish, and there was no greater source than that which emanated from the companies that were exploiting the Internet "revolution." The *new age* of the online *information superhighway* had finally arrived. The figurative poster child for this new age was a new class of company simply and collectively referred to as the *dot-com*. The dot-com company was a magical business model touted as the driver and the exemplar of the *New Economy,* an economic ecosystem where information was the product. The prevailing wisdom of the day asserted that the rules governing the development of markets for New Economy products and services would be radically different. New Economy companies were unparalleled models of business efficiency that would lay waste to Old Economy business models, which had clearly outlived much of their usefulness. Authors and consultants everywhere wove a prophecy of doom for many of the Fortune 500. "Many of them simply don't 'get it,'" asserted numerous self-anointed New Economy pundits. They opined that a new generation—the Internet generation—was now being spawned, born to point their browsers in an unceasing quest to learn, shop, and connect with others online. The industrial and financial dinosaurs that had roamed the earth since the industrial revolution were now laden with inefficiencies and would soon be *disintermediated,* an uncertain fate that did not sound appealing. Those clever enough to exploit this *paradigm shift* would make tons of money as a result of consumers' relentless desire to point and click.

"We're going to use our first-mover advantage and build brand early to aggregate and quickly monetize eyeballs," enthused one young, Armani-clad dot-com CEO clearly impressed not only with these phrases but also with himself for having uttered them during yet another Internet conference that feted not only the latest crop of Internet-based companies but also those who "got it"—indicated by being asked to participate in various panel discussions on stage—and even those who ostensibly did not and were relegated to the audience but were eager to "get it" as well. Adding to the popular lexicon, another celebrated idea of the time was the concept of *Internet time,* a new, completely subjective measure describing the pace at which Internet businesses evolved versus their Old Economy brethren. *Digitization, cyberspace, stickiness, walled gardens,* and a variety of other terms stormed into our everyday speech—the new patois of the Internet generation.

Then a rather annoying thing began to happen, and rather quickly too. In March 2000 the music stopped. The metaphorical New Economy balloon filled with Allan Greenspan's irrational exuberance finally burst. The equity markets, abused as never before and fed up with all the hype, concluded that many New Economy companies were of the species *Ideus stupidus*. And what of monetizing eyeballs, building brand early, and filing S1's after the second round of funding and well before product beta testing and actual revenue generation? What of Internet time? Such time had come and gone.

Many New Economy companies were much more adept at marketing a good story then a good product, more adept at going public than staying that way. Meanwhile, the once vanquished Fortune 500, mostly composed of Old Economy, old guard companies, had caught up to the newcomers by using the same technologies and processes, but underpinning them with proven value propositions, strong brands, established value chains, and seasoned management. The victors appeared to be the vanquished. And the technological mass hallucination that we all experienced over the past several years now turns out, as it were, to be a kind of a bummer.

HOW'S YOUR MEMORY?

Now we are back to a language that all of us "get." Some, understandably, use it more vocally and shrilly than others.

"Wall Street doesn't understand our space. We need to reposition our products and the company—and we need to do it now!"

"We need to rethink our business plan or we're not going to get our next round of funding!"

"Our market cap has declined by two-thirds! We need to develop a new marketing plan for the next board meeting."

"We need to train our executives [formerly our middle managers] and our middle managers [formerly our new hires] how to develop and execute more effective marketing and sales strategies."

All the preceding quotes are real, picked up from conversations with various executive staffs over the past year. It's time once again for the business equivalent of heavy lifting.

While it may now be the most challenging of business climates, has anything fundamentally changed (besides our collective net worth)? Not a lot. For those of you just joining us, it's called a *business cycle*. As mundane as that may seem, for many of us it is back to business as usual, i.e., creating, fielding, and communicating a demonstrably valuable product or service and doing so in a compelling, competitive way. During all the fun of the last decade, some of you might have forgotten all the details about doing this rather difficult work. For others, the memory of the last technology recession may stir coincident memories of your senior prom, cramming for that organic chemistry final, or your first job as a newly minted MBA.

Coping with an economic downturn is always tough, but many organizations face some particularly thorny challenges. After an unprecedented run of uninterrupted business growth, many management teams must now confront issues that they had previously only read about. Slowing demand for products and services, intense competition, and surly, now profoundly disillusioned shareholders have wreaked havoc with many companies and their previously unassailable business models, of which many were so proud. A widening gap between what customers and investors now demand and what companies can actually deliver has once again placed an extraordinary premium on understanding how markets develop and are likely to develop going forward.

Well, let's take a deep breath and try to put this all in some perspective. The New York Yankees don't forget how to play baseball during the off-season. But they still report to training camp in spring. Similarly, we in high tech have been playing a game in which winning, for many of us, was simply the norm. Welcome to a new season. While many may feel unfairly treated in the current environment—having to postpone their scheduled wealth attainment—there are many others more insightful who continue to view the high-tech industry for what it is, and always has been: the most fascinating, volatile, vexing, and ultimately uncompromising business in the world. And unlike Wall Street, we actually make things!

THE INTERNET IS DEAD. LONG LIVE THE INTERNET.

The mad rush to capitalize the first widespread deployment of the Internet is over. Now we can get down to the serious business of capitalizing *on* the Internet. It is a marathon, not a sprint. We must now forsake *Internet time* as a measurable pace or usable work rhythm. In our parlance, Internet time was a synonym for *tornado time,* representing the highest possible speed of change, one that occurs when the pragmatist herd breaks away from the old paradigm and stampedes to the new. It is absolutely a real phenomenon, but it is short-lived, existing in a much larger context of *life cycle time.*

Life cycle time describes the shifting rhythms of technology adoption from the beginning of a market to its end. We have identified this market-evolution model as a series of different stages, each with its own imperatives for creating shareholder value. In some stages, the goal is to move swiftly; in others, it is to extend the moment as long as possible. There is no one steady beat, no single setting of the metronome that can keep companies in sync. To move less swiftly, however, does *not* imply that one must think or plan less swiftly. The stages of the life cycle are not time-predicated, and therefore life cycle time is also subjective. We do know that technology-enabled enterprises tend to move more swiftly rather than less. So too must the technology-based organizations that serve them.

And so we come back to the basics, specifically, the very first exercise we do in any of our consulting engagements: getting consensus with the management team as to what stage of the life cycle each of the component technologies that make up their offer is in. That leads to an overall life cycle placement for the offer itself, and that placement in turn drives every other strategic and tactical decision made—until the next stage in the life cycle is reached.

GET INTO A TORNADO? SORRY... IT'S TIME TO CROSS THE CHASM.

This may seem a bit disingenuous, since both books actually work together to advocate the life cycle thinking outlined above, but in spirit, the dawning of the new millennium marks a period for letting go of *tornado illusions* and embracing *chasm truths* learned painfully beginning in March 2000. The most important chasm truth, we believe, is that there is a form of natural selection for companies that can accumulate their own power, granting them more power as partners and customers are attracted to their success. In this process the most universally recognized form of marketplace power is dominant market share. Therefore, the core chasm prescription is to find a market you can dominate and then dominate it as fast as you possibly can.

To guide this effort (and perhaps reacquaint you with our theories), this book presents a series of models, tools, and frameworks that leads management teams to address the key issues in this process. What's different from previous efforts is that this book is intended as a "field guide" to thinking about, creating, and executing strategy. The book is organized around three major sections, the first devoted to reviewing how high-tech markets develop, the second to specifying market-development strategy, the third to considering go-to-market programs in light of the various life cycle stages. It is, in effect, an organization's blueprint for getting new offerings into the marketplace. This blueprint is most often interpreted by the marketing organization and function, but by no means should it be limited to this organization.

The back-to-basics focus that managers need to reenergize themselves, their organizations, and their markets carries a straightforward prescription:

- Focus the entire company on the product (or service) marketing plan,
- Ensure that execution is flawless based on basic go-to-market imperatives,
- Direct these imperatives toward dominating a target market,
- In order to increase market-share power for the company,
- Thereby creating a sustainable platform for increasing shareholder value for investors.

It is all about formulas that can be—and have been—used to win. There are no trick plays anywhere.

THE CHASM COMPANION

Part One

How High-Tech Markets Develop

This section reviews the key principles governing each inflection point on the Technology Adoption Life Cycle and explores some key mistakes or missteps that organizations make at each point.

Back to the Basics

The ideas and concepts outlined in this book are built in part upon theories of high-tech market development first discussed in *Crossing the Chasm*, originally published in 1991, and *Inside the Tornado,* published in 1995. My partner, Geoffrey Moore, authored both books, and in them he defined and refined a vocabulary and framework for understanding how and why high-technology markets develop for *discontinuous innovations,* and why these markets evolve as they do. Over the years we have used our experience in consulting with technology-based organizations, both large and small, to hone these concepts further, adding to an ever widening body of work. We have added, modified, borrowed, and discarded ideas based on these experiences. And we are grateful that many of our clients are willing co-conspirators.

Since continuous innovations still account for a significant portion of modern economies, it is hardly surprising that much of the language of business and the specifics of modern marketing theory and practice continue to reflect this fact. Yet, the fastest-growing sectors of these same modern economies are now driven by *dis*continuities—disruptive technologies that force changes in both strategy and behavior that are often counterintuitive to both buyer and seller. Thus, a knowledge and practice *gap* exists, a condition that is completely understandable when you compare the number of patents issued between 1900 and 1970 with the number issued since 1970. It is exactly this gap that high-tech organizations face every day. They must make sense of developing markets and business practices where, to paraphrase a line from the *Star Trek* TV series, "no one has gone before."

Since the basic function of business strategy is to create wealth for shareholders, employees, and society, we start our investigation with some basic principles and observations—some long held, others gleaned from the technology market meltdown recently witnessed.

We begin by trying to make more sense of what has transpired during the recent past.

One way to describe the excessive valuations in the technology sector in the run-up to the year 2000, particularly those surrounding the Internet, is that investors fell under the spell of *category power*. Historically, when whole new paradigms—underpinned by discontinuous innovations—have entered the sector, they have driven massive transfers of valuation, much of which accumulates in the market-leading companies. Internet investors anticipated this trend and bid up the stocks of any company with a good story about how it would ride this latest hyper-growth category to wealth and power.

We are reminded of the old proverb "Many are called, but few are chosen." Now we want to examine the results of a few quarters of competitive performance before bidding up a stock. Instead of jumping on the bandwagon of companies declaring victory based on a declared *strategy* of pre-emptive market leadership, the markets wait to see if victory (a) has been achieved, (b) can be sustained, and (c) is worth anything once both conditions are satisfied.

The implications for management teams are straightforward enough. Quit fooling around (or fooling yourself) with strategy or business-model experiments and go make some money. Do this by focusing on your core business. Do it by selling something for cash to customers who pay their bills. Launch a new and exciting product or service. Penetrate a new market with a valuable value proposition. And when competition appears, show that you can hold it at bay not through discounts but through differentiated value.

SHOW ME THE VALUE

Those of you who have read our most recent books, *The Gorilla Game* and *Living on the Fault Line*, may recall the concepts of *Competitive Advantage Gap*

(GAP) and *Competitive Advantage Period (CAP)*. GAP is the value of your company's differentiated offerings when compared with those of your direct competitors. CAP is the length of time that investors anticipate you can sustain that differentiated advantage. In the investment climate prior to March 2000, all the emphasis was on catching the next technology wave. This represented a focus (some would argue an obsession) on CAP, manifested as a fear that the current advantages enjoyed by the status quo would be summarily wiped out by an emerging new category—the now legendary New Economy. While understanding CAP potential remains important, nowadays the emphasis is on demonstrating results in the present rather than in the future. We live now in a world dominated by GAP, the power to win business through differentiated offerings in viable, demonstrable, and compelling categories. Our first return to the basics should be dominated by that thought.

The implications of this for management are far-reaching. In surveying where to invest scarce resources for competitive advantage, The Chasm Group uses a *Competitive Advantage Hierarchy* model that isolates four general domains where companies can focus attention. They are:

- differentiated offerings—denoted as *offer power*
- market segment domination—denoted as *customer power*
- value chain leadership—denoted as *industry power*
- new category participation—denoted as *category power*

Competitive Advantage Hierarchy

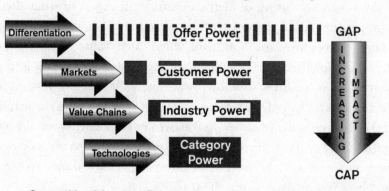

Competitive Advantage Drivers   *Competitive Advantage Effects*

Category and industry power, i.e., the strength and importance of the value chain you operate within, have a greater effect on CAP and the long term; while your customer power, i.e., the number and type of customers that you have captured and the offers you have fielded to capture them, have more impact short-term on GAP. Investors currently feeling burned by new business models are turning away from new category participation, value chain domination, and other heady visions of the future. "Show us some differentiated offerings that make money today," they demand.

SHOW ME THE MONEY

To be sure, value chain domination holds forth the promise of immense competitive advantage sustainable over long periods of time. It has long been the driving force behind the valuations of such behemoths as Cisco, Intel, Microsoft, and SAP. No one doubts that it is a great prize and worth much sacrifice to gain. But investors have learned that as a sustainable outcome for any particular company, it is improbable. And so they are prepared to search for other safe harbors as they seek more reliable returns from their increasingly scarce capital.

When the focus was almost exclusively on value chain domination, investors eagerly sought news of emerging partnership announcements that would signal value chain formation and provide clues as to which companies were accumulating the most marketplace power. Both Amazon and Yahoo! validated their investors' expectations by demonstrating value chain power recruiting numerous partners in excess of what their direct competitors could demonstrate. But such auspicious beginnings would later temper investor optimism when such value chains, once formed, proved nowhere near as valuable as advertised, at least not in the short term. As companies, notably Amazon, called again for more patience and capital in order to demonstrate their true values, investors decided they had no more of either. In the current climate they are simply making that most basic of all requests—*Show us the money!* Partners do not pay money; customers do. Show us the customers, what you plan to offer them, and how you intend to keep them.

In this context, customers with large budgets to spend are preferable to those of more modest means, which translates into higher valuations going to companies with large-enterprise customers than to those focused on small-business or fickle consumer markets. But in all cases there is a focus on liquidity, on the ability to generate initial order and repeat business such that investments in fixed costs and customer acquisition can be paid down. Thus the need to quickly understand the dynamics of market development—the shifts in focus that now seem almost preordained—and do something about them, not because of Internet time per se, but because that is what investors are looking for, and what they want to see now.

In 1999, the toughest hire in Silicon Valley was a great vice president of business development. This rare bird combined the savvy of a salesperson with the power-brokering skills of a lobbyist and was sent out into the world to spin a coalition of partners into a value chain. Every key announcement was greeted with an escalation in stock price. As stock currency grew cheap and plentiful, acquisitions became the preferred substitute for organic growth, further distracting investors from the dramatic outflow of cash from core business operations. *Strategic alliances* became the focus, the buzzword *du jour*.

In demand now is someone who can recruit and lead a direct-sales force selling into enterprise customers offerings that have an average selling price into the hundreds of thousands of dollars, with large deals going over $1 million, and even higher in special circumstances. The call is for someone who has closed a quarter, has closed dozens of quarters in fact, making quota. Such rainmakers are not to be found among any recent business school graduates, or in the outflow of people from dead or dying dot-coms. Instead, the sales organizations at big systems houses like Hewlett-Packard, Sun, and IBM, along with large consultancies and integrators like Accenture and EDS, are the breeding grounds in which recruiters will now be trawling.

SHOW ME THE MONEY *NOW*

In the era just past, most companies, notably the dot-coms, sought to validate their valuations by treating the *lifetime value* of a customer as their primary asset—an asset that could be booked like any other. This is not a bad idea per se, but it is subject to interpretation and abuse. What lessons can we learn?

1. "Eyeballs" are not a reliable indicator of, or proxy for, customers. Orders may be. The real issue is not trial, but repeat orders. Will or can customers switch from one vendor to another?

2. Any projections of future returns from current customers should include a churn rate validated by actual customer behavior. Total available market statistics are far less relevant than those representing the total *addressable* market—the relevant part of the market, which can be appealed to over and over again and will behave in the desired way.

3. Customer-acquisition costs are paid in present dollars; lifetime value is paid out in increasingly future dollars. Such future returns must exceed those gained by simply putting the same money in government-backed bonds.

4. "Irrational exuberance" has now been wrung out of the public markets, and decidedly so. We find ourselves getting back to the future, and realize that the tide will turn decidedly bullish once again—and not soon enough for most of us.

5. Our industry will emerge different in the next up-cycle. Seeking to understand those differences begins now.

But maybe the biggest lesson was recognizing the sheer magnitude of the capital needed to achieve the lofty lifetime goals investors and management were pursuing. In all of these models it takes a long time and a lot of money just to get to breakeven, and investors are now seeing that the model works only if customers can be persuaded to supply part of the needed funding through advance funding of their own, i.e., buying and continuing to buy. The mission we now embark on is to understand how to get customers to do exactly that.

2

The Basis for Strategy Decisions

High-tech companies, whether they know it or not (and most of them do), base their most fundamental strategic decisions on a model that is now older than most high-tech companies themselves. That's right. Apple, Intel, Microsoft, Cisco, Dell, Hewlett-Packard, and literally thousands of companies besides are devotees, acknowledged or not, of a model that was first postulated in the late 1930s and advanced in the 1950s by researchers at Harvard University who were interested in how people—indeed, communities of people—consider and adopt *discontinuous innovations.* We call this model the *Technology Adoption Life Cycle,* or TALC for short. Because this model is seemingly so accurate and, as a result, so pervasive within high technology, it is the foundation for this book, as it has been the foundation for two previous books authored by my colleague Geoffrey Moore. The life cycle model is the fundamental basis for how we at The Chasm Group think about developing and executing strategy—specifically what we will call *market development strategy.* While the following may be old news to some, it is nonetheless useful here to review some basics.

THE NATURE OF DISCONTINUOUS INNOVATIONS

To start, let us consider the nature of a discontinuous innovation. What is it? How does it come into being? How should we react to it?

What *it* is, is typically obvious to everyone. It's the automobile or the telephone of the early 1900s. It's the machine gun or battle tank of World War I, or the atomic bomb of World War II and the Cold War. It's the minicomputer of the 1960s, and the microprocessor and personal computer of the '70s and early '80s. It's the relational database and distributed computing. It's the genetic sequencer. It's the electric car. It's the Internet and the dot-com. As of this writing, it's application servers which underpin other e-business infrastructure applications.

What attributes do these very different innovations have in common?

First, they all represent significant, even radical, departures from the status quo. Second, these innovations were not merely new or different from what preceded them. They reshaped (and are reshaping) fundamentally the field of human endeavor—whether it is communications, transportation, warfare, information processing, treatment of disease, or how we buy and sell things. These innovations do not alter an otherwise level playing field. They crater and scorch it. Suffice it to say that discontinuous innovations—and the benefits they promise—often render what preceded them irrelevant and obsolete. Do you remember when you last bought a typewriter?

If a discontinuous innovation changes everything, correspondingly, a *continuous innovation* changes very little, much to the relief and benefit of the buyer and user of the continuous innovation. Why? Simply for the reason that the continuous innovation requires little or no behavioral change on the part of anybody. Users, in particular, feel virtually nothing except the specific and typically modest benefit associated with the so-called innovation. This means that they are built upon the infrastructure and standards already in place at the time. Think of a continuous innovation as the "green bleaching crystals" in your laundry detergent. Why are they there? The advertising promises "whiter whites and brighter brights." And I don't even need to buy a new washing machine; I only need to buy the new detergent. It's the same, only *better*. Now *that's* the kind of product I've been looking for.

Conversely, consider the price that discontinuous innovations extract. From the users of the innovation to the infrastructures necessary to support them, all will be subjected to a kind of *discontinuity shock*. Unlike continuous innovations, discontinuous innovations require end users—and the marketplace itself—to change fundamentally. Such change may be felt in the way people and organizations obtain and utilize such innovations. Or in the way such innovations are supported and/or incorporated into systems. Or in the way such benefits are delivered and sustained. Suffice it to say at this point that discontinuous innovations disrupt current value chains, but they must also result in new value chains if they are to survive. More about value chains in later chapters.

Most important, discontinuous innovations represent *risk*, sometimes profoundly so. Risk to the investors bankrolling the innovation. Risk to the first buyers who bravely cast their fates and their budgets into the unknown. Risk to the infrastructure providers who must come together on sometimes little more than a hunch to create what will become, in effect, a life-support system for the innovation. And so on. Thus, to be successful in the business of high technology means being able to recognize the *sources* and *impacts* of discontinuity and manage them accordingly.

You may think you're in the high-tech business—software, hardware, networking, services, biotech, whatever. In fact, you're in the discontinuous innovations business. Which means you're in the most risky business on earth.

▶ THE ELECTRIC CAR JOLTS CALIFORNIA

In the mid-1990s both General Motors and Honda introduced an electric-powered car in the California market—southern California to be more precise, arguably the car capital of the world. The GM car, the EV-1, in particular displayed a "forward-looking" design, which might be viewed as unusual depending on your design aesthetic. Both cars featured a DC-powered motor that required some very sophisticated battery technology—and some very expensive batteries. The motor is unnervingly quiet and very responsive. It also requires a complete charging every seventy to one hundred miles, depending on how much you have demanded of the motor. Those with a lead foot need to be prepared to not venture farther than they could safely return to their recharging facility—typically their home—or risk walking the rest of the way. Kind of like a pilot calculating the point of no return on a flight across the Pacific.

Both cars were introduced with the usual fanfare. Lots of advertising, particularly of the *brand* variety along with the typical hoopla surrounding a product that promised some unique environmental benefits—for example, no tailpipe emissions, which are in the Los Angeles basin the major cause of photochemical smog.

Of course, there was another more obscure reason why these cars were introduced into California. The California legislature had passed some rather onerous legislation that, in summary, required a small percentage of the total number of automobiles sold by any manufacturer wishing to sell in California to be of a nonpolluting variety. These percentages must be realized by the middle of this decade, or so requires the legislation. However, the practical effect of this legislation is to *mandate* that a certain percentage of automobile buyers obtain nonpolluting (at least by conventional measures) cars, and ostensibly be pleased to do so—and to mandate the build-out of the infrastructure necessary to support the vehicles.

While the marketing surrounding these cars was palpable, consumer reaction has been notably tepid. After all, why in the land of the automobile, in a culture that celebrates freedom by virtue of the practically unfettered ability to go anywhere by car, would you want a vehicle that required a complete change in thinking, behavior, and supporting infrastructure? Why, indeed?

The electric car that was touted to go practically everywhere seems now to be going nowhere. Consumers have stayed away in droves. The automobile companies' responses, while well intentioned, have mostly been of the "See, I told you so" variety; while those of various governmental agencies and environmental groups can be summarized as "People just don't get it."

The industry quite correctly has reasoned that it must redouble its efforts to convince car buyers of the benefits of an electric car. More advertising rendered by ad agencies who pray at the altar of "the brand." More dealer training. More publicity. And so on. After all, as Frank Sinatra sang, "If I can make it there, I'll make it anywhere."

In fact, consumers do "get it." They just don't like it. A car buff's enthusiasm aside, most consumers behave quite rationally about something as serious as purchasing an automobile. And they behave relative to the lessons of the Technology Adoption Life Cycle. In the car capital of America, perhaps the world, where the car not only supports a lifestyle but also is representative of that lifestyle, the last thing anyone is looking for is radical change. Let the next guy worry about smog, many people reason; I want to be sure that I can pull off the Santa Monica freeway at 2 A.M. and fill up the car with fuel.

Thus, while electric cars appear fine for the U.S. Postal Service following a predetermined route day in and day out, most Southland drivers rely on the petroleum-based engine and the automobile it powers for their livelihoods, their recreation, and ultimately in the urban landscape that is Los Angeles, their freedom. The entire market infrastructure—consisting of vast numbers of service stations—to competitive car insurance rates, the mechanic on the corner, the Automobile Club of Southern California—all of these elements are based on sustaining, even optimizing the status quo.

The issue is not one of consumers relating to the brand values associated with the EV-1, or consumer psychographic distinctions that might determine the optimal advertising and media plan. Rather, it is an issue of infrastructure and the risks, both real and perceived, of adopting a product that a current infrastructure does not support. Why take the chance? Indeed, is there any incentive or motivation for current stakeholders in the infrastructure—the same players mentioned above—to support such changes to the status quo? As might be said, zero to none.

As it comes to pass, California's energy problems notwithstanding, the electric companies have the incentive but not the real estate. The oil companies have the real estate but not the incentive. The future now appears to be *hybrids*—cars powered by both gasoline engines and electric motors.

What is the lesson learned? If you introduce a discontinuous innovation that requires customers to change their behaviors and current infrastructures to accommodate these new behaviors, initially you walk alone. And no amount of marketing hyperbole can, in the short term (and perhaps in the long term), overcome this basic fact.

◄

THE SIX PHASES OF TECHNOLOGY MARKET DEVELOPMENT

This book describes a hypothetical journey, that of taking a discontinuous innovation from its inception, when it challenges the status quo, to the point where the innovation *is* the status quo, to be challenged by yet another upstart. Along the way, I will describe the various forces that will affect adoption, and the strategy imperatives necessary to accomplish each transition.

Applied to market development strategy, the TALC model postulates that when a community or marketplace is faced with a discontinuous innovation—one that has the possibility and likelihood of necessitating an infrastructure shift—customers for the innovation will self-select themselves into groups according to their attraction or aversion to risk. We will focus on six fundamental phases of market development, considered in the following diagram as *inflection points*. Each inflection point represents a fundamental change point in how a technology market will develop, and therefore how we must change in order to capitalize on each new phase.

Technology Adoption Life Cycle Model

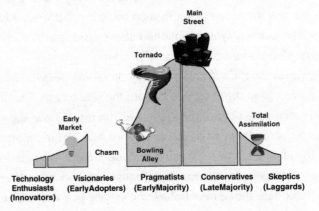

The model describes metaphorically each inflection point and its dominant citizenry as follows:

The Early Market: The gestation period of any discontinuous innovation, characterized by both excitement and uncertainty in the minds of both vendors and customers. This phase is under the sway of technology enthusiasts (also referred to as innovators) and visionaries (also referred to as early adopters).

Technology enthusiasts operate on the principle that a discontinuous innovation is, at its core, superior to what is currently available. Their motivation is thus to seek out such opportunities, explore them, and pronounce them fit or unfit for general consumption. Simply put, they are the first customers for anything truly new.

Visionaries see discontinuous innovations for what they can be, particularly if they can be harnessed early to begin a new paradigm—one that visionaries can exploit to significant competitive advantage or leverage over that to which the market is now wedded. Given their numbers, visionaries provide the first real impetus to a fledgling market because their significant economic clout drives vendors to further commercialize their efforts. Visionaries also are the first group to extol the virtues of the innovation both in word (their vocal support) and in deed, by virtue of their considerable investment in the new way.

Taken together, technology enthusiasts and visionaries constitute the first or *early market* for a discontinuous innovation. There are no other customers other than these two groups at this stage of the TALC.

The Chasm: A pause of indeterminate length in market development, when the early market interest has waned and when there is no preordained or natural customer among the mainstream market for the discontinuous innovation, owing to its immaturity and lack of widespread deployment.

The Bowling Alley: Resumption of market development consisting of specific customer segments who are adopting ahead of general market adoption based on their desire to address specific problems, and on vendors' willingness to provide segment-specific solutions to such challenges.

This phase is driven by those *pragmatists* (early majority) who are willing to shed their natural aversion to discontinuity in order to achieve specific benefits not available from the current paradigm or infrastructure. Pragmatists at this stage are interested in evolution, not revolution. They are interested in what the innovation does reliably and predictably rather than what it promises to do at some future point. They also require demonstrable evidence that their early moves (at least for them) will pay off and that people they would typically reference—other pragmatists in similar situations—will also proceed, albeit cautiously, in this direction.

The Tornado: A period of market hypergrowth caused by pragmatists adopting en masse a new infrastructure that renders the previous paradigm obsolete. Remaining pragmatists now flood into the market. These customers are highly influenced by the market-leading solution and the company that sponsors it, and will tend to behave as a pack. Their behavior is reinforced by third-party companies now embracing the market-leading solution further validating the pragmatists' decision to adopt an emerging value chain. The previously discontinuous innovation is now deemed *safe and effective.*

Main Street: A period of relative stasis during which demand for and supply of the no-longer-new product are in relative equilibrium. Thus, the market development challenge is to provide aftermarket offers that extend the paradigm now adopted.

Conservatives (the late majority) now extend this market development phase. This group does not embrace the promise of competitive advantage but rather is concerned about being left behind—being put at competitive *dis*advantage. Conservatives embrace Main Street markets, as they are price and option sensitive and feel that by waiting for this phase in the cycle, they can attain the benefits of the new way without unduly subjecting themselves to any remaining risks that may still lurk in the wings.

Skeptics (laggards) also begin to take notice of the emerging status quo but will continue to prefer that their purchases be completely risk free. They are not an attractive market for high-tech vendors and may decry the emergence of new markets as just another high-tech marketing scam perpetrated on those who neither need nor want anything remotely thought of as new.

Total Assimilation: A final period reflecting the end of the Technology Adoption Life Cycle—but not the end of the product category. Final adopters, the skeptics, now adopt the new paradigm unconsciously or as a matter of course, but may do so in ways whereby the original innovation is not apparent or is obtained as a *service.*

Going forward, we shall see how these inflection points and the market dynamics exhibited by each of these customer groups at each point should influence the development of effective market strategies, summarized by the following assertion:

▶ *Winning strategies will change as we move from inflection point to inflection point and will, in most cases, reverse the prior strategy conceived and executed.*

Let the journey begin.

3

The Early Market

One has to look out for engineers—they begin with sewing machines and end up with the atomic bomb.

—MARCEL PAGNOL

How do you make God laugh? Tell him your plans.

—WOODY ALLEN

Developing an early market for a discontinuous innovation may seem quite straightforward. This chapter considers both the basics as well as some of the intricacies. This is important because we are now embarking, so to speak, on our great journey eastward across the TALC, and our time, money, and reputation are now at stake. It is here that we first put ourselves in harm's way.

First, an entrepreneurial organization or company with a breakthrough technology must develop the technology such that it can be purchased as a "thing." The point of this initial product is to enable, at least partially, some new, exciting, and compelling application or process. Prior to and during this phase, entrepreneurs will build and refine a *business plan,* ostensibly detailing how the new innovation will be brought to market. Typically, these plans follow a formula and are now available as software templates. Buy one or download one through the Internet and you, too, can fill in the blanks.

Your *marketing plan* should outline the steps necessary for seeding the product among technology enthusiasts who will, of course, see the immediate advantages of this new approach over what is now available. The techie's enthusiasm will find its way into the office of the deep-pocketed visionary who will, in turn, appreciate how implementing this new *vision* will result in order-of-magnitude advances, with numerous benefits accruing to those who can implement such a vision first.

Nothing to it really. On the other hand, let's first observe how entrepreneurs and their respective organizations typically get it wrong.

If our consulting experience is a faithful guide, *the typical early market plan will be full of unfounded assumptions and/or faulty in its conclusions.* Market size projections will be grandiose. Notions of the *total available market* will be carried to an extreme—sometimes ridiculously so. Assertions as to why people will buy the new product will be naive or based on questionable premises. Assumed initial customer acceptance will influence future product development in order to attract vast numbers of new customers, but such assumptions miss by the mark by any number of measures: time, cost to develop, resources required, necessary supportive infrastructure, demand creation requirements, and so on.

In short, the plan will be developed and worshiped for what it is: an ultimate how-to manual for creating a completely new market that will enable us to get rich in the process. After we've all read it, and we get down to the actual work of implementing it, we will soon find our initial thinking on the shelf with last year's telephone book.

"We have met the enemy, and he is us."

The good news is that the plan itself does not really matter all that much, since the ultimate *strategy* for developing the market, at this stage, does not really matter all that much. "What?" you cry. Certainly every prudent businessperson is going to make important decisions like launching a new product, creating new markets, and tapping vast amounts of untapped wealth—not to mention using other people's money to do it—with the diligence and clear thinking that such important pursuits demand. The problem is that these plans often focus on the wrong things.

In fact, early market efforts can go off the rails almost right from the start. Such false starts are typically characterized by three fundamental flaws in our thinking:

1. **We fail to build the proper foundations for actually going to market.**
Sometimes companies have little real expertise in bringing new, discontinuous products to market. This situation is exacerbated when organizations hire or task the wrong people. Either they have little experience bringing new products to market, or they have the wrong experience—that is, their previous efforts have been in categories or businesses that differ significantly from the one now contemplated. Since to be human is to approach new tasks based initially at least on how we did things previously, we tend to repeat our mistakes happily pursuing a completely new destination, safe in the knowledge that our previous modus operandi got us to our last destination.

   This devotion to doing things "the way we've always done them" is further compounded when it is institutionalized to "that's the way we do things around here." The resulting confusion and consternation when things don't work as planned cause organizations to reevaluate their entire plan, typically after a painful process of self-examination that usually follows a process similar to that of grieving, described variously in four stages: denial, anger, acceptance, and resolution.

   The point here is that this introspection and its outcomes eat up valuable time—time that could be better leveraged earlier by really confronting these questions in a serial fashion starting with:

   - Do we have the right objectives?
   - Do we know what tasks must get done right and well to meet these objectives?
   - Do we have the right processes in place to support the tasks?
   - Do we have the right people in place to do the work?

   This fundamental dilemma is taken up in Geoffrey Moore's latest book, *Living on the Fault Line* (HarperBusiness, 2000).

2. **Our expectations do not align with our planned investment.** In *Crossing the Chasm* the case is made for seeking smaller rather than larger market segments initially because they are, by definition, easier

to dominate. The larger a segment is, the more customers a competitor must win to be considered a market leader. This becomes extremely problematic when a new market entrant is proposing to attack a large market; that is, one that appears attractive because of large numbers of available customers. Available customers rapidly morph to prospective, probable, even planned customers when subjected to unrealistic or otherwise optimistic spreadsheet exercises. One of the most common mistakes we see—a mistake destined to result in teeth gnashing and tears—is confusing the *total available market* with the *total addressable market*. They are not the same.

I suggest, therefore, as a sanity check against your doubtless potentially terminal optimism that you consider a different *what-if* scenario. For our example, consider the total available market represented by pet owners in the United States, a segment that until recently was eagerly pursued by numerous, otherwise clever entrepreneurs who believed the Web and e-commerce to be perfectly suited to satisfy Fido's and Fluffy's (and their harried yuppie owners') quest for the latest in designer pet food, bedding, and chew toys. Research tells us that Americans spend $23 billion a year on pet products and services. That's a big market! (I know what you're thinking: "If we could get just five percent of that market . . . hell, even one percent, we'd have a huge business!") An estimated 58 million Americans—nearly 60 percent of all households—own some 212 million pets.

But consider. Is the total available market likely to be much smaller when you consider how many pet owners have a PC—indeed, a home PC—*and* are connected to the Internet, *and* are surfing regularly on the World Wide Web, *and* can do so at anything other than the agonizingly slow rate of conventional modems? Now consider what the market looks like when the question is asked, "How many of these pet-owning surfers will actually buy things for their pets via electronic commerce?" as opposed to visiting their local pet shop or, just as likely, their grocery, warehouse, or pet warehouse store (e.g., Petco). Now consider how many people will do this on a *trial* basis only. What will be their repeat rate? How many will become site loyal?

Can you see great big numbers becoming much smaller numbers—in a big hurry?

Now consider what each site-loyal customer will spend over a given period of time and how much must be invested to reach these people and keep them. Consider the cost of shipping forty-pound bags of dog kibble. Consider also various *confounding factors,* including competitive reactions from the large chain stores that will pressure their manufacturers, distributors, and franchisors for all manner of concessions in an effort to protect their bricks-and-mortar businesses from the onslaught of e-tailers. What about other e-tailers who pursue the same market? If pet owners want to shop online, will they choose a specialty site or opt for a well-known retailer's e-commerce site? Will one site's advertising have the significant and unintended consequence of drawing shoppers to the site of its competitors due to the similarities in names? ("Let me think. Was that promotion for Petopia, Pets.com, Petsmart.com, or Petstore.com?") Is there any wonder why this particular form of e-retailing has gone to the dogs? (Sorry.) What were they thinking? What perfect conditions for a market shakeout. And shake out it does—witness the unlamented demise of the online pet retailers. (I did love the advertising.)

And so it goes. All these considerations, as well as many more, become the real basis for the size of this hypothetical market, defined not by its sheer potential size, but by what we can really address, win over, and sustain.

Suddenly the picture is a lot murkier and perhaps just a bit less attractive than when we just thought about the cool technology and new business model that was to be our path to riches and fame. Such are the vagaries of early market planning.

Finally, we encounter the final indignity. The new innovation is not really that great after all.

3. **Can we articulate, deliver, and sustain the real value such that it stands a good chance of winning over visionaries in sufficient numbers as to warrant our efforts in the first place?** Promising new products can die during the time between initial adoption by technology enthusiasts eager to see what all the fuss is about—and subsequent adoption by visionaries pursuing a number of sometimes conflicting initiatives to advance their company (and personal agendas)—because the benefits of the innovation are unclear, confusing, contradictory, or too risky as opposed to other choices. As such,

the product fails to capture the imagination of the visionary. This failing then further negates the chances that the product will be rolled out as part of a visionary's new *system*—that is, whatever he/she contemplates as "my next move" to gain significant competitive advantage.

Worse yet, visionaries tend to reference other visionaries, and so the now-struggling product category is seen as intrinsically flawed as well. The sponsoring vendor, and perhaps its early competitors as well, are now muttering collectively, "I coulda' been a contender." The innovation never gets any real traction with the one group, visionaries, who actually represent the first *real* market. At this stage, people associated with the project are cutting their losses, leaving behind the original team of innovators who have been banished along with their wares to an older, underutilized, and probably "off-campus" building where they will toil on in relative obscurity.

Naturally, given the patience and attention spans of most high-tech management teams, this entire experience probably transpires in less than two years. This may not be a bad thing, under the proviso of "fail early, fail cheap." In any event, the conspirators are named; the blameless are blamed; the guilty are absolved; and the bank accounts of hopeful investors or shareholders are diminished.

▶ SEPARATING THE GOOD PLANS FROM THE BAD
by Nancy Schoendorf, co–managing partner, Mohr, Davidow Ventures

A business student at a lecture I was giving once asked, "I understand the concept of venture capital funding, but what does a VC *do* all day?" It's an excellent question. Different VCs might give different answers, but I can almost guarantee that reading plans ranks high on every VC's to-do list.

As venture capitalists, we're entrusted with investing other people's money, a responsibility we take seriously. Our firm specializes in early stage investments, which means we meet entrepreneurs at their most formative stages. So we try to be rigorous and thorough in our evaluations of the plans that cross our desks.

We look at the people behind the plan; their technologies and the products that might emerge from those technologies; the market the fledgling company plans to enter; the entire competitive landscape; the customers expected to buy what the company will sell; the channels for getting products to these customers; the organization and partnerships surrounding the business; the financial requirements to bring the vision to fruition; the risks; and any other miscellaneous information that might point to success or failure, or give us a gut feel about the worthiness of the plan.

Of course, we read many more plans than we fund. Sometimes it's hard to pinpoint exactly what is so good about the plans that do get funded—after all, if the process were too formulaic, there'd be no art or suspense to it. On the other hand, it's easier to isolate where the majority of plans go wrong.

Let's call these the three fatal flaws.

Fatal flaw #1: *The market identified in the plan isn't good enough.*

Sometimes, once you take the plan's dreams and flights of fancy about the market opportunity and whittle them down to a realistic scale, the addressable market simply isn't big enough. Here's one major hint, at least for early stage investments: If a business plan defines the potential opportunity using, for example, Forrester Research charts, the idea is either irrelevant or too late. Available markets destined for big-time success are typically defined by bottom-up rather than top-down numbers.

Sometimes the market is properly defined, but the business plan hasn't clearly identified the problem it solves or hasn't provided a compelling solution. Other times, the business plan doesn't realistically address the competitive landscape or how barriers to entry will be erected and sustained.

Other times, we simply don't believe the business plan's assumptions about how strongly the customers in the potential market care about the solution proposed. Does the plan propose a vitamin or a painkiller? Vitamins may be positive and wholesome, but we invest in painkillers because those are what customers care enough about to spend money on first.

Fatal flaw #2: *The company lacks strong entrepreneurial vision and drive.*

No business plan can overcome the absence of a strong entrepreneur, or the founders' lack of deep knowledge about what they're trying to do and intense passion for their venture. As VCs, we can help tend a fire to keep it burning brightly, but it's not our job to strike the match or even chop the wood. The people behind the business plan need to demonstrate their desire to breathe life into their plan and to embody it every day.

Some VCs, especially those investing in later-stage rounds, cite an incomplete team as a fatal flaw. Because our firm specializes in early stage investments, however, incomplete teams are almost a given. We see it as a tremendous opportunity to use our contacts and marketing expertise to fill in the gaps. As long as there's at least one founder with sufficient technical skill and entrepreneurial fervor, we are delighted to roll up our sleeves and help build a complete, winning team.

Fatal flaw #3: *The plan is sent to the wrong kind of VC.*

Despite some people's view of venture capital firms as indistinguishable entities filled with virtually interchangeable individuals, there's a huge difference between outlooks, expertise, and focus among different firms.

Business plans need to be targeted at the right kind of VC. A venture capitalist specializing in late-stage rounds can't afford to fund some of the "out there" ideas that an early stage investor might embrace and nurture. On the other hand, a late-stage investor might be willing to put up more cash or take a more hands-off role, which could be preferable for some companies. An early stage investor is more likely to take an active role in the development of the company being funded. From a nascent company's perspective, the way to choose the right early stage fund is to evaluate the VC's resources and expertise in the plan's particular market area. So matching the plan to the investor is a crucial, and often overlooked, requirement.

In the final analysis, avoiding these three fatal flaws still won't guarantee that a business plan gets funded. A plethora of other obstacles can cause a business plan to stumble. But *not* evading these flaws will lead surely to failure.

As for what VCs do when they're not reading business plans, speaking for our firm, we're out working our tails off to make these companies as successful as they can be.

◀

What to do? Evaluate realistically whether or not the innovation truly is a breakthrough. Does it offer order-of-magnitude benefits over what is now possible, without resorting to untested, cold fusion–type approaches? Or does it offer more modest benefits, thereby aiding or augmenting an existing paradigm already well understood and in use?

If it's the former, then one *killer application* must be pursued relentlessly, sponsored by those visionaries who buy into the promise and thus will deploy it as part of their businesses. If it's the latter, then expectations must be reset and existing business models must be examined and leveraged as appropriate. Unfortunately, there is very little middle ground. And in fast moving high-tech markets, there are precious few moments to dither over our choices.

▶ IRIDIUM FALLS TO EARTH

In 1998, Iridium was launched to the marketplace, and I mean that literally. Over sixty satellites were put into low Earth orbit for the purposes, at least initially, of carrying voice traffic—accessible through a handset—literally from anywhere to anywhere. And it was a glorious thing to behold. Five billion dollars were invested by a consortium of companies and governments, including Russia and China, led by Iridium's chief proponent, sponsor, and investor, Motorola, a company renowned for its technological prowess but also regarded as lacking marketing ability and sophistication. Ironically, Iridium showcased both conditions.

Today, Iridium is in bankruptcy. The company acquired fewer than forty thousand customers worldwide while spending a stunning $100 million in a global advertising campaign to attract them. The top marketing people have been cashiered along with the CEO. Iridium restructured itself—a corporate euphemism for activities born out of dire circumstances, directed either at attracting people willing to spend good money after bad; or figuring out a way of going out of business without too many people, particularly plaintiff's attorneys, noticing. Not finding the former, it succumbed to the latter.

How did they err? Let us count the ways.

First, and most notably, Iridium did not work the way people expected.

The system was supposed to let you call anyone from anywhere. To make such a call, of course, required the user to be outside, positioned so that nothing blocked the line of sight between the handset's antenna and an orbiting satellite. This meant that users could not be in buildings or in cars! This is the killer application? This is the order-of-magnitude improvement over the status quo that will draw visionaries like bees to a field of new flowers? To make matters worse, the vaunted and time-honored *demo,* revered by technology enthusiasts everywhere, didn't always work. *Quelle surprise!*

The handset itself resembled the walkie-talkie depicted in World War II movies. There was also a kit full of accessories and adapters that came with the handset. Because the handset weighed about one pound, you couldn't really clip one onto your belt (and keep your trousers up in the process). And it was too large to fit in a shoulder bag or briefcase with a laptop PC, a PalmPilot, a mobile phone, and other dedicated devices that no self-respecting techie would be without. So how were you going to carry the damn thing? (Perhaps an Eddie Bauer model with its own backpack?)

Did I mention the price? Iridium's price initially was a staggering $3,000 for the equipment plus operating charges that approached $7 per minute. Later, Iridium dropped the equipment price to $1,500 with a corresponding reduction in airtime charges. I don't know about you, but my last mobile phone cost about $70, with airtime running at approximately $0.10 per minute. It clips on my belt and I get to use it in buildings and cars!

Finally, Iridium's marketing planning and execution was, for the most part, decentralized among its numerous partner organizations. These regional organizations, called *gateways,* were expected to drum up demand for the phone and service in their local markets. They didn't. When the global marketing campaign was launched, most local distributors were starting with few, if any, customers to serve as references. Moreover, recalling an old adage long respected within the advertising business—namely, that nothing hastens the death of a bad product faster than good advertising—Iridium's advertising generated lots of prospect inquiries—reportedly over one million after the first few weeks of the campaign. Lacking the proper channels and sales infrastructure to follow up, these potential leads went down the proverbial rat hole. They were not heard from again.

Wireless enthusiasts hoped that Iridium would rise again. The company, or what was left of it, tried pursuing the pager market and the wireless phone business, promising North American subscribers that they would never have to speak to foreign operators or worry about international dialing codes. I guess there must be a unique and compelling benefit there somewhere.

◄

On a more positive note, let's consider some key questions we need to think about when planning for early markets:

- Who is the "first" set of customers?
- What do these customers need to know to become interested in or attracted to the new technology and product?
- How will the new product create and deliver value?

THE FIRST CUSTOMER

Early market customers are the first technology enthusiasts looking to test the technology, followed, importantly, by visionaries gauging whether or not the innovation can really be tamed, mastered, and utilized to put them out front. What techies lack in funding, they make up for in commitment and influence, perhaps even exuberance. **Visionaries, on the other hand, are whom you target in strategy and program development.** They represent real money and real influence with other visionaries—typically, of course, outside their own competitive set. Therefore, begin by seeding technology enthusiasts with the product so that they may educate and influence the visionary. But make sure that your identified visionaries are highly placed within their organizations and have the clout to influence their firms' adoption of something that will remain fraught with risk for the foreseeable future.

Early markets typically form around individual customers rather than customer segments. Such customers do not want to be seen as part of a herd, nor do they wish to be herded. Rather, they intend to use the new technology to differentiate themselves from the herd. Not surprisingly, we can sometimes peg where an innovation is on the TALC—for example, in the early market—if there are a number of high-profile customers who appear from many different market segments.

TO DEVELOP THE EARLY MARKET, WHAT DO THESE CUSTOMERS NEED TO KNOW?

Technology enthusiasts, for the most part, are interested in new technologies for their own sake. Techies need to know that the new innovation is a breakthrough—is "cool"—and thus warrants time and energy to investigate it. "Who knows? It may even be useful," they might be heard to say. Visionaries, however, will subject the innovation to considerably greater scrutiny, asking themselves these questions:

- Will the innovation deliver significant, sustainable advances over what is now available? Is a sustainable *killer application* likely to emerge that will result in order-of-magnitude benefits, thereby potentially reshaping the competitive landscape for those who can employ it successfully—and be the first to do so?
- Will it distance me from competitors by creating barriers to entry owing to its complexity? (This can be considered as a head start for visionaries.)
- Are the purveyors of this innovation likely to demonstrate and sustain a whatever-it-takes commitment to advancing the innovation, based notably on the desires of those who adopt it first?
- Can I have personal influence on the direction of both the innovation itself and the company that brings it to market?
- Will other people whom I respect adopt it for their own advantages as well?

As part of their due diligence, visionaries will also consider the overall question of whether the new innovation is likely to initiate the formation of an entirely new value chain or will supplant an existing element of the value chain. Thus, to understand the visionaries' quandary, we must first understand another fundamental model of high-tech market development: *the value chain*.

HOW WILL THE NEW PRODUCT CREATE AND DELIVER VALUE?

Markets are made up of value chains. For most high-tech markets, a typical chain looks like the following figure:

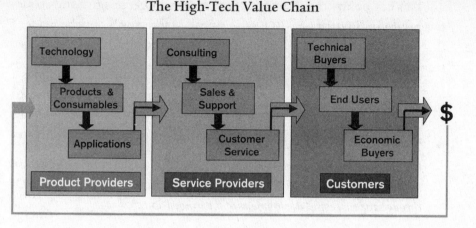

Purveyors of high-tech innovations must concern themselves with (from left to right):

1. Developing a novel technology.
2. Forming a product out of this technology.
3. Building an application and/or system that exploits the features and benefits of the technology and product.
4. Delivering the new application, determining how it will be sold, supported, and nurtured. The four boxes in the diagram thus can be considered the *vendor domain.*

The *customer domain* consists of three potential buyers, all of whom can be one and the same person or can be three separate people:

1. The technical buyer, who takes title to the application and systematizes it further such that end users can use it.
2. The end user who will actually use the new application.
3. The economic buyer who sponsors the acquisition of the new application and commits the funds for its purchase.

The value chain can be likened to an electrical circuit whereby if any one of the "gates" does not close, the "light" will not go on. The light in this case is the *economic return on the total original investment.*

This last point—that economic buyers actually get positive and attractive return on investment (ROI)—is critical. Markets will only be made if the return associated with the purchase causes additional purchases throughout a given customer community or *segment*. Absent actual return, there is no reinvestment and no additional purchasing, and thus a market will not be made for the new product.

▶ *Therefore, early markets form when, and only when, new technologies become solutions that can be delivered, supported, and sustained through an appropriate channel—and economic buyers receive demonstrable ROI through the successful deployment of the innovation.*

Bear in mind that ROI is calculated for the sum total of the investment necessary to obtain a given benefit. For example, my return on investment for a given personal computer application includes the cost of the personal computer (should I need to obtain one), the cost of the software application, and any start-up or ongoing support that I may require to enable me to use the application. This total cost consideration will become a crucial factor when we consider our move to the mainstream market.

Consider also that whereas continuous innovations leverage existing value chains to sustain themselves, discontinuous innovations must form *new value chains* in order to be adopted. The stronger the existing value chain, the more difficult it will be to dislodge that chain. This is the initial hurdle—and a high one at that—that new technologies and products must surmount.

LEARNING TO WORK BACKWARD

Thus, one of the first keys to high-tech market wisdom is to learn to read the value chain like a Hebrew text, from right to left, instead of vice versa. The first goal of marketing should be to follow the money—or, more accurately, to find it in the first place. We then endeavor to devise a system whereby we move it to our own pockets. The only way to do this legitimately is to *earn* it, through effective value creation. This is done, in effect, by working *backward,* ensuring that there is a predictable, if not smooth, transition through every step of the value chain, bearing in mind that hiccups along the way will have adverse consequences.

Using a systems approach to value creation, we have also learned another important lesson. As products move into *self-sustaining* markets—that is to say, as the ROI associated with a new product becomes predictable and can be reinvested in a pervasive way—technology providers tend to lose control, often even when they hold strong patent positions, as with xerography and laser printing. Thus, the closer you are to the right-hand side—that is, the side of the chain where the money is—the better your chance for getting or improving your share of it. Many technically driven entrepreneurs and the companies they spawn have been content to make great technical discoveries on the left, never developing the capacity to engage in the marketing morass on the right. This may be appealing to some—marketing can be exhausting and depressing, to say the least—but such contentment is obtained at a substantial, often ruinous price.

DECLARING VICTORY IN THE EARLY MARKET

Most, if not all, business-to-business markets are driven by the ultimate economic buyer making money. If you adopt this view, you can always identify ways in which some class of economic buyer is either losing money or missing out on a moneymaking opportunity. Once that becomes your focus, you can map a path back to the technologies that can correct this customer condition. This means that marketers must truly understand the dynamics of value creation, first by understanding the true nature and scope of the customer's current problem. This understanding must result in true solution creation, rather than just creating platitudes or empty promises as part of a promotional campaign. It is also extremely good practice that will sustain us during the travails and tribulations that we will encounter when making the passage to the mainstream market.

▶ CONSULTING 101: FINDING THE BREAKS IN THE CHAIN

Want to be a consultant to the high-tech industry? We won't debate your undoubtedly questionable motives or psychological profile here. Instead, and suffice it to say, the modern art and science of management consulting is shrouded in myth, theory, dogma, and *black box solutions* ad nauseam. Led by the large management consulting firms and the business schools whose graduates man the production lines, consultants engage in a never-ending quest to *add significant value by providing sound analytical insights and creating best-practice solutions for client competitive advantage.*

Sound intriguing? Now you, too, can learn to do this in your spare time!

Seriously, the high-tech value chain represents one of the most useful tools, not to mention thought processes, that one can utilize to assess both high-tech market opportunities and problems (the latter usually referred to as *challenges*). How can you make it work for you?

Recall that value is created when a given *technology* becomes available and accessible through *products.* These products are then assembled into *whole products*—that is, solutions that serve specific customer needs. The solutions are then made available via packaging, sales and promotional materials, documentation, and training to the appropriate *sales channel.* The sales channel then sells the solution to an organization where title may be taken by the technically competent—for example, an IT organization. This department then installs and supports the solution so that *end users* can perform their duties in a more effective or efficient way, thereby causing the *economic buyer,* typically a ranking executive who sponsored the purchase, to receive an attractive return on his or her investment (ROI).

What we know is that any time there is weakness or an actual break in the value chain, ROI will not be realized, or, as importantly, its *expected* realization becomes questionable or unclear. Such problems spell big trouble for each constituency profile represented in the TALC. How? Each constituency tends to focus on a key transition point represented in the vendor domain.

For example, technology enthusiasts sniff out the weaknesses inherent in the technology itself and its transition to product. They concern themselves with this almost exclusively since their technical reputation is at stake, and they're likely to have to fix—perhaps continually—technology defects and deficiencies.

Visionaries will examine whether the product's inherent benefits are sufficiently breakthrough such that replacing their current systems and technologies with this new stuff will provide fairly immediate and sustainable competitive advantage. Their fixation with the *product-to-solution* part of the value chain owes to the rather significant choices they must make. Do I commit my company to this direction or to that? What will give me the biggest bang for my buck?

Pragmatists are examining this transition point as well, but for different reasons. He or she wants to know whether this new value chain will actually harden sufficiently such that it stands a good chance of replacing existing paradigms, albeit in a predictable, evolutionary manner. If the pragmatist must adopt the new chain or paradigm due to insurmountable problems associated with existing systems, will the new chain deliver, unequivocally, the ROI it promises?

Conservatives are looking at value chains as a way of examining how to achieve maximum value in adopting what is now a clearly safe and sane technology. The transition point under the conservatives' microscope is that between *system* and *sales channel.* Quite simply, where can I get the best deal for the longest time from the most predictable, stable source with me dictating or influencing significantly the terms and conditions of the relationship and/or exchange?

Skeptics, true to form, do not want to be exposed to new value chains, preferring instead to look for products that fit completely into existing paradigms or can be outsourced altogether to service providers.

Finally, to really understand high-tech value chains, it's useful to reflect once again on some more notable market failures, or "markets in waiting," during the past five years or so.

Consider such fanciful and promising technologies that flopped initially as actual products or applications: Apple's Newton, artificial intelligence, speech recognition, smart cards, and biometrics come to mind. The technological underpinnings of each of these were laudable. Yet each failed in its initial incarnation, each stumbling from one step of the chain to the next. Bad engineering? Bad marketing? Yes. But more likely, bad value chain management. And while some of these today are now flourishing, the cost of failure to the initial investors and their champions is breathtaking.

Now, let's get back to your fledgling education as a consultant. What's the first thing the consultant does?

Find the break points in the value chain! Often, organizations can't (or won't) see that something is amiss, sometimes egregiously so. Next, we look at what needs to be done to fix that which is broken. Then we examine whether the organization assigned (or sentenced) to fix the problem really can do so. Finally, we consider stopgap measures that might be undertaken to address or avoid immediate marketplace unpleasantness. And we try to do all this without making the client feel too bad, too angry, or too stupid in the process.

4

The Chasm

All great changes are irksome to the human mind, especially those which are attended with great dangers and uncertain effects.

—John Quincy Adams

In 1991, with the publishing of the first edition of *Crossing the Chasm,* Geoffrey Moore introduced a new term into the lexicon of high technology: the chasm. (By the way, chasm is pronounced *kasm,* like "kitchen," and not **chasm,** like "children.") The chasm metaphor was used to describe a sort of market development twilight zone, devoid of Rod Serling to be sure, but just as strange and unfathomable as the stories told in his American television series of some forty years ago.

The chasm is born out of a simple yet extremely important idea: namely, that for any given discontinuous innovation, an early market will develop more or less as expected; followed by a period during which sales may stall, recede, even plummet; followed, in turn, by a period where sales will resume. However, this recovery period will not be at an expected or even hoped-for rate, but at a rate coincident with the number of customer segments possessing specific attributes that now turn to the innovation for specific reasons.

We can illustrate this metaphorical chasm as a gulf separating technology enthusiasts and visionaries who constitute the early market from the

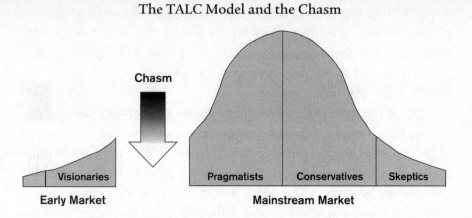

The TALC Model and the Chasm

mainstream market comprising pragmatists, conservatives, and skeptics.

As a practical matter, there are a number of specific dynamics that play out during a chasm period. The first slap in the head is that we do not anticipate this predicament. But, in fact, as the rate of discontinuous innovation introduction has accelerated, chasm events now seem pervasive throughout our high-tech world, and the TALC model we have turned to for salvation now appears to lead us astray in its predictive ability. For example, it is of no use in helping us time our market development. Make no mistake, time *is* an implied dynamic throughout the TALC; however, the model itself references population distribution and the psychographic attributes associated with various segments that comprise a population. But *the TALC is not about time!* It is only our own impatience to develop a market for our new widget quickly and efficiently that leads us down this garden path.

Moreover, because we did not plan for the chasm, its effects are not in our plan, either. Thus, for a time, anyhow, we bumble along hoping things will get better, hoping this will all go away. Compounding our folly, we may even engage in activities guaranteed to prolong the chasm period and thus our agonies.

At the same time, competitors who may not be able to introduce a similar market innovation of their own join ranks to preserve the status quo. In so doing, they raise the FUD specter—*fear, uncertainty,* and *doubt*—

about the future prospects for the new technology and the purveyors of it. This can have a chilling effect on the intruder's ability to raise additional rounds of financing, build alliances in hopes of building out a new value chain, and so on. But the largest impact of FUD is on future customers. It can play out in two ways.

First, if the competition is only minimally successful in raising legitimate issues about the viability of the new category, interested early adopting pragmatists, seeing no real "gotchas" to this new paradigm, may come to the fore, effectively shrinking the gap that hopeful visionaries could utilize to their advantage. This early adoption by the herd unnerves the remaining visionaries who now search for other, even more discontinuous solutions. At the same time, those pragmatists who *are* affected by the FUD arguments from the status quo search for reasons to stay on the sidelines. And they find them. There may be plenty of pragmatists running *special* or *pilot projects,* using the new technology, but there is nothing really in production. Thus, both groups—visionaries and pragmatists—effectively abandon the new technology in its infancy. Left on its own, the technology drifts to the fringes of the overall market or passes into obscurity.

All of which brings us to the next point: *pragmatists do not trust visionaries as credible references.* In the early market, most of our initial work is focused on winning early converts to the cause. First customers are just that: first customers. For most discontinuous innovations, they will not be like our future customers.

Although pragmatists and visionaries are adjacent to each other on the TALC, they may be likened to the various ethnic factions composing the populations of the Balkan States in Europe. The values, customs, lifestyles, even language upheld by each of the various groups vying for power or control of their own destinies make it practically impossible for one group to communicate *effectively and meaningfully* with another.

The table on the next page summarizes these two groups' attitudes and demeanor relative to discontinuous and/or early market innovations.

We have witnessed numerous examples of visionary/pragmatist abandonment, from expert systems and computer-aided software engineering (CASE) tools to the early personal digital assistants, frame-relay networking, so-called network computers, at least initially, and genetic fragment analysis. Each of these promising technologies turned out to be a promise unfulfilled. Many chasm technologies and products linger on, but the

VISIONARIES	PRAGMATISTS
Intuitive	Analytic
Seek revolutionary advances	Seek evolutionary advances
Contrarian	Conformist
Self-referencing	Reference others perceived as similar
Avoid the herd	Stay with the herd
Risk-taking	Risk-averse
Motivated by future opportunities	Motivated by current problems
Seek what is possible	Pursue what is probable
Will seek best technology	Will seek best solution or vendor

—adapted from Geoffrey A. Moore, *Inside the Tornado* (HarperBusiness, 1995)

costs they engender to perpetuate them typically far outstrip any real revenues, not to mention the opportunity costs associated with sticking with a loser, rather than backing winners.

Since market success is possible only when innovations cross the chasm, management teams demanded that all their products achieve this feat. "The TALC predicts this eventuality so let it be now" resonated through many an executive management team meeting. Happily, many companies now realize that chasms are indeed strange places and that the promise of mainstream markets may be more than just a little challenging to reach. However, we shall cross that chasm when we come to it.

Let's recap:

1. Chasm periods do not always develop during the life cycle of a new technology, but the more discontinuous the technology is, the more it deviates from the status quo—either in real or perceived terms—the more likely it is that the conditions for a chasm period will develop and subsequently occur.
2. Chasms typically affect all market entrants sponsoring products that manifest the discontinuity, and not just one vendor's product.
3. Chasms can persist for indefinite periods. Given the pace of innovation, product categories that remain in the chasm for longer than two

years can be considered lost in the chasm, sometimes irretrievably so.

4. Chasms are *not* the result of bad technologies or bad products per se, but rather of *incomplete* technologies or products. This, in turn, inhibits the creation of a compelling and attractive value chain. Weak value chains do not attract suitable levels of market investment to advance because the projected or actual ROI is difficult to understand and forecast.

5. Chasms *do* result because the customers who have adopted the product early on simply do not serve as satisfactory references to people who have yet to adopt.

▶ DOES ANYBODY REALLY KNOW WHAT TIME IT IS? DOES ANYBODY REALLY CARE?

One reason we fall prey to misinterpreting the Technology Adoption Life Cycle may be related to our own individual interpretation of and comfort with *time as a concept* and how it affects, even runs, our lives. Previously, I spoke of technology vendors using the TALC as a device to time their market development activities. We are trained to run our businesses with a keen eye for timing investment to payback. We don't want to over- or underinvest such that our time to payback, internal rate of return, or other measure of asset utilization is off ratio. So it is no surprise that we search for models that will help us forecast. Americans, in particular, seem to have a notable preoccupation with models and will create them to define or postulate a desired outcome. In my time as both client and consultant, I, too, searched for tools that would help me define and predict my environment. Our devotion to the models described in this book is an outgrowth of my search, and that of my partners, for rational explanations to seemingly irrational events.

When helping a client to diagnose a condition or problem, we naturally turn to the Technology Adoption Life Cycle. I have always been struck by how differently three organizations—engineering, marketing, and sales—speak of the time necessary for markets to develop as they themselves planned.

In my experience, engineers typically expect markets to take quite some time to develop fully. After all, they reason, some of this discontinuous stuff that they invented took them a long time to control and master. Many engineers seem to feel that it is reasonable, even preferable, that organizations should adopt a more mature, long view about their businesses. They complain, sometimes bitterly, that they feel pressured by marketing and sales management to bring a new technology to market before it is completely "baked."

I have witnessed firsthand how many of their breed will seemingly dawdle until deadlines become onerous before actually getting close to finishing, let alone being able to actually ship the final version of something. I admit to being somewhat sympathetic to this condition owing to my own tendencies toward procrastination. I therefore postulate that most research and development (R&D) and engineering organizations operate tacitly on an "infinity minus one day" time frame. The "minus one day" refers to the day actual sanctions will be imposed should the deadline not be met. Not surprisingly, Silicon Valley engineering departments' consumption of pizza, Coca-Cola, and other caffeinated beverages reaches new zeniths just prior to the one-day deadline.

Sales organizations, on the other hand, seem almost the polar opposite in their time orientation. During our workshops and situation assessments, salespeople routinely complain that the market for new product X will never meet projections because (1) they are too high to begin with; (2) it will take too much time to develop the market profitably; (3) there are numerous deficiencies in the current version that will take months to sort out; and (4) X is not what their current customers want now. The final reason typically is of the "Why bother?" variety, since the market will be captured or otherwise undermined by more nimble-footed competitors whose sales organizations operate with both greater autonomy and more support.

"I can't spend a lot of time with this stuff searching for a market and still make a living," these salespeople are heard to say. And, like Bill Clinton, we feel their pain. Not surprisingly, therefore, sales forces that often display a collective attention span similar to that of a five-year-old boy expect things to develop quickly—and if they do not, the same salespeople will just as quickly marshal their arguments to justify a significant forecast reduction.

When the market does not develop as either group expects, we, along with senior management, turn our collective attention to the group now responsible for this insult—the marketing department—perennial fall guys for TALC misinterpretation.

How did this rush to judgment come about? Well, marketing organizations do something every year that puts them precisely in the bull's-eye. They write an annual marketing and budget plan detailing the revenue forecasts and spending plans of the organization in general, and for the new product specifically. The net effect of this plan is to make a prediction—and record it for posterity—how things should go for the coming twelve to eighteen months. In some instances, a really *strategic* marketing plan is conceived, preceded typically by an off-site meeting at some resort facility, that forecasts with a .8 probability what the next three years will look like. In any event, when asked how long it will take the market to develop, marketing's usual answer will be "twelve to eighteen months or so." Why? "Because that's what the plan calls for."

This devotion to carefully analyzing and documenting how the market will develop leads inexorably to the following soon after the market fails to behave as expected (they are given in order of occurrence): (1) more off-site meetings with a correspondingly high utilization of slide presentations that strive to explain, in detail, the obvious; (2) further planning sessions with attendant documentation to account for what went wrong and what we will do about it *now,* to fix things before they get really out of control or somebody really vocal or important notices; (3) a complete (and massive) new set of PowerPoint presentations and other merchandising materials that reposition the offending product from its insolent initial prospects to those more to our liking or orientation ("We need to support the field through this challenging transition that we have always known would occur"); and (4) the inevitable hunt for the guilty with coincident reorganizations or purges resulting in some people leaving the organization "in order to pursue other, more entrepreneurial opportunities."

Thus, I submit for your consideration that marketing departments always get it in the neck when markets don't develop in a timely fashion. Why? *They wrote the plan!*

◀

5

The Bowling Alley

Marketing is like bowling, except you wear better shirts.

—GEOFFREY A. MOORE

The territory we call the *bowling alley* lies just at the other side of the chasm. You might think of it as the place where our discontinuous innovation, now perhaps suitably humbled during its time navigating the chasm, once again makes landfall. It is here that we will develop and execute our *market penetration* strategy designed to take us into the pragmatist "heartland." We will discuss how to build this strategy in Part 2. In the meantime, let's review what we know—and need to know—about bowling alley market development.

First, why "bowling alley"? The origin of the metaphor is based on considering the first pragmatist segment to be won over as a kind of headpin. Bowling devotees know the key to success is striking the headpin in such a fashion that the combination of the rolling ball and the pins falling into one another causes the maximum number of pins ultimately to fall. The more pins that fall, the more points you receive.

So it is with high-tech marketing. Developing a viable market in the bowling alley is accomplished through what can also be called *niche* market development. The niches are identifiable customer segments arrayed in tenpin fashion owing to each segment having a *referential relationship* with its neighboring segment. This relationship is based on two ideas that are the key to understanding how bowling alley markets develop: *shared applications* and *word-of-mouth referencing.*

The bowling pin model can be depicted as follows:

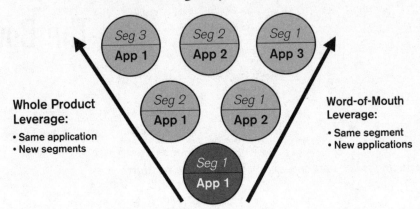

Bowling Alley Model

Shared applications in this sense means that two similar but not necessarily identical segments could use the same application. In some instances, these two groups or individuals, say a marketing director and her financial analyst, might literally share a PC spreadsheet application or graphics package. The reason the application can be used by two similar groups is basic: The application achieves the same goal—solves the same problem—experienced by both groups. This, then, is the power of whole product leverage.

Word-of-mouth referencing here means that these same two groups might seek each other out in order to gain more information about such an application. They do this because they each believe that the other group has experience with the application, insight into how the application works under various scenarios familiar to each, and, summarily, an educated point of view concerning the ultimate efficacy of the application and from whom to obtain it. In our example, then, the marketing director, wishing to do some analyses that call for the use of a spreadsheet, seeks counsel from her financial analyst, whom she knows uses spreadsheets every day, albeit not necessarily for identical reasons. The financial analyst, in this case, is a *trusted source of expert knowledge* about an application that while common still retains some degree of risk and uncertainty as perceived by the marketing director, owing to its complexity and, perhaps, user interface. This is the power of word-of-mouth leverage.

While the example may seem a bit commonplace and obvious, it underpins a hugely important idea for mainstream market development, that of *segmentation.* In order to develop a bowling pin market development model, we must take seriously the mission of dividing a market into its component pieces.

MAKING SENSE OF SEGMENTATION

The discipline of consumer marketing, notably that of packaged goods marketing (that is, the items you and I buy in our local supermarkets—from shampoo to canned peas), is rooted in consumer segmentation. Packaged goods marketers constantly seek to understand the various demographic and psychographic attributes of their customers and prospects. Demographics—the science of grouping people by attributes such as gender, age, race and ethnicity, education, and income—is a well-understood practice. As direct-response marketers will tell you, the database, data warehousing, and search engine capabilities now at our disposal make it possible for us to target our audience literally on a home-by-home basis.

Psychographic segmentation attempts to aggregate consumer segments by, for example, their values, behaviors, beliefs, and lifestyles. Both these forms of segmentation are highly appropriate and conducive not only to the development of demand-generating functions like advertising, but also to the creation of new products targeted at specific groups and subgroups of customers. Having worked in packaged goods, I can tell you that people rarely get up from their desks, let alone make important marketing decisions, without checking first for what the most recent research says about the subject!

If only it were so easy in high tech.

While demographic and psychographic data are important and useful in understanding and targeting various groups for advertising, as an example, we are still left with many questions unanswered as to how we will develop our market on a pin-by-pin—or, more accurately, a niche-by-niche—basis. Through years of being disappointed by the shortcomings of various qualitative and quantitative research approaches to determine customer segments, it became apparent to me that conventional descriptions and definitions of customer segments, like those noted above, needed to be reconsidered in a far more practical way.

Accordingly, we define a *segment* as follows:

▶ *Any self-referencing group of people with common needs, wants, problems, or aspirations that could and would be likely to use a common or similar application.*

The idea that segments self-reference each other is critical to understanding how bowling alley markets develop. However, as a general rule, segments reference each other in high-tech markets specifically as a way of *managing and mitigating risk*. Risk is inherently present in virtually all high-technology markets and can assume four forms:

- **Adoption risk:** the risk that a chosen solution or application will not be useful or deliver positive ROI because it is too difficult to use, requires too much behavioral change, or its benefits are not substantial enough.
- **Solution risk:** the risk that a chosen solution or application will not be able to be easily replicated, supported, and sustained because it is hard to assemble, deploy, or otherwise does not integrate well into existing systems.
- **Marketing risk:** the risk that a chosen solution or application will be difficult to source, purchase, or obtain support for.
- **Business risk:** the risk that a chosen vendor will remain viable and thus able to advance the innovation beyond its early versions.

Prospects in general, and pragmatists and conservatives specifically, reference people they trust and, not surprisingly, those they perceive to be most like them. It's also apparent that risk mitigation is not strictly a function of price—that is, whether something costs a little or a lot. Consider, for example, how many times you have bought a relatively inexpensive high-tech product, like a simple home/office software application or a peripheral product for your personal computer, only to retire it to the shelf in frustration because you can't use it properly. Thus, the acid test is whether each of the four forms of risk noted above can be successfully predicted and accounted for, and thus we seek out people like us who have gone before us.

Demographic and psychographic data alone do not, in my opinion, offer sufficient insights into how birds of a feather *might* flock together when presented with high-tech adoption choices. Instead, our first segment—the head bowling pin—determines our initial approach. Each segment, corresponding to the remaining bowling pins, is derived from our headpin based on the attributes associated with that segment.

LET'S GO BOWLING

Our goal in the bowling alley is to continue our chasm-crossing strategy in the hopes that our new product can win adoption in market niches. If we are successful in attracting these niches to our cause, we stand a chance at winning widespread adoption with potentially all pragmatists comprising a given market. While we can take some solace for making it this far, our ultimate goal is the tornado.

So why can't we go there right now, directly to the tornado? First, pragmatists typically remain with current value chains (or paradigms) until they are no longer viable or until they are forced to move. Second, while a group of pragmatists now believes that your new product is legitimate, other pragmatists, exhibiting the referencing behavior described previously, are asking themselves in effect, "What is in it for me, and people like me?" Not finding the immediate answer, they tend to remain at rest, waiting for a *generalized* product that can and will be adopted by the pragmatist fraternity as a whole.

Bowling alley niche markets typically represent profitable and sustainable customer franchises that will allow us to develop our next product versions based not on the demands or musings of visionaries, but on the studied needs of the pragmatists now implementing our new value chain into value chains of their own. Our challenge at this point is concentrating *solely* on building out our value chain based on our chosen bowling pin model.

Do not get distracted here! Niche markets have several unique characteristics that, if ignored, result in vendor frustration. They include:

- Niche markets may need highly tailored applications based on specific requirements.
- Niche customers do not weigh alternative solutions on the basis of the strength of the technology or product itself, but rather on how complete each alternative is compared to each of the others.
- Niche customers evaluate alternatives based on demonstrable measures, notably return on investment (ROI).

As a result, niche customers seek out a single vendor who can deliver a highly application-specific solution that addresses particular issues unique to the needs of the niche. For perhaps the first time, these niche market pragmatists are heard to say:

"I don't care about all the technical mumbo jumbo or which product is supposed to be better. I just want to know that whoever we choose knows something about our business . . . can prove it through their proposed solution . . . and has done it before successfully, in situations just like ours."

BECOMING A LEADER

At this stage of market development, we see the pragmatist *herd* mentality begin to emerge. Niches involved in early mainstream markets typically are not large enough to support multiple vendor offerings, nor are they really looking to do so. Instead, competitive alternatives are now being screened based on the criteria listed above. Thus, in order to prosper, you must win this competition and cause to be expelled all those who would challenge you.

"Sure," you say, "all my competition will just go away." Well, they just might. If our experiences with many different product categories in bowling alley markets can be generalized, we find that few companies actually navigate this market as successfully as they otherwise might, particularly if we measure success by the key bowling alley metric, *segment,* rather than market share.

Consider again the strategic imperatives of the bowling alley. Since you have reached this point in the TALC, you have an innovative product that is highly prized by your current customer base, consisting primarily of technology enthusiasts and visionaries. In order to win over pragmatists segment by segment, you must focus your efforts on those you can persuade first to adopt your product because it solves a pressing problem that they now experience—a problem that if ignored will cause even greater pain going forward. You earn this group's business by replacing its aging, now crippled application or system (read *value chain*) for your own. This is only possible because you have completed your product—that is, made it whole based on your knowledge of the customer's problem and your overarching commitment to solving it. Word gets around! It seems now that other pragmatists, now referencing the segment(s) you have been focusing on, consider your approach not only effective but safe and desirable as well. These customers now award you even more business. Better still, you are now labeled as *vendor of choice* for this application—the "vendor di tutti vendors." This imprimatur now puts other competitors on notice and further discourages other market entrants from competing for your segments.

Lest your head swell at this point, remember that you are not considered a *product* leader but rather a leader in a specific *application* market. You have won this market but not necessarily the product category as a whole. Nevertheless, this is an extremely important win. Unlike a tornado market, in which product categories serve as the reference points, leaders in bowling alley markets might be considered future product leaders in training, poised to compete in the tornado should it emerge. If it does not, you have built a potentially long-lasting business among grateful customers who trust you and sing your praises.

THE POWER OF LEADERSHIP

Market leader. Sounds good, doesn't it? It sounds good to pragmatists as well. For pragmatists are interested in pursuing evolutionary approaches to their business and technology infrastructures. This is why they prefer markets that are self-organizing and self-selecting, resulting in a market leader. Conversely, markets without clear leaders are anathema to pragmatists because such markets appear as unstable, unpredictable, and therefore unattractive.

Once a category market leader does emerge, it serves to validate not only the market leader itself but also the category in general. Evidence of this validation now appears in many forms, from third parties ensuring that their offerings are now compatible with those of the leader to the various pundits and gurus now extolling the merits of this new market to other pragmatists now adopting similarly. Customers in the adopting niches now regard their judgment and subsequent purchase as even more fortuitous because a market is now being made for this innovation, thereby ensuring good return on investment—probably, even more than originally considered or hoped for. This newly functioning value chain now attracts even more players eager to contribute to this newly emergent (at least among pragmatists) market in an ever-expanding effort to feed from the same trough.

Of course, many of these entrants will be loath to support other, lesser-known competitors or platforms for the simple reason that while the market seems to be burgeoning, it is still comprised of niches. As such, there is probably not the bandwidth nor payback to support different approaches. Sponsoring vendors of other application approaches or platforms become increasingly *marginalized* because pragmatists are now herding about their chosen market leader.

▶ "THEM THAT'S GOT SHALL GET, THEM THAT'S NOT
   SHALL LOSE . . ."

The most notable and perhaps the most costly example of the *marginalized product syndrome* of the past decade must be IBM's OS/2 operating system. Remember it?

The story begins in the mid-1980s with the vast majority of PC users still slogging along with autoexec.bat, C:\> commands, and other anachronisms associated with MS- or PC-DOS. Some of us, of course, had seen the light— or couldn't bear the pain—and thus were using Apple's Macintosh operating system. Noting an inexorable trend toward graphical user interfaces (GUIs), first pioneered by Xerox and sustained by the Mac's success, Microsoft introduced its initial versions of Windows. Incorporating a Mac-like graphical user interface (remember that lawsuit?), it was an order-of-magnitude improvement on DOS—when it worked. Not to be outdone, IBM introduced OS/2, its related but competitive answer to Windows and its designated heir to the DOS throne. It, too, exhibited a number of eccentricities, all of which provided us Mac users great delight on our way to becoming even more insufferably smug.

DOS persisted as the clear market standard until Microsoft could finally field a stable version of Windows called 3.1. Early adopting pragmatists pronounced 3.1 "safe and effective," causing DOS devotees to move to it in droves. Microsoft further upped the stakes by preannouncing Windows 95, an OS that would not be built on top of DOS but would instead represent the next generation of PC operating system. IBM, meanwhile, gloated that its latest version of OS/2 could "do Windows better than Windows, and DOS better than DOS." Unfortunately, users decided that it could do neither. Application developers, tired of being both cajoled and bullied by each camp to support their approach, in addition to supporting DOS and Macintosh, decided they had heard enough.

Market dynamics now took on the flavor of elective politics. On election days, the news media stage all kinds of so-called exit polls in an attempt to call the winners and the losers prior to the completion of actual polling and vote tabulation. So it was with Windows and OS/2. The pundits called the race early, and developers validated this prediction with their support. There was room enough for two GUI-based operating systems—Mac and Windows—but not three. The ultimate expression of this conclusion was now evident in starkly apparent terms. You could walk into your local computer or software dealer and find three floor-to-ceiling racks of software applications based on DOS, Windows, and Macintosh. The OS/2 rack consisted of a few shelves, and the pickings were meager, indeed. The situation at this point was irreversible for IBM.

While it is hindsight at this stage, I often wonder how things might have turned out if IBM had abandoned the desktop battle in favor of competing on grounds more to their tradition and strength. For example, what would the competitive landscape look like now if IBM had recast OS/2 as a *server* operating system, since the client/server computing paradigm at the time was beginning to show signs of significant and persistent vitality? Where would Microsoft NT be, or the various flavors of UNIX? IBM was counseled to pursue this direction many times by many different sources. But, unfortunately, revenue and unit shipment promises had been made and the die was cast, the mold now broken. IBM went on to invest literally billions of dollars trying to salvage OS/2, later to effectively abandon it when a new management team asked some embarrassing and obvious questions.

Intrinsically, there was nothing really wrong with OS/2. Simply put, OS/2 failed to garner market support because pragmatists saw no advantage to such an outcome.

◄

This example serves to underscore the prime directive of the bowling alley: *You must build a dominant presence in each bowling pin segment.* Those of you with longings for the tornado will celebrate the day you committed to this goal. Those who engage in a haphazard approach to this pursuit will similarly mark their decision as perhaps the dumbest thing they and their organizations ever did. The reasons will become glaringly apparent when we review the dynamics of market tornadoes. What is dominant market share? We think of it as winning approximately 40 percent of our target in twelve to eighteen months. Such dominance virtually assures that any competitors are not able to achieve this number. Of course, this is a guideline, not a rule. By the same token, coming in second or third in the race is not a preferable option. Put simply, to invoke word-of-mouth referencing among pragmatists, pragmatists need to make sure you're the winner. That is who they feel safe buying from—and it's what they tell their friends.

If a segment can't account for this level of business because it's already well served by another vendor that has established itself as a market leader, or if the segment is otherwise unwinnable by you during this time frame, it's best to choose and pursue a different segment. All of which brings us to some final thoughts concerning this aspect of market development.

PICKING AND CHOOSING

In the bowling alley, we are asking customers to get off their duffs and do something. For them, this involves advancing into the unknown, ahead of the herd, putting hard-won budgets—and perhaps promising careers—on the line, all because their current processes just aren't working very well. *Currently,* that is.

If you were that customer, wouldn't you seriously consider waiting a bit longer? Perhaps you might pursue some incremental measures to minimize the discomfort rather than suffer the shock and dislocations sure to be visited on you by new technologies and systems. "Certainly, we should study the problem a bit more to be sure that we're attacking the cause and not just the symptoms," you write thoughtfully in your e-mail to the committee that has formed to examine a problem that most committee members wish would just go away. "Why do these things always happen to me," grumbles the IT director as he puts out one fire only to be faced with another about to go out of control in another part of the organization. And, if you are a good pragmatist, you would be justified both in your feelings and in your response to this new challenge.

If this is the natural state of things, why do most organizations act surprised and frustrated when customers behave this way? Why are we baffled when, following our persuasive sales presentation, customers don't immediately display the desired Pavlovian salivation response coupled with the signing of a letter of intent?

Simple. In the bowling alley, you are asking people to act against their best instincts and do something they really don't want to do. Great, I hear you say; how can we avoid the bowling alley altogether and go right to the tornado? Even in the mythical Internet time, tornadoes can't develop unless the conditions are just right. First, we need a whole product solution that can be generalized. Then we need a whole lot of pragmatists wanting to move our way. How can we at least get started?

Simple again. Just pick the right customer segment to start with. You can recognize them by their **compelling reason to buy your product** (this condition, by the way, should not be confused with your compelling reason to *sell* the product) and by the **absence of any other vendor making a concerted effort to serve the real needs of that segment.**

But wait! Isn't that what we tried to discover in our chasm-crossing strategy? Right again. If you have successfully crossed the chasm, you already know and are prepared for the bowling alley.

Step up there and roll a strike. Do it now. The weather may change at any moment. But, before it does, let's recap the key principles associated with the bowling alley.

1. You must segment your intended market to determine a practical if not optimal bowling pin array. The segment array is determined by two key leverage factors:

   - How easily will your whole product solution migrate from segment to segment?
   - How likely and readily will one segment reference another segment?

2. Segments should be identified in priority based on:

- How compelling their problem is, which implies the degree of urgency they may feel to move to alternative paradigms
- Whether they are currently served by other competitors or potential competitors
- How rapidly you can deploy a whole product solution tailored to the specific needs of the segment in question
- How demonstrable superior returns on investment can be realized by your new approach

3. The customer domain of the value chain must be considered, specifically the economic buyer. It is the economic buyer who will ultimately put up the money to solve the problem and will ultimately suffer the consequences should the problem persist.

4. The goal in bowling alley market development is segment or niche domination. Domination is measured by market share accruing to a particular segment. This argues for targeting segments when such domination can be achieved rapidly. The larger the segment, the more difficult it will be to dominate, as measured in both time and resource allocation.

5. Bowling alley market development does not result in immediate gratification for vendors, is difficult to plan for and execute, and, in a time-driven, time-obsessed business culture, is typically avoided if possible. This avoidance can often result in the creation of a market for someone else more willing to expend the patience and resources niche market development requires.

6

The Tornado

Whenever people talk to me about the weather, I always feel certain that they mean something else.

—OSCAR WILDE

In spring, Mother Nature visits upon the midwestern region of the United States—the tornado. It is a phenomenon of nature so powerful, so destructive, yet so paradoxically fascinating that legions of so-called tornado chasers literally risk life and limb to record and measure the nature and course of its fury. You may recall a popular movie called *Twister* that chronicled the exploits of just such a group. In high tech, we have our own breed of tornado chaser—from venture capitalists to job-hopping executives to market timers looking to invest at just the right moment—who seek the metaphorical, and elusive, tornado.

And so should you.

Market tornadoes can be just as destructive as the real thing, for they obliterate old paradigms with uncompromising finality. During the process, product categories and the companies that represent these new paradigms are lifted from their niche and/or nice-to-have status to that of must-have. Along the way, one company typically is thrust into the position of market leader based on its dominant market share. This leader, if publicly traded, will also enjoy a breathtaking market valuation based on such market leadership. It becomes de facto the company now tied uniquely to the real and perceived benefits of the product category. All other market entrants rushing to cash in on this massive showing of customer largesse will be consigned to secondary roles. It is a form of *natural selection* in action.

But, if tornadoes are destructive, they are creative as well, generating new wealth where none was present before. For customers, tornadoes institutionalize a new infrastructure upon which businesses and organizations will be redefined and reengineered. Tornadoes affect us all. When they happen, they are pervasive; yet they are also elusive and unpredictable as well.

All of which prompts us to wonder about the forces that change a market figuratively blowing as a steady breeze to that of a gale-force wind. Like meteorologists, we ask, "Why and when do they happen?"

Let's review the basics.

THE WINDS OF CHANGE

In nature, tornadoes are spawned fundamentally through significant imbalances in atmospheric pressures. When winter turns to spring in North America, the waning though still frigid Canadian winter generates massive amounts of cold air carried aloft by the jet stream. When these air masses dip southward into the heartland region of the United States, they may collide with a similar mass of moist warm air pushing northward from the Gulf of Mexico. Because these two masses—one sinking, the other rising—are at different pressures, their meeting is quite dramatic. Violent thunderstorms, golf-ball-size hail, and tornadoes are often the result. These atmospheric behemoths literally feed on themselves and can dissipate as quickly as they started once equilibrium is restored.

To understand the dynamics of market tornadoes, we must understand pressures of a different sort; namely, those that are exerted on the people we task with managing our basic infrastructures. These are the poor souls whom we trust to develop, install, and maintain the underlying technologies of our businesses, from IT platforms to scientific and medical instrumentation to telecommunications switches to myriad other *systems* that we rely on to support our respective trades. These systems seem as if they are always in need of modification or replacement, and the people who mind them are always under pressure to make them all work better, faster, and cheaper.

Along comes a new way of doing things, a discontinuous innovation that has proven its mettle in niche markets, one that promises to change fundamentally how business, even life, will proceed in the future, holding out the prospect of a new age of prosperity and competitive advantage for those wise enough to adopt it. Of course, the IT people have heard this before. Of course, it is their responsibility to investigate, something that they usually are quite interested to do. Yet all their instincts say it is too soon to adopt, too soon for the next paradigm shift.

As this investigation proceeds, in a classic consumer as well as human response, these members of the early majority—pragmatists, as you recall—begin to reference their peers as never before. The question at hand: *Is it time to move yet?* Their responses are like those of herd animals, suddenly nervous because something unknown, perhaps dangerous, has been detected at the periphery of their senses.

Moore sums up the IT community's response eloquently.

> If [they] move too soon, they incur all the trials of early—which is to say premature—adoption, devoting precious resources to debugging systems that a few years later would come already debugged, committing themselves to write in-house protocols that end up being incompatible with the eventual de facto standards, and stretching themselves thin running systems in parallel until the new paradigm is reliable and robust enough to shoulder the load alone. If they move too late, they expose their company to competitive disadvantages as others in their industry operate at lower cost and greater speed by virtue of their more efficient infrastructures. Worst of all, if they move way too late, as often happens to conservatives, they run the risk of getting trapped in end-of-life systems that, with alarming rapidity, become almost impossible to maintain as the staff and the companies that used to support them move on.[1]

Indeed.

Thus, managers face a classic dilemma. If they move too soon, they risk exposure to potentially unacceptable levels of adoption and solution

---

1. Geoffrey A. Moore, *Inside the Tornado* (New York: HarperBusiness, 1995), p. 65.

risk. If they move too late, they risk being subjected to potentially dangerous levels of market and business risk, measured *not* in terms of technology but in terms of the damage suffered in their own industry at the
hands of their faster-moving competition.

The herd's response to this dilemma is one of constantly monitoring
what other members of the herd are doing. Or, extending our meteoro-
logical metaphor, the herd is constantly watching the weather. As such,
the herd actually creates the atmospheric conditions for a tornado
through their collective behavior, played out in the following manner:

1. *They begin to move together to adopt the new infrastructure or paradigm.*
2. *They move at approximately the same time.* When organizations adopt
   the *new* to replace the *old,* most prefer to reduce as much as possible
   the transition time for such an exchange. This is done in order to
   minimize the disruption to the organization at large and to eliminate
   having to maintain two infrastructures in parallel, not to mention
   building temporary bridges between them.
3. *They show strong preference for the offering of an emerging market leader. If a
   market leader is not apparent or fails to emerge, the tornado may prematurely
   end.* Picking a common vendor ensures a clear reference point for the
   establishment of de facto standards. This is a basic ingredient to one
   vendor's achieving not only market leadership but also market dominance. Market leaders serve as safe harbors for pragmatists trying to
   avoid unnecessary risks. Should a market leader not emerge, the pragmatist response can be that of waiting it out until such time as one
   does emerge.

Thus the tornado begins. Once it begins, it is virtually unstoppable.
Similar to those in nature, a market tornado follows its own unpredictable course. Our only certainty is that the landscape will look
markedly different at its conclusion.

FOOLS RUSH IN

During tornadoes, customer demand vastly outstrips a given industry's
ability to provide supply. The good news is that the financial implications
of this backlog can be extraordinarily gratifying. For not only does it rep-

resent a massive sales opportunity in and of itself, it also represents an even larger follow-on market opportunity. Now it is no longer a question of "Will they buy?" but "From whom will they buy?" At this point, we now make our acquaintance with a particular breed of tornado chaser—namely, those competitors who rush into the market eager for a chance to fulfill this now insatiable customer demand.

These Johnny-come-latelies are hardly welcomed by those now gorging themselves at the table, however, because these recent arrivals show their lack of manners through such behaviors as discounting, cloning, creating or expanding new distribution channels, becoming an OEM, and the like. What's more, many caught up in the tornado will resort to promotional campaigns of dubious veracity pitting them against everyone else, but mostly the market leader. Advertising claims—some factual, some fatuous, and all obnoxiously intrusive—spill from every medium imaginable. If market tornadoes make a sound the way real tornadoes do, it is the shrill wail associated with an ever-escalating battle of who can shout the loudest, for the longest.

Life gets more exciting for marketing departments as well. Suddenly, marketers who struggled previously to focus their promotional efforts and resources on extolling both the merits of their own offers as well as the category itself, now find themselves having to defend their turf from the onslaught of potentially dozens of new competitors now claiming a stake in this gold rush. In the end, we are forced once again to change our thinking and actions going forward. And the battle, as it were, now turns to that of winner takes all. No quarter given, no quarter asked.

DARWIN WAS RIGHT

During a market tornado, the most important dynamic playing itself out is that of the pragmatist herd choosing who will lead the product category—*for the life of the product category!* Since tornadoes are about complete infrastructure swap-outs, buyers have a significant stake in seeing that a single, powerful *sponsor* leads the category. Such a leader will be joined by two or three attractive alternatives that also appear robust, with perhaps an additional clone or two of the leader added in to keep the leader somewhat price competitive with the others. For the most part, the herd looks no further; it has no interest in any market model other than this one.

Since members of the herd are in constant contact with one another, this behavior is signaled and replicated over and over again.

The herd behaves this way for some basic but often ignored reasons. First, during a time of great uncertainty and turmoil, pragmatists do not want to complicate their lives or the lives of their organizations by looking either at too many competitors or at those who appear weak or insignificant. The analogy here is biological. In many animal species, ranging from insects to primates, males of a species will fight with each other during breeding time in order to establish their dominance within a territory or family unit. Winners of these contests become the breeding partners of choice. In this way, nature attempts to predispose females to produce offspring with potentially more favorable genetic outcomes. Males on the losing sides of these contests typically receive very few invitations for their services, and they may be shunned or driven out entirely.

Second, the pragmatist herd also desires that the infrastructure transition happen as smoothly as possible, with minimal disruptions. Since infrastructure choices dictate how entire *systems* will operate, minimizing the number of choices ensures that all the vendors who are needed to make the system work will have standards by which to design their complementary products and services.

Finally, fewer rather than more choices actually simplify life after the tornado. Because infrastructure swap-outs are complicated, expensive, and disruptive, it is hoped that the new infrastructure will be lasting, potentially for many years. The last thing pragmatists or conservatives are looking for at this stage are a bunch of upstarts trying to start the whole cycle over again. Thus, tornado markets act as *self-organizing systems* creating various classes of market players—what we call gorillas, chimps, and monkeys.

PRIMATE PECKING ORDERS

At the end of a tornado, customers exercising their buying power in various ways have imposed a new order on the participants. The market share leader is now nominated by the market to be the *gorilla*. Other gorilla candidates who achieve a modest, perhaps even impressive, level of market share success—but do not reach that of the gorilla—assume the persona (well, not literally!) of a *chimpanzee*. Chimps are sizable and intelligent in their own right, to be sure, but they lack the power and perhaps a kind of market majesty that the gorilla now possesses. Trailing both are the numerous other competitors who scrambled into the fray looking for a piece of the action, often cloning exactly what the gorilla is offering. We call these competitors *monkeys*. They may thrive during a period of hyper-growth, but they will exit the tornado with no greater market power than they had at the beginning.

Once these roles have been assigned, they rarely, if ever, will change *over the life of the market*. Here's why.

The advantages enjoyed by the gorilla are based on its power, both real and perceived, over a value chain. This power is exercised at the *solution* level. The gorilla's proposed solution, one that customers have now flocked to, can be considered an *architecture* that other products and systems will reflect as they in turn are adopted by customers as part of an infrastructure swap-out. Since the gorilla controls this architecture, it is de facto *proprietary* in nature. Yet we can say that it may also be *open* as well if the gorilla encourages and facilitates other vendors in the chain to integrate their products with the gorilla's product in order to forge a complete solution—a whole product—for the target market. When such a powerful value chain forms with the gorilla at its center, the resulting solution typically conveys very *high switching costs* if, once the solution is adopted by customers, a subsequent swap-out would be so invasive and costly as to be unthinkable. Grabbing customers by their architecture ensures that their hearts and minds soon follow. We have witnessed this time and again through the actions of companies like Applied Biosystems, Cisco, Intel, Microsoft, Oracle, and SAP—gorillas all in their respective categories.

Chimps also thrive during the tornado and will thrive beyond it, but they must play a more cautious game. Chimps feature a proprietary architecture as well. To use a voting analogy, they won in local elections and went on to post impressive numbers in the regional primaries. But they lost to the gorilla in the general election. Certainly, the chimps keep the customers that they win, for their customers are also locked into a proprietary architecture. But the ability of chimps to achieve market scale beyond the limits of their own customer bases is, for all practical purposes, nonexistent. Business partners will play with chimps but rarely at the expense of compromising their own gorilla commitments, especially if there is a significant difference between the gorilla's market opportunity and that of any particular chimp. What's more, there is usually more than one chimp in a given market.

As a result, the chimp typically faces two competing options:

1. Attack the gorilla directly in an attempt to change the course of the tornado to its favor.
2. Focus on its niche markets in an attempt to achieve gorilla status within these niches.

History teaches us that the first option is foolhardy, possibly fatal, and typically diminishes rather than improves the lot of the attacking chimp. Yet it is exactly what we see happen again and again.

There are two powerful market forces that blunt the chimp's attack. First, a chimp may assume that there are still customers to be won. If this is true, then the tornado is not really over, and chimps can legitimately compete for this new business. Category growth rates are indicators of the wisdom of this challenge. Sadly, they are typically trailing indicators. Thus, when the chimp is ready to make its attack against the gorilla, typically armed with a new, presumed best-of-breed revision of the product, there are many fewer customers now willing to buy. Moreover, those that have bought competing architectures can hardly be considered valid customers. Thus, to whom does the chimp sell? Its own installed base. But many of these folks have just bought as well.

Second, and to make matters worse, it is the gorilla's architecture that other organizations such as application providers, peripherals manufacturers, service providers, and distributors have chosen to throw most, if not all, of their resources to. These vendors are willing to support the chimp just so long as the chimp knows its place and behaves accordingly. Thus, the dynamics of the market now overwhelmingly support the gorilla—and most folks want it this way. IBM's OS/2 fiasco is living—well, actually dead—testimony to the folly of trying to overthrow the gorilla—in this case, Microsoft. As previously noted, the market as a whole decided that it would tolerate and support two, and only two, personal computer operating systems going forward: Windows and Macintosh. It would not support a third regardless of its credentials or pedigree.

This underscores the importance of competing vigorously in the early stages of the tornado, but also argues for a realistic fallback strategy—indicated in the second option above—that can be implemented should it appear that gorilla status is eluding us, at least this time.

GORILLAS IN THE NICHE

Pursuing and locking up niche markets, particularly those that are either related closely to the ones pursued during the bowling alley or left unserved by the gorilla, is the chimp's sensible choice. The goal here is to capture as many acolytes as you can by virtue of some special thing you do or can provide, in order to claim local gorilla status. The virtues of gorilla power will accrue to the chimps that can execute this strategy well.

Oracle, a chimp in the enterprise resource planning (ERP) market and never one to give up a gorilla contest willingly, executed well against its own installed base and is viewed by some as leading overall in Web enabling ERP customers with, for example, customer relationship management (CRM) applications. Correspondingly, the Internet's influence, particularly embodied in e-commerce applications, caught SAP somewhat flat-footed, forcing the gorilla to play catch-up. The moral: *Never forsake your own customers for those of your competitor*. Envy has no place in the tornado.

FEUDALISM RETURNS

Clients ask whether there can be a gorilla without a tornado. No. Can there be a tornado without a gorilla? Yes. We see them emerge in markets built around nonproprietary or legislated standards. Cellular phones, fax machines, DRAM, modems, biological reagents, and the like are all examples. A strong leader can emerge during the tornado phase of these markets, but there is *no architectural control* inherent in the category, so the market share leader—the *king*—can't exercise this form of power over the market at large. As a result, high switching costs are less apt to develop. Therefore the king's hold on the market, while tangible, is somewhat tenuous. And a king's hold on the kingdom requires 24/7 vigilance.

Consider the PC market once again. IBM was dethroned by Compaq, which, in turn, has been dethroned by Dell so that the kingdom now is really a fiefdom, ruled over by a number of *princes*—the equivalent of a chimp. Dell achieved its prince status solely by virtue of its business model, and because this model is so desirable to customers, Dell is emerging as a king. Other competitors either can't or won't emulate Dell's business model to the same level of excellence or efficiency. But they could. And I bet Michael Dell knows it.

While princes have few built-in defenses against others in the kingdom, unlike the chimp, they can assault a king directly or merge with another prince to precipitate a market coup d'état, provided the combination is powerful and compelling. Expect to see numerous coups such as these in the business-to-consumer e-commerce market. Conditions in this market overall, and in some categories in particular, will never favor a powerful king on a sustainable basis. There are too many alternatives, too much risk, too much smoke, and too many mirrors within the P&L statement. Even current kings like Amazon and AOL are dispatching legions of emissaries trying to improve and expand their influence over a fickle consumer.

Finally, we consider the downtrodden—the *serfs*—who, as in medieval times, exercise little power over their own destinies and exert no influence individually. Taken collectively, however, serfs provide a valuable role by serving customers in the low end of the market when they can't qualify for more exalted positions. Serfs also do well in commodity markets, where their cost structures, business models, or distribution systems are attractive to certain customer segments.

Summarizing, at some point in the tornado, you will wake up one morning, look at your reflection in the mirror, and see one of the above. Your ability to "deal with it" will determine whether your future is one of a promise fulfilled or a legacy denied.

COMPETING IN A TORNADO

Experts from many fields tell us that it is nearly always preferable to follow a prescribed set of behaviors when faced with a moment of uncertainty, be it merely frustrating or potentially life-threatening, than to get creative and/or follow our own instincts. Actors in the midst of filming a scene will ask for their lines. Football teams run set plays that are practiced and well documented. Airline pilots rely on their instruments rather than their senses when flying in inclement weather.

A market tornado is no exception. Simply put, there are some things that you absolutely must do during a tornado if you are to enjoy a favorable outcome. In keeping with our emphasis on doing the right things quickly and well, organizations do not have the luxury to dither over how to proceed when the tornado sirens scream.

Let's review.

During a tornado, you must assert your superiority in every possible way. This means pursuing as many customer prospects as possible to build market share, as well as pursuing and attacking your competition on every front, every day. It also means streamlining your business operations to cause the *most products* to find the *most customers* in the *shortest time* possible. More specifically:

1. *You must shift the focus of competition from serving specific customer segments completely to that of doing whatever you can to showcase your strengths and highlight your competitors' weaknesses. The ultimate goal of such positioning is market leadership, both actual and perceived. The key success metric shifts from market share within these specific segments to overall market share for the category as a whole.*

   Customers are not trying to decide *if* they're going to buy but rather from whom they will buy and when. Thus, you must take every opportunity to hasten this decision in your favor. There are very few strategic nuances associated with this endeavor, so don't look for any. During a tornado, we have found that Dame Fortune—and the financial markets—do not smile on those who opt for grand strategies carefully researched and planned, but instead favor those who can execute brilliantly, flawlessly, and quickly. Netscape had a grand strategy. Bill Gates pivoted his entire company with one memo, and Microsoft completely co-opted Netscape's value proposition as a result of Gates's call to arms. IBM consolidated its entire advertising account with Ogilvy & Mather and executed one worldwide campaign positioning the company as the leader in e-business. During the same period, Hewlett-Packard twiddled its collective thumbs, continuing instead with a series of fragmented and banal messages about its products and future intentions. As a corollary to the HP reference (and any large corporation, for that matter), tornadoes rarely reward organizations who slavishly manage by consensus, matrices, or any other *groupthink* model, either by culture, design, or default. There simply isn't time to debate ad infinitum what an organization should think, do, or say, let alone give everyone input to the process, when there are hordes of customers eager to give you and all your competitors one opportunity with which to satisfy their cravings.

KEY LEARNING ▶ ▶ ▶ ▶ ▶ ▷ ▷ ▷ ▷ ▷

Lest you get ahead of yourself by exercising all this competitive zeal, tornado marketing, a zero-sum game effort, typically works *only* in the tornado. Recall that in early markets, competition is usually in the form of an old way of doing something, which is to say that it barely exists at all.

When you are stuck in the chasm or working your way out, competition takes the form of either overcoming pragmatist inertia or competing on the basis that you have a whole product well suited for the needs of specific groups, whereas your competitors are trying to be all things to all people. Since you represent a new and, to most pragmatists, unproved way of doing something, attacking your competition directly serves to undermine confidence in the category as a whole. These efforts, typically bombastic, provide little of substance to pragmatist prospects searching for real reasons to help them justify what now seems a leap of faith.

As we will see, waning tornadoes deliver a once hyperkinetic market to Main Street, where companies will derive their growth and profits yet again from their installed bases. Attacking your competitors at this point is typically fruitless because *their* customers have just lived through the tornado as well, and thus are probably girding themselves for new challenges not related to your product category.

2. *You must standardize your product offering as much as possible, reducing its complexity, time to deployment, services required, and so on, as well as making it compatible with relevant industry standards, thus ultimately preparing it for commodity status. The ultimate expression of this intent means getting the product to a point where the buyer can now assume all future responsibility for the product's installation, deployment, and use.*

While you may think that actively managing your product to commodity status is marketing heresy, or perhaps, commercial suicide, consider further how customers might be thinking. While you're convincing everyone who will listen that your new widget is guaranteed to save the world, your customer is busily weighing the merits of your widget against all the other widgets available during this widget tornado. Thus, when we consider the customer, it's now useful to focus almost exclusively on the poor souls who must procure the new infrastructure and install it, get it up and running, and support it when it breaks. And do this all under the duress of management howling to have it done "yesterday." From our value chain model, we call these poor souls the technical buyers, and better known in many cases as the IT department.

Imagine their plight in being forced to move to some new infrastructure, let alone having to select the right one. For example, alternative A promises best-of-breed technology cut from the bleeding edge. While attractive, closer examination reveals that A will require efforts akin to the first splitting of the atom in order to install and deploy. While A is elegant, complete, robust, et cetera, et cetera, it is also exceedingly complex. Alternative B, on the other hand, seems more modest in its capabilities, perhaps owing to its heritage as a niche-oriented solution. B is not considered best-of-breed by the pundits who pronounce on such matters. However, it appears to be a damn sight easier to get up and running. Moreover, its niche heritage may have contributed to the formation of a small but knowledgeable group of partners who can provide complementary products and services to further augment its value. To be fair, A enjoys similar relationships, albeit more focused around taming or mitigating A's inherent complexity. Your choice in this example is *best technology* versus *faster time to deployment*.

Which do you want to buy?

Neither alternative, however, presupposes that *product quality* can be sacrificed. You want the product to stay sold and not be returned for credit, which is to the detriment of your market share goals, not to mention your P&L statement. With customer word-of-mouth referencing at a fever pitch, you also cannot risk the lasting damage if a reputation for poor quality becomes tied to you like a tin can on a cat's tail. A whisper campaign concerning your quality issues, aided and abetted by your competitors, can lengthen your sales cycle just at the time you can least afford it.

Is there a short answer to the quality issue? Yes. Quality is not a point of difference during a tornado. It is the price of entry to the game. Poor performers are weeded out quickly because there are likely to be extremely viable alternatives. A practical outgrowth of this advice can also be felt by the engineering and product management organizations during a tornado. Namely, since we will not differentiate on quality during the tornado, we will not fuss with or otherwise obsess on advanced or arcane features or functionality that is likely to compromise our quality standards. Some high-tech vendors speak proudly of their *six sigma* quality, no doubt a laudable goal. Just be sure of two things: that you're not shipping five sigma quality when the market wants six, and that six sigma quality does not result in six months too late.

3. *You must drive your price down as much as possible.*

Recall that in the bowling alley, people are motivated to solve broken business processes that will cause real problems if left to persist. They are, as we say, "bleeding from the neck." Because of this condition, pricing in bowling alley markets is, and should be, set to value. (I will pay just about anything to stanch such a hemorrhage.) The overriding goal during a tornado, however, is dominant market share. Our thinking about pricing must be reset based on this singular goal. It is also good practice, realizing that the next market phase, that of Main Street, will continue to be price sensitive throughout the remaining life of this technology wave.

Key to your understanding is that while the herd is moving to a new infrastructure, it is also beginning to evaluate such an infrastructure as a commodity that can and will be served up by a variety of vendors. While pragmatists will look for reasons to purchase from *leading candidates,* they are also mindful that one can be played off against another. Price concessions thus can be had by the skillful pragmatist who knows that he or she has little power in moving to the new category but still retains significant power as to whom they will pledge their allegiance, particularly in the early stages of the tornado.

More important, however, is the emergence of the *conservatives:* those members of the herd who are now moving behind the pragmatists in lockstep. These are the people who do their Christmas shopping the day before Christmas because of their belief that there will be bargains to be had. And bargains are what many conservatives are looking for. We win their business by hitting price points, lowering them as we go, in an effort to stimulate every conservative possible to part with his or her money. The point here is to *be the first* to hit the next lower, strategic price level that generates the *next* price-sensitive customer group to take action. In this way we reach new customer bases, thereby giving us immediate market share and the chance for follow-on business in the months or years to come. When market leaders follow this dictum, they leave little maneuvering room for competitors. Such action fosters and reinforces the leader's market hegemony, forcing competitors to retreat to the safety of the segments they may have previously won or to the unattractive domain of forever playing catch-up in a market that will be a source of steadily diminishing returns to all but the winners.

On the other hand, if you as an emergent market leader—or at least a candidate for this appointment—fail to take such action, you leave an important flank undefended, and thus your market leadership credentials can be open to challenge if category *clones* should emerge. If category cloning is not possible, you still remain at risk of alienating the next big wave of buyers—that is, the conservatives who have remained on the sidelines until prices and values are more attractive.

4. *You must make your product as widely available as possible.*

Remember that tornadoes are characterized by a significant imbalance of supply to demand. In actual fact, this may not be the case for some product categories. It would be hard to conceive of not being able to acquire enterprise resource planning (ERP) software during the mid to late 1990s, which was tornado time for this category. On the other hand, deployment of these systems was really paced by the availability and resource dedication of service providers like Accenture and PwC, without whom deployment of this class of software was virtually impossible.[2]

---

2. The ERP category is one of the few examples in which complexity was not significantly reduced but buffered by service providers who, contrary to most experiences, were able to ride a product category through the tornado. Since complexity could not be reduced significantly at the product level, this was, and continues to be, a major impediment to an ERP tornado in markets other than Fortune 500 or *Financial Times* 100 companies globally. Midsize and smaller enterprises simply can't afford the level of services necessary to buffer this complexity.

Consistent then with reducing overall product complexity in order to build faster time to deployment, smart marketers will also expand their distribution channels in order to be on the shelf when the customer is ready to buy. As any packaged goods marketer will tell you, out-of-stocks are a brand manager's worst nightmare. Despite all the advertising and promotional dollars spent to support such products, we know that actual brand selection is often made at the actual time of purchase. No shelf presence thus guarantees no in-store consideration and, subsequently, no purchase.

We in high tech also have to get it right—the first time. When vendor A's offering is widely available, and vendor B's is not, due largely to the distribution strategies and programs subscribed to by each, vendor A stands a significantly better chance mathematically of being adopted sooner by a wider group of audience than vendor B. After all, vendor A is available when customers want the category almost immediately. Vendor A looks more *attractive* to customers because more people sell and support it, which further engenders the perception that vendor A is more of a *standard* than vendor B. And since vendor A is more widely distributed, chances are that the myriad complementary products and services that inevitably chase tornadoes will disproportionately favor vendor A as well. Suddenly, vendor A looks like the safe choice simply on the merits of its availability.

Finally, we shall not pass this way again anytime soon. At the end of the tornado, customers' bellies are full. There will not be another opportunity to dislodge vendor A for many a day. Its infrastructure has now been installed in potentially many more sites than vendor B's simply because it was there. And customers are loath to part with their infrastructures on a whim, as we have found out previously. The customers you win during the tornado are the customers you carry pretty much for the life of the category. There will be few chances after the tornado to win more.

▶ A CHANGE WILL DO YOU GOOD

In the early 1990s the client/server, distributed-computing tornado was raging. Fueled variously by the relational database vendors and a new stable of applications written to take advantage of these now reliable platforms, new business models that favored decentralization, the proliferation of the UNIX operating system, and, perhaps, the promise of this weird new thing called the Internet, customers ran into the arms of the hardware vendors who could sell them things called UNIX servers.

For Sun Microsystems and Hewlett-Packard, it was a time of renewal, great hope, and a whole lot of money besides. Both companies realized that their respective direct-sales forces could not satisfy the number of calls, let alone orders, that such a tornado was producing. So both expanded dramatically their third-party distribution channels to include many different channel providers—from value-added resellers (VARs) who previously focused on the technical workstation market to PC dealers who demonstrated a particular application expertise and were eager to move up the food chain. It was not long before HP and Sun suddenly looked like de facto standards and the winners of the contest.

Envious of this success, and perhaps a bit outraged by it, traditional data center computing vendors like IBM and Unisys pursued strategies ranging from better technology to OEM partnering to price-cutting. Unisys, in particular, was left at the station. While praised for its computing expertise, solid products, and domain knowledge, it imposed on its customers and prospects a business and selling model derived from its mainframe business—a model designed to benefit Unisys, and virtually no one else. While the company pursued halfhearted attempts to expand modestly its distribution, any real attempts to overhaul it were aggressively thwarted by— you guessed it—its direct-sales force, which viewed such efforts as a "take-away" and "competitive" and thus thoroughly counterproductive to its own interests. Factions within the company argued that their relative lack of success was largely due to Unisys's product offerings not being competitive on a feature/functionality basis. This was an assertion that was not supported in fact or in market perception. Having been relegated to the backbenches by IBM during the heyday of the mainframe, Unisys watched as the tornado roared past again, surviving only by dint of its service and system integration expertise, its hardware reputation and position now marginalized. While Unisys regained some of its footing, consider the opportunity cost imposed on an otherwise fine company when it mistrusts itself and thus searches for reasons not to do the right thing—and finds them.

◀

What have we learned based on previous tornadoes? One obvious notion is that customers buy *you* during a tornado! Your product, your reputation, your standing with Wall Street, your chairman, your technical service representative, your shipping clerk and accounting system. Any sign of weakness, real or otherwise, is exploitable by your competition, and rest assured it will be exploited to your great detriment. It is the herd moving. Once it finds or creates a path, the herd follows it blindly.

Oh yes, and they also buy your advertising.

5. *You must communicate all your points of advantage, in the most relevant way, to the widest audience of target prospects possible.*

Marketing communications in general, and advertising specifically, has rarely been a core competence of most high-tech organizations. Many high-tech companies are extremely adept at developing and selling the most innovative technologies and products imaginable, but they show their utter ineptness when it comes to talking about them in meaningful and memorable ways. This deficiency can cause problems at any stage of the life cycle, but it can be positively fatal during a tornado.

The reasons are rather simple.

If I don't hear about you, or recall your message, it follows that I won't know much about you. If I don't know much about you, I can't really assess your merits as part of my consideration set. Thus, you're never really on my radar screen. Or, more academically, you are not highly relevant to my purchase decision. You lack *saliency*. There's no reason to investigate further since I'm under pressure as it is. Why make life more complicated?

The tornado is not about shopping, it is about buying. We can invoke the law of unintended consequences here. If you don't communicate the who, what, where, why, and how of your value proposition—or communicate it poorly or without much commitment—you are actually telling prospective customers that relative to other alternatives, you are not as attractive. Prospects may draw the conclusion that you are, most probably, a minor factor in this market, without much influence or staying power. The major players all seem to be making lots of noise about themselves on a sustained basis. Those that aren't must somehow be deficient or, at best, less successful than their more aggressive brethren. This speaks volumes to the risk-averse herd looking for a leader, perhaps even a savior, to bring it to the promised land.

Thus, as part of your tornado strategy, you must be prepared to devote ample resources to getting the message out. And not just in fits and starts, but on a sustainable basis, until the tornado is no longer.

▶ MADISON AVENUE FINDS SILICON VALLEY

During the early to mid-1980s, seemingly a lifetime ago (and during which many of you were probably experiencing your first date), we demonstrated how the power of highly effective advertising—effective because of its strategy, execution, and significant investment—could be brought to bear during a tornado. The product category was the personal computer—a marvelous new invention that owing to its two killer applications, word processing and spreadsheets, was now a must-have for people in many different walks of life. For those of us at Apple during the same time, it also represented a time of great opportunity and great peril. We faced a multitude of competitors, from a newly upstart Compaq to traditional computing titans like Texas Instruments to offshore competitors such as NEC to some other interesting start-ups like Kaypro, Altos, and Eagle. And we also faced a giant, IBM, a company more like an environment than a competitor.

Although we were young, rebellious, ambitious, and arrogant—not to mention flush with the spectacular success of the Apple II in specific market segments like education—we grew increasingly uneasy as many of these upstarts began not only to bring out interesting products but also to capture shelf space with the fledgling PC retailer channel. As a market leader, we still wielded enormous clout with the channel. An Apple Authorized Dealer medallion was a highly coveted prize and not awarded to just anyone who could occupy space in a strip mall. However, like any good merchant, many of these same dealers sought to hedge their bets. Instead of carrying the two obvious brands, Apple and IBM, why not add a third and possibly a fourth brand to the mix as well? "We're just responding to customer demand" was the collective answer voiced during dealer council meetings, "but we're still loyal to Apple." Sure, but for how long? And how about the dealer's salespeople? Would they be as loyal and motivated as well? Or would they just sell what the customer wanted to buy? What effect could this brand proliferation in the dealer's shop have on customers seeking Apples but *switched* at the time of purchase to another, probably less expensive brand?

We decided not to wait around and find out. Working in our favor were two things that at the time were almost unique to Apple as an organization. First, Apple's relatively flat and decidedly nonhierarchical organization fostered an abiding sense of collaboration throughout the company. There were, of course, the usual palace intrigues, but people felt like they could dream up a new way of doing something and go directly to people like Steve Jobs, Bill Campbell, Michael Spindler, and John Sculley to secure both funding and sponsorship. Committees convened to say no were eschewed at Apple. They wasted both time and human bandwidth. Weak ideas were shot down fast, typically by your colleagues, who asked, sometimes relentlessly, "Is that the best we [meaning you] can do?" Second, a small cadre of managers had been recruited out of the consumer marketing and advertising fields, tasked with developing and executing such demand-creating programs as advertising, sales promotion, and merchandising, as well as the overall look and feel of Apple the company, and Apple the brand. We were given what seemed like almost unlimited resources and authority to do our jobs. And, looking back, for most of us then in our twenties, big jobs they were.

It was clear to some that we could not out-tech our competition. We could not demand that our dealers carry only our stuff, nor could we ask them to provide us with more favorable treatment. Nor could we provide them more favorable treatment in return, or offer terms to some but not others. *All we could really do was cause customers to want our stuff more than they would our competitors'!* What's more, we knew we did not have to knock off the big guy, either, only the wanna-bes who were trying to establish themselves.

How? By outmarketing them. We would develop a sizable promotional *footprint*. We would create superior advertising, then run it in major consumer publications like *People* magazine and major business periodicals like *Fortune* and *BusinessWeek*. Our ad agency produced some breakthrough TV commercials and ran them in network prime time, at significant weight levels in top-rated programming. To accomplish this, of course, required us to triple our promotional budget to an unheard of level (for us), exceeding a whopping $30 million. Oh, by the way, we would also tie in a Christmas sales promotion that would provide coupons good for rebates on popular peripherals, most of which we made, as well as popular software titles, all of which we didn't. Naturally, we went out of our way to inform our reps and dealers that we would be doing all this, well, just because we wanted them to be successful, to show just how much we valued their efforts, commitment, and shelf space. We also noted that many of the other companies whose products they carried were not making the same commitment. "What a pity," we said, "guess they're just not up to it."

At this point you might say, "Well, duh!" How obvious. This is done day in and day out in the world of consumer marketing.

Except that in high tech, it wasn't. With the exception of IBM, whose PC division at the time was led by some mavericks of its own, the rest of the industry was caught flat-footed, reeling over the new price of entry to the PC business. What's more, their competitive responses were either too clumsy, too equivocal, or too late. Dealers, knowing a good thing when they see it, and subsequently watching the revenues of Apple, IBM, and even Compaq (back when its name described its product) all soar, did what all savvy merchants do—sell and stock what the people want to buy. Adios, Texas Instruments. So long, Sony (at least for now). *Arrivederci*, Atari. *Que será será*, Kaypro.

And then there were three.

Well, perhaps a few more. But this first PC tornado irrevocably changed the competitive landscape. What's more, the first global battle (there would be many more to come) had been won with marketing savvy, not superior technology. The PC business would exit the decade with fewer players than when it began, and life in the high-tech world would never be the same again.

◀

Of course, we learn these lessons over and over again until we get them right. Which reminds me . . .

COMMON TORNADO MISTAKES

Blowing it during the tornado (forgive me!) is easier than it would seem. "Shit happens," as the saying goes. In our experience, bad things happen

to good people during tornadoes through the commission of two fundamental sets of mistakes. Not surprisingly, each is related to the other.

1. *Vendors ignore, deny, or otherwise try to control a tornado.*

    Ignoring a tornado or, worse yet, denying that one is happening is
    plainly and tragically irresponsible. To do so denies both the organi-
    zation and its shareholders the most fundamental form of wealth cre-
    ation: providing a highly valued product (or service) to a potentially
    huge customer base that craves it. What's not to like here?

    What's not to like for some nearsighted executives and their boards
    of directors is the potential for losing control of the technology, the
    product, the channel, and/or the market itself. The temptation among
    such types is to apply the economic laws they may have learned in uni-
    versity—for example, when a product is in high demand, you can raise
    revenues and margins through (a) raising prices; and (b) controlling
    supply. Sounds OK so far. Except that when tornadoes hit, demand far
    outstrips supply. When a vendor tries to further restrict that supply
    through what they may believe are artful means—limiting distribution,
    raising prices, onerous licensing terms, and so on—the market searches
    for alternatives. In fact, customers fairly demand them. And make no
    mistake. It is not the category they are rejecting. It's you.

    Moral: Do not let control freaks dictate your tornado strategy.

2. *Vendors add features, functionality, or infrastructure that is once again discontinuous, either in real or perceived terms.*

    There is a huge temptation to build into your product every last
    bit of benefit you can at the early stages of a tornado. After all, didn't
    you just read that you are supposed to compete vigorously using
    every point of advantage you can muster? True. But this does not
    mean that such advantages come at a price of reintroducing disconti-
    nuity back into the market that is now evolving precisely because dis-
    continuity has been drastically reduced from previous levels—or,
    more likely, eliminated altogether. Engineering's main—and arguably
    its only—task during a tornado is to streamline the product in what-
    ever way(s) will make it faster to deploy, easier to use, cheaper to oper-
    ate, more convenient to service, and more efficacious as to its
    promised benefit. It should not try to outengineer its rivals.

Consistent with not overengineering your product, you must also design out as many *service-oriented* requirements as possible. Those that can't be designed out must be streamlined as above. The rationale here is that services cost money and may take time. The market is looking to optimize the expenditures of both during a tornado. Vendors, having designed specialized services in during the bowling alley to win over specific segments through value-added domain expertise, are now very content with the margins that such services provide. When services need to be part of the product because the product can't be sufficiently standardized, or when margin-hungry organizations try to sell some bogus *needs analysis* study prior to actually selling the product, they do so at their own peril during a tornado.

Lest you think that sources of discontinuity are limited strictly to engineering or professional services organizations, think again. Marketing's job is to announce all your benefits to as many people as possible while denouncing competitive efforts. It should not be planning new features for specific segments and then promising actual delivery, although such an effect can be gleaned through clever packaging. Rather, marketing's key job during a tornado is shortening the sales cycle as much as is humanly possible. Period. And for all you marketers enamored with branding, the tornado is when that starts to matter, because selling the category is now moot.

The sales department's job is to sell and close, both early and often. It should not be demanding that customers buy in the manner in which the company wants to sell, but instead it should aggressively deploy programs to reach buyers it would not or could not ordinarily reach.

Anything that stands in the way of these fundamental efforts is likely to be seen as standing in the way of customer adoption. That, in turn, can be seen by customers, partners, channels—virtually anyone in the value chain—as discontinuous; that is, a significant change from some status quo. All these folks, but particularly customers, develop options, and they will exercise them accordingly.

Moral: You do not get another chance during a tornado.

7

Main Street

There is a hook in every benefit, that sticks in his jaws that takes that benefit, and draws him whither the benefactor will.

—JOHN DONNE

And finally, the party is over. It is now the morning after. You know you had fun, but why do you feel so bad now? And where (and when) did all the people go? All you've got now are a lot of empties and a sizable mess that now demands your attention.

What do we wake up to when the tornado ends? Though market tornadoes can persist for several years, they usually end as they began, with a number of warnings that herald their departure. Of course, like the party animals we are, we ignore these warnings. Why spoil the fun by letting reality slip through the front door? Metaphors notwithstanding, how do we know when the party's really over?

- Projected revenue targets for the category are now being missed, and further declines now seem almost a certainty. *And, as a result . . .*
- Projected profit targets for the category participants are now either not being met or under significant pressure. *And, as a result . . .*
- The share prices of the companies participating have been cut, in some cases drastically. Wall Street is now turning up its nose to the

category in general, and in some cases thumbing its nose at specific companies that it once was enamored with. *And, as a result . . .*

- Employee turnover, particularly at the executive staff level, is now on the rise. *And, as a result . . .*
- The remaining executives and their boards are in a state of shock, denial, or paralysis as to what to do next.

What has happened?

Market equilibrium is once again established with supply now having caught up with demand, and demand is now waning significantly from its previous levels. The market is now reaching the *assimilative* phase of the Technology Adoption Life Cycle, and, for the first time, growth rates are beginning to resemble other industry markets served by continuous innovations.

THE WINTER OF OUR DISCONNECT

Does assimilation mean the end of growth? No. Just the end of growth as we have known it previously. Customers, in a fit of gluttony, have gorged themselves on the new infrastructure and are now pushing back from the table. More to the point, we are again *running out* of customers, similar to our early market experience. Pragmatists are now preoccupied with *implementing* this new infrastructure rather than just acquiring it, so the buyer profile now shifts to that of the conservative. The previous status quo has now been replaced with a new status quo. The paradigm is dead. Long live the new paradigm. In fact, conservatives are now rubbing their hands with glee as they realize that the price tag for the category, previously too rich for their taste, is dropping significantly. "Now I can get the attention of these darn vendors who previously didn't have the time to return my phone calls," muses the conservative, "not to mention even offer a significant discount. What's more, everyone knows how to do this stuff, so there should be little risk in deploying it. I'm glad I waited."

Our problem is that this growth slowdown is both unexpected and, from our point of view, unwarranted. It forces us once again to rethink how we're going to play this new game, and what changes we will need to make in order to play effectively. Trust me. Such changes will not be welcome or easy to do.

Main Street challenges high-tech organizations like no other point on the Technology Adoption Life Cycle. Everything about it seems so wrong. Revenue growth is modest, even flat, when compared to the dazzling growth rates of the past. No longer can we advance our cause by conquering new territory, getting new business. It seems like there's none left to get. Restless executive staffs now facing lowered revenue and profit expectations go on the prowl for the next big thing. Wall Street analysts change their opinions of both the category and the company, modifying their recommendations from that of *strong buy* to *accumulate* or *long-term buy,* or the dreaded *hold*. These phrases are euphemisms. In a practical sense, they are indicators that the once high-flying shares of these tornado participants appear now to have fallen to earth and are not expected to gain significant altitude again any time soon. Monkeys and serfs now surmise that their best times may be behind them, and they lament further that they're now somehow typecast. In sum, the current market dynamics bore everyone concerned. Everyone, that is, except customers.

Encountering this new dynamic, high-tech companies typically leave a tremendous amount of money on the table by veering away from Main Street markets and toward anything that faintly resembles early markets and tornadoes. This is certainly an error in judgment. Main Street is a natural part of the Life Cycle landscape. It is a time of renewal; a time for reintroducing ourselves to our customers. A time once again to seek an intimate understanding of their needs and desires. It is also a time and a source of enormous profitability. But first, we must learn figuratively how to walk down the street itself.

DOWN ON MAIN STREET

When the infrastructure paradigm—now no longer new—is deployed and operating, the demand/supply imbalance that characterized the tornado is shifting as well, from one of excess demand to excess supply. Our metaphor is derived from the idea that the new infrastructure can be found (and acquired) on every main street, high street, *strasse, platz,* boulevard, and shopping mall across the land. Thus it should be no surprise that future commercial relationships between buyer and seller now favor the buyer.

Going forward, there are two market archetypes that will comprise

Main Street: a commodity-like market that extends the paradigm to additional locales; and a differentiated or value-driven market that appeals to various segments of the market that may be searching for additional things they value—for example, specific features, functionality, and the like—that are currently not available in the commodity offering. Competition will form similarly, spanning a range from low-cost providers to highly differentiated offerings that build on the infrastructure in *continuous* ways. Concurrently, the customer domain of the value chain bifurcates as well, emphasizing the technical buyer or purchasing group searching for the lowest bid, and the end user now searching for additional benefits. The economic buyer, if different from either the technical buyer or the end user, is now no longer a factor since the economic return on investment of the category is no longer in doubt.

Vendors now must shift their ruthless pursuit of market share to a relentless pursuit of the most profitable customers located *first* within each vendor's own installed base. There are two key measures of such profitability:

- How much will a given customer buy over the life of the category?
- What premium will a given customer pay for a differentiated offering?

Obviously, ideal customers are those who will both buy the most and pay the most. And Christmas comes but once a year. It makes sense, therefore, to adopt a more realistic approach to our Main Street strategy in order that we make business decisions that in effect self-select for one metric or the other.

THE COMMODITY APPROACH

Vendors who are driven by volume-oriented metrics and who are participating in markets that are undeniably commodity-like—for example, components, disk drives, or consumables—are probably well served to pursue those customer segments that will buy lots and lots of the category over its natural life cycle. While this may sound obvious, it is an optimal strategy only if you can meet several key strategic, tactical, and operational fundamentals:

1. You must have some demonstrative share of the market. You need not be a gorilla or a king, but you should recognize that monkey or serf positions call into question your long-term potential and viability.
2. You must enjoy superior and sustainable economies of scale in sourcing, manufacturing, and servicing your product.
3. You must have low-cost channels of distribution that customers can transact with efficiently.
4. You must be able to operate profitably on low and/or declining margins over a prolonged period.

If you think that this sounds unfamiliar to most North American and European producers, and sounds more like the market model pursued by many Asian vendors, you would be correct. Historically, Asian producers have been able to capitalize variously on lower operating costs, governmental subsidies, beneficial trade barriers and tariffs, and artificially low costs of capital to pursue the lowest-cost provider role in Main Street markets. However, it is also a strategic direction that Hewlett-Packard is able to pursue vigorously in the ink-jet and laser printer market.

Typically, a Main Street commodity strategy appeals to two customer constituencies—conservative economic buyers and purchasing agents. Conservatives seek low prices because the category in question may not hold that much intrinsic value to them (a concept that supports our contention that not all innovations, particularly those in the IT world, are strategic to customers or provide competitive advantage). Purchasing agents, on the other hand, are compensated based on their ability to obtain goods at the best terms and conditions. They begin their low-price search when the category is sufficiently stable and standardized, and thus demand can be bid out.

We have found that for many high-tech markets, notably software, a low-cost provider strategy is difficult to optimize. In fact, in the age of the Internet and e-commerce, this approach may be either irrelevant as a strategy or a fundamental cost not of entry, but of continuance. So another Main Street strategy is necessary if vendors are to sustain themselves in a world that now seems completely homogeneous. Happily, we learn the lesson here from the world of consumer marketing.

During the tornado, the optimal market development strategy is appealing to and capturing as many customers as possible, as quickly as possible. Often, there is more hype than actual substance associated with these efforts as vendors engage in a marketing *shouting match* attempting to lure wide-eyed and eager customers through their figurative, if not literal, doors. In some categories, the scene that plays out reminds us of a carnival barker extolling the wonders to behold behind his curtain, for those wise and adventurous enough to venture inside.

When the dust settles, we have now a vast number of customers who have paid their money and are just as eager to begin reaping the benefits of a category that they hope will sustain them for many years to come. Our Main Street market development dilemma thus remains. How do we attract those prospects that have held out during the tornado? And how do we get our own installed base to either expand or, at the very least, buy the next version of the product?

Eschewing a commodity approach, the answer in the *value-driven approach* lies within the installed base itself. Far from being homogeneous, this group is likely to consist of many different subsegments, each with specific attributes common to a particular segment but unlike other segments that comprise the market as a whole. Our mission on Main Street must be to reconnect with these customer subsegments, discover their needs and latent desires for additional value, and create specific offers that meet such needs. Increasingly, this is referred to as *mass customization*. The strategy for reaching these subsegments has been described as *one-to-one marketing*.

Most consumer markets are driven by mass customization, but we in high tech tend to avoid it since it typically does not celebrate our long-held views of what constitutes engineering breakthroughs—that is, the discontinuous innovation. *Main Street customers do not want discontinuity!* Recall our discussion of the electric car. While it's true that I might want significantly better fuel economy and also want to feel good about my "green" approach to driving, I'm not willing necessarily to give up on an infrastructure I've come to rely on. Unfortunately, by the time we get to Main Street, we have probably lost sight of who our customers really are and what they really want. Thus, our first instinct is to reinvent the category. Like our mothers who know what's best, we give the market discontinuity whether it wants it or not! After all, it didn't know it would want the new paradigm before we provided it, and look at all the fun—not to mention money—we've created in the process. Plus, this Main Street stuff is boring, anyway.

Well my friend, your headstrong ways will likely cause you problems. The value-driven strategy *is* based on engineering additional benefits into a given product. But such benefits must meet two key tests. Do customers really want such features? And will they really pay for them? Not surprisingly, many of the benefits that customers covet on Main Street seem to the industry to be rather modest and ho-hum. Often, customers see additional value in the form of new industrial designs—for example, a smaller footprint for a printer or CPU. Or value manifests itself as ease of use, ease of service, or ease of acquisition. Perhaps the value is based around demographic considerations—for example, products designed by and for women, or products designed for those with physical limitations. *Whatever the case, our engineering efforts must not result in any discontinuity to either end users or the distribution channel, and such efforts must not be so extensive as to require a significant increase in pricing in order to recapture an increased cost of goods.*

▶ NO WONDER THEY CAN'T DRESS

In the early 1990s, IBM's once-mighty PC division was suffering the effects of a mighty fall. IBM's MicroChannel debacle—a classic example of introducing discontinuity at exactly the wrong time—as well as the failure of OS/2 to gain much, if any, market traction significantly dampened enthusiasm for the business among both consumers and many IBMers alike. Company executives insisted that the problems were those of positioning and branding, and they called on numerous consultants to wield their marketing alchemy.

Well, they were right, but for different reasons. There was a branding problem. IBM's market offerings at the time—notably the PS/2 and its lamentable sibling, the PS/1—tended to cost more than other brands, and they were also quite unappealing visually. In fact, they looked downright cheap. Certainly, they did not measure up to what you would expect from IBM.

In years past, IBM warehoused samples of every computer the company made or contemplated making—from mainframes to workstations to personal computers. A number of the more interesting models had been directed out of IBM centers in Italy and Japan, countries and cultures recognized for cutting-edge industrial design. An IBM design director once explained that some of the more radical (and totally cool) designs were not destined for the marketplace. "Certainly, the company could really rewrite the rules of the game with some of these beauties," he mused. "Nobody has done anything interesting in PC form factors since the Macintosh."

He went on to explain that several innovative designs were contemplated, but they first had to proceed through a gauntlet of engineering reviews. Innovative designs just didn't seem to pass muster. "Why?" I asked. He went on to explain that since the current PC form factor was the so-called stack of pancakes with a monitor on top, those in charge thought that the new form factors *did not look like computers."*

◄

Remember also that products, as they evolve through the Technology Adoption Life Cycle, have most likely had features and functionality built in that people either don't value or don't realize are there. Consider, for example, most television remote controls. They are now "universal control devices" capable of managing your TV, VCR, DVD player, stereo system, and God knows what else. Except we don't know—or can't remember—what buttons to press in order to use all these features. Don't you wish they would make these things with just a few buttons that would do what you really want? Apply this desire to hardware or software products and systems, and you develop the basis for high-tech "lite" products—that is, products that are not as full featured as the standard offering. To certain customer segments, this absence of features may translate to "lack of complexity," "easy to use and maintain," or other positive benefits associated with the user experience. Do we do this in high tech? Rarely.

It remains then to determine once again who and what are the relevant segments within the market and then build *whole product +1 (or −1) offerings* to serve such segments. Packaged goods marketers worldwide have successfully extended their products and brands through such +1 programs. Shampoo manufacturers reach dozens of different customer segments that may have only one attribute in common: hair. There are shampoos that condition your hair; those that fight dandruff; those intended for dry, oily, or thin hair; those formulated for people who color their hair; and so on. All of us (at least those of us who wash our hair) gravitate to the one that we think is right for us. We may even pay significant premiums to obtain a single benefit, or promise of a benefit, even knowing as we do that virtually all shampoos are formulated using the same basic ingredients. This is the power of *differentiation* and, when done right, the power of branding. You would think that as consumers exposed to such offers day in and day out, we would somehow be more proficient in applying similar ideas to our own high-tech challenges. Some companies like Intuit and Microsoft are quite good at this. Intuit's Scott Cook and Microsoft CEO Steve Ballmer are both Procter & Gamble grads, and Microsoft's former chief operating officer, Bob Herbold, spent most of his career with the Cincinnati-based firm.

But, in reality, most high-tech companies still have a long way to go in understanding that +1 marketing is not specifically a function of providing objectively considered *utility* through scheduled releases, but rather seeks to put the customer at center stage instead of the almighty product.

BACK TO THE FUTURE

It's useful to think about Main Street market development in a context similar to that of the bowling alley. Both are based on identifying and developing niche markets. However, there is one striking difference: the absence of a well-formed *supportive infrastructure* in the bowling alley, and, conversely, the proliferation of such an infrastructure on Main Street. So much so that we take it for granted. In the bowling alley, part of our whole product assembly process included recruiting partners and allies who might supply key missing components in order to form our whole product solution, plus the addition of a distribution channel that could deliver such a solution while also adding value. Things worked well for all parties because there was sufficient margin such that everyone could make a living.

Main Street markets typically do not provide for such allowances. Thus, your +1 program must be delivered almost exclusively by you. This does not preclude the creation of *virtual* partners and allies: organizations that would come together on a *promotional* basis to elevate or differentiate a given offer from competition. It does mean that such partnerships are probably short-lived, however. Few wish to remain at the table when the food and drink have all gone.

Competitively, your +1 offerings typically need not be positioned against your competition, but they should be positioned against any status quo commodity offering, *including your own!* "But won't such a thing cannibalize our own product line," I hear you say, "and shouldn't we be going after our competition?" No, and not necessarily.

Product cannibalization in high tech is one of the most irrelevant issues ever to be put on a meeting agenda and agonized over. On Main Street, we are seeking to hold our customer base in the bosom of customer satisfaction—so they won't leave us, and so they will buy more things from us. As part of this strategy, we provide +1-driven offers to segments seeking, and willing to pay for, additional value. Failing this, we commoditize our product as much as possible, making us the low-cost provider. Typically, however, we find that organizations that pray to the false god of cannibals try to execute both these strategies simultaneously. In so doing, they usually shackle one strategy to the other and then try to manage them both, demanding that each strategy either explicitly or tacitly provide for the successful outcome of the other.

This is a fool's errand. It is also completely unnecessary. Main Street customers gravitate to the value propositions *they* find most compelling. Therefore, to maximize customer satisfaction among your customers, *each* of your offerings should be *maximally attractive*. We achieve this by letting each compete against the other. By differentiating your offers based on what you know about customer segments, you increase the number of customer segments you can potentially engage over a significant amount of time. The Tide brand manager at Procter & Gamble develops strategy based on what is best for Tide, rather than on what is best for Tide and won't hurt Cheer. P&G knows that its success is dependent on selling as much laundry detergent to as many customers as possible. Each brand stands—or falls—on its own merits. So let the best offer win, for it will anyway.

Finally, going after your competition at the expense of your own installed base is fraught with danger. In a market where products convey a level of architectural control or lock-in, it is sheer folly. Such a strategy assumes that customers are once again going to switch part of their infrastructure to accommodate a new product that promises new benefits. Why would they ignore the switching costs associated with such an endeavor? The short answer is they wouldn't and they don't. Yet high-tech organizations continue to pursue such a strategy as a way of somehow defeating their (and they assume the market's) sworn enemies. Such was the strategy that Informix pursued in the mid-1990s when, in a fit of Oracle envy, the company announced and shipped a new and very discontinuous object-oriented database as the successor to its venerable and very competitive relational database. People weren't buying. "Why don't you improve on what you have," cried the installed base. Informix thought it was.

Almost at the same time, Novell was following a similar path. Envious of Microsoft, and spiteful of that company as well, it launched Netware 4, a significant improvement compared to the known, loved, and installed Netware 3. The ads proclaimed the seemingly magical powers associated with the new version. They did not mention the significant level of discontinuity that organizations, most perfectly happy with 3, would encounter trying to master 4. Novell's customers weren't buying, either. To make matters worse, customers fed up with Novell's preoccupation with Microsoft bit the switching-cost bullet and jumped to Microsoft, installing Windows NT. This, of course, was Novell's worst nightmare and ironically part of what 4.0 was designed to prevent. Failing to meet earnings estimates, Informix and Novell were both scalped by Wall Street. Both companies turned over management teams. Novell subsequently refocused its efforts on its "core business." Informix, having struck a deal with the Securities and Exchange Commission (SEC), decamped from Silicon Valley to Massachusetts, and later to Armonk, New York.

In markets where switching costs are not a significant issue, the wise marketer builds virtual switching costs, tempting customers with attractive terms and conditions, ease of acquisition programs, repeat or long-term purchase programs, and the like, all in an effort to manifest as much customer loyalty as possible. These things, if done even half well, usually work. Why? It's not the technology. It's the business model we become accustomed to as repeat customers. We may prefer a vendor solely by virtue of how we interact with them—as, for example, Dell. We may like a certain vendor's sales and support programs. Or we may enjoy something as subjective as one vendor's clever advertising or another vendor's charismatic founder.

Importantly, you should think of your +1 programs as potentially encompassing all these things. Virtually any type of offer has the potential to both reintroduce and reinforce a customer's commitment to your product and, far more important, to your company. This is both the essence and the goal of Main Street.

LIFE BEYOND MAIN STREET

The TALC models the adoption of discontinuous innovations. Main Street represents the completion of the cycle in the sense that discontinuity is no longer present in the product category. It does not represent the end of the category itself. On the contrary, we can now describe the category in terms of a *product* life cycle represented by the following diagram.

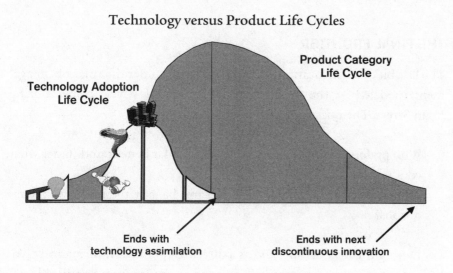

Technology versus Product Life Cycles

Technology Adoption
Life Cycle

Product Category
Life Cycle

Ends with
technology assimilation

Ends with next
discontinuous innovation

While not precise, the difference in the shapes of the two curves represents the uncertainty associated with the product life cycle. Its height represents all possible purchases from all buyers. Its length or persistence is dependent upon the next discontinuous innovation that will replace the category as a whole. Once again, consider the PC market. The fundamental technology is no longer discontinuous. Yet we have no clear picture as to how long this market will persist. Most likely, if Moore's law of very-large-scale integration continues to operate, it will be a very long time indeed. The shape of the product life cycle curve then is dependent upon the very market it represents.

Increasingly, however, customers, while desirous of the benefits that many of these same product categories deliver, now have more stuff to manage than time or resources allow. Thus we see the growth of outsourcing through companies, such as EDS or Jamcracker, that will provide the necessary platform—or plumbing, if you prefer—to support virtually any business process. We used to call these companies *service bureaus*. Today, we call them ASPs (application service providers). Customers moving to this kind of outsourcing are saying, in effect, that they want the benefits that many continuous as well as discontinuous innovations provide. They do not, however, want the responsibility and attendant cost of trying to manage it all while also trying to stay abreast of the latest developments.

They may also be saying something potentially more profound.

THE FINAL FRONTIER

The last bit of segmentation we will need to do under the rules of engagement modeled by the Technology Adoption Life Cycle comes during Main Street. The questions are rather simple:

- Who prefers the product form of a particular benefit and under what conditions?
- Who prefers the service form of the same benefit and under what conditions?

During the next decade, and as a direct result of the information revolution in general and pervasive influence of the Internet specifically, we are likely to see many types of industries discovering what is *core* to their business and what is *contextual*. The IT department for many organizations will be the focal point for this particular analysis, for it is this department that is at the forefront of a new global economy.

Core-versus-context (or "chores," as I now call them) issues will be debated around a central thesis: *What do we do, such that when we do it very well, the result improves our overall valuation, most often reflected in our stock price? Correspondingly, what do we do, such that when we do it well, the result has virtually no effect on valuation, and if we do it poorly, our valuation is diminished?*

If the product category is core to my business, I may wish to devote a significant amount of scarce resources—now recognized increasingly as human resources, management attention, and time—seeing to it that the product category continues to meet my needs going forward, since I will use the product to differentiate my own offering to my customers. On the other hand, if the product is really just *hygiene*—that is, I have to have it to operate my business, but the outcome of such an operation does not or cannot affect my valuation—I may choose to forgo devoting scarce resources in this direction and pay someone else outside my organization to devote their resources to its management. In other words, one person's context can be another person's core.[1]

This last idea gives rise to the final differentiation effort associated with Main Street as the Technology Adoption Life Cycle moves to the assimilation phase. Do we pursue differentiating our product because it is core to many of our customers' businesses, and because we have a significant stake in driving the category forward as gorillas, kings, chimps, or princes? Or do we pursue a strategy that morphs the final revision of the product to that of a service (and thus we become a service provider)? Or do we do a combination of both? Our ability to connect with and understand our customer base, combined with keen and realistic insights into how and why our category has made its way this far, serve both as guideposts for our next important decision as well as a harbinger of things to come.

RECAP

We have made it through the tornado to the promised land of Main Street. And we have done it realizing that there is more to life than just tornadoes. (Besides, that kind of excitement can kill you.) We have realized during this transition that virtually everything we did in the tornado is now dreadfully inappropriate for Main Street.

To recap the main points of this section, market forces before, during, and subsequent to hypergrowth—the tornado—impose different market

---

1. Geoffrey Moore's latest book, *Living on the Fault Line* (HarperBusiness, 2000), details this dilemma and all its implications.

growth models that in turn drive different market development strategies. We can illustrate the four basic growth models as follows:

Market Development Evolution

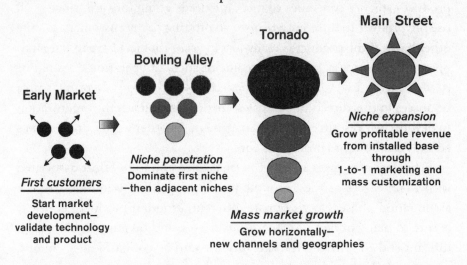

Early Market

First customers

Start market
development—
validate technology
and product

Bowling Alley

Niche penetration
Dominate first niche
—then adjacent niches

Tornado

Mass market growth
Grow horizontally—
new channels and geographies

Main Street

Niche expansion
Grow profitable revenue
from installed base
through
1-to-1 marketing and
mass customization

In the _early market_, adoption occurs through visionaries pursuing discontinuous innovations for the purpose of securing competitive advantage within their own categories. Prolonged or overly obsessive segmentation of the market is not necessary. These so-called new paradigms hold some breakthrough benefits when wielded correctly; however, they hold the promise for disrupting significantly existing infrastructures. As such, they will be avoided by those people who hold a continuing stake in the status quo.

The goal of early market development therefore is to _seed_ as many visionaries as possible with the new technology—and do anything to make them successful—such that the technology can be validated in real-world conditions, and such that these early customers can and will extol the virtues of this new approach.

In the _bowling alley,_ adoption is a function of how well a _killer application_ can be crafted for a particular customer segment (the beachhead segment) seeking to remediate a specific and compelling problem. Adoption among other, similar segments or niches will hinge on whether a whole product solution can be sufficiently tailored for each segment in the absence of an overall, generalized supporting infrastructure. Because creating such whole products for each niche is expensive initially, only those who will enjoy a strong economic return on their investment are likely to opt for this new approach. Accordingly, you need to seek niches that have a strong and compelling reason to buy. Obviously, segmentation is a prime requisite for whole product success. Finally, bowling alley market development requires focus. The key to success is leverage across other segments that can take advantage of a similar or identical whole product application and infrastructure. You must resist the temptation to wander off to new, noncontiguous segments that do not relate to your previous efforts.

In the *tornado,* however, this focused strategy should be abandoned in favor of generalizing the whole product solution as rapidly as possible. Now, mass adoption of the new paradigm and its corresponding infrastructure will cause demand to far outstrip supply. Winning the maximum number of new customers during this phase is the key to your future on Main Street, where the size of your addressable market will be governed for the most part by the size of your installed base. The tornado is a winner-take-all market that rewards those companies that can expand as rapidly as possible to reach new markets. Segmentation here is counterproductive to such efforts unless overall market expansion is the result.

Finally, the tornado subsides and the focus shifts from winning new customers—there are far fewer to win—to building more and more profitable business from the customers you have already won. Profitability on *Main Street* is a function of additional margin earned through providing additional and specific benefits to customer niches willing to pay for them. Once again, thoughtful segmentation is key to pursuing your +1 product strategy. Alternatively, vendors may pursue a low-cost provider direction.

Now that you have familiarized yourself with each of the four major types of markets, and witnessed how each is coherent in itself but contradictory to its neighbor on the TALC model, how can you use this information to help you succeed? And do it efficiently?

Turn the page.

Part Two

Developing a Strategy

This section provides a set of analytical models and tools forged out of The Chasm Group's consulting practice. Employing this Strategy Development Toolbox enables the rapid development and deployment of market strategy. The models are built on the theoretical precepts found in the preceding section.

▶ *Introduction*

No man is able to make progress when he is wavering between opposite things.

—EPICTETUS

Every year we have to wager our salvation on some prophecy based on imperfect knowledge.

—OLIVER WENDELL HOLMES

Too often, organizations commencing strategy development end up spinning their collective wheels because the process they follow is either arcane or archaic. Perhaps equally frustrating, the entire exercise usually takes too long. The result is typically a thick sheaf of PowerPoint slides that, while comprehensive in facts and historical analysis, delivers little by way of actionable "Now what do we do?" recommendations. When marketing organizations specifically try to take shortcuts to improve their time to market, results suffer as well, often because the strategy is based on poor or unfounded assumptions. One client laments, "We spend way too much time on strategic *planning*, rather than strategic *doing*."

Moreover, for most technology or technology-facilitated markets, making strategy decisions is a high-risk, low-data endeavor. This condition vexes all of us, and thus we turn for salvation to the *pundits* and *gurus* who wax eloquent about the promise of a new technology or product. Yet despite all the well-intentioned output of even the brightest technical and market analysts, much of their information is of the trailing indicator variety—historically derived, but you project it forward at your own considerable risk. In fact, market forecasting for some categories would cause even the most jaded carnival fortune-teller to blush. Figures seem to grow and grow, one assumption based on another, until it all comes crashing down in a market and market-capitalization meltdown reminiscent of Chernobyl.

Now well-reasoned quantitative analysis has its place, if for no other reason than your chief financial officer (CFO) will demand it. But successful market strategies in high tech can't be based solely on data. The fact remains that people respond differently to discontinuities, be they customers, partners, or high-tech organizations themselves. If strategy is to be implemented successfully—in other words, going from *strategic planning to strategic doing*—it must be developed, understood, and committed to by many different constituencies, including customers. The need for rapid and decisive responses to a shifting and ambiguous marketplace, and the need to gain teamwide commitment to these responses on a sustainable basis, requires new strategy creation alternatives to the traditional and time-consuming process of market research, quantitative analysis, diagnosis, and prescription. You need to follow a process that tempers or melds *analytical reason* with your and your organization's own *informed intuition*.

We believe that following a specific process utilizing the tool set described in this chapter delivers *quickly* a strategy statement that clarifies your thinking while at the same time focusing on those issues and assumptions that will underpin how you actually execute the strategy. This method also provides a "know before you go" approach in that the statement can be held to the appropriate qualitative and quantitative scrutiny, modified as required, and translated easily to relevant go-to-market programs.

PLANNING TOOLS

These tools are designed to aid you in developing your strategy based on where your product category fits within the TALC framework.

- **Life Cycle Placement:** Identifies where a product category is on the Technology Adoption Life Cycle.
- **Discontinuity Analysis Assessment:** Examines the sources and impacts of discontinuity.

STRATEGY MODELING TOOL

- **Market Development Strategy Checklist:** Nine elements that constitute a strategy statement.

Each of these elements represents a set of assumptions (which is all strategy really is) that must be addressed—and must be validated—if success is to be predicted. To address issue number two, for example, depends on the assumption stated in number one, and so on down the list. The list allows for speculation as well as analytical objectivity.[1]

1. Who is the target customer? What is the description of the ideal customer?
2. What is this customer's compelling reason to buy?
3. What is the whole product solution that fulfills this reason to buy?
4. Who are the key partners and allies who might be a part of a whole product solution?
5. What is the optimal, value-adding distribution scheme?
6. What is the price of the solution such that a measurable ROI can be realized?
7. Who, what, and where is the competition?
8. What is the optimal positioning for the product/service?
9. What is the next target segment that can/should be addressed?

---

1. One of the most fundamental challenges for most marketers is being open-minded enough to be *wrong*. In fact, being wrong is preferable initially so that we can "get wrong out of the way" in order to open the possibility of being *right*.

Finding Your Place on the Technology Adoption Life Cycle

LIFE CYCLE PLACEMENT TOOL

DESCRIPTION

The first exercise in virtually all high-technology strategy decisions should be determining where the product category as a whole is positioned using the following TALC diagram as reference.

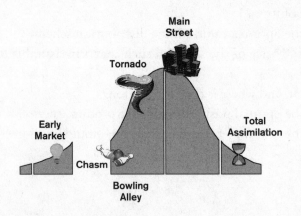

While making the right choice is usually based on judgment rather than fact, there are some keys that we can use to get us started in the right direction. Given a product category, consider placement based on the following:

1. **The Early Market:** Customers are visionaries under the influence of technology enthusiasts. The product is still immature, even though it may incorporate some type of existing technology. Often, a complete solution must be built from scratch for each customer, which may include a significant amount of systems integration unique to that customer's requirements. The press and the technical analyst community extol the merits of the category in glowing terms, positing it as the "next big thing."

2. **The Chasm:** Early market commitments now absorb all discretionary resources such that you cannot offer any more specials to visionaries. Pragmatists, however, do not see the references or the evidence of a whole product that would make you or the category a safe buy. Sales cycles are now rather lengthy, and most that do close are for pilot projects. Journalists and analysts are no longer as interested in the category as they once were and/or begin segmenting the overall category into product/solution species, some of which they still regard as viable going forward.

3. **Bowling Alley:** The product category reemerges but is now endorsed by pragmatist customers within the confines of one or more niche markets. Sales within these confines are predictable with good margins. Outside these confines, there are only opportunistic sales, often at significant discounts. Significant customization of the product solution may still be necessary outside of specific niche markets now forming. Specialist press and analyst communities now follow the category in the context of their particular area of interest or niche orientation.

4. **Inside the Tornado:** The product category is now enjoying broad appeal across a wide variety of market segments. This market acceptance is now drawing numerous vendors who can supply this category of product. A fierce market share war has developed and price discounting is becoming rampant. A market leader has emerged, establishing de facto standards, and this company may enjoy both better margins and shorter sales cycles than its competitors. Media coverage, for the most part, focuses on the market leader and its closest challengers. The technical analyst community now focuses on the strengths and weaknesses of each competitor.

5. **On Main Street:** The hypergrowth era is over. Market growth slows as the market saturates and matures. To expand further, some competitors are now modifying their standard offerings to appeal to niche markets. Other competitors compete on price alone. The market leader may still enjoy a margin premium but is under pressure to reduce price. Media coverage addresses primarily the market itself, rather than the product category, and the various players participating in the market.

6. **Total Assimilation:** The category now represents the final implementation of a given technology, and possibly is the last of its product type as well. While the benefits of the category may linger, often in the form of a service, product-based markets are now based on a new category of technology. There is little if any press or analyst coverage of the category. It is old news both literally and figuratively.

DISCUSSION AND IMPLICATIONS

Quite simply, placing the product category in its proper place on the TALC model is the first step in developing an appropriate market strategy. Significant resource expenditures will hinge on this choice. So let's make sure we understand what we're trying to accomplish.

Discontinuity manifests itself in two ways. *Paradigm shock* describes the amount of disruption likely to be experienced by buyers, be they technical buyers, end users, or economic buyers. The electric car story cited in chapter 2 is just such an example. Drivers will need to adopt new behaviors to cope with the limited range of an electric car, as will mechanics, insurance companies, public utilities, and even the employers of people who drive such vehicles. It is this paradigm shock that is currently holding back this innovation. In some cases, the shock can be fatal.

A second, more positive dimension of discontinuity is *application breakthrough,* the resulting benefits experienced by buyers that translate notably to dramatic returns on investment. For example, while the Internet can be considered as a significant breakthrough, applications such as e-commerce software, customer relationship management, and sales force automation all utilize its framework. These applications are delivering huge returns to both end users and the infrastructure vendors that support and extend them.

Taken together, application breakthrough and paradigm shock represent the accelerator and brake pedal, respectively, of technology adoption. The following diagram expresses both these concepts as x and y axes on a coordinate plane.

Discontinuity and the Life Cycle

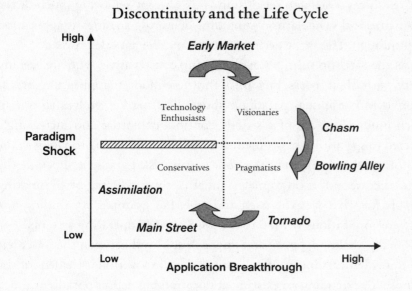

You interpret this model as follows:

The innovation life cycle starts in the upper left quadrant, where paradigm shock is significant and application breakthrough, while promising, is not yet apparent because such applications have yet to be deployed in a meaningful way. This is the realm of a technology enthusiast's personal interest or pet project. An early market emerges for the technology if technology enthusiasts pass on their recommendations to fellow techies and to visionaries.

These visionaries take the early market forward through the deployment of the new product category in the form of a new application. Such applications deliver significant benefits to the visionary, thus warranting the pain of their adoption in the form of paradigm shock. However, pragmatists are likely to not be so moved, preferring applications that minimize this shock.

Accordingly, proceeding to the lower right quadrant requires reducing this shock, possibly at the expense of some application breakthrough, such that pragmatists can proceed with confidence knowing that the new application provides a specific solution—and thus alleviates a specific problem—not only to warrant adoption but to pursue it. As the adoptive segments proliferate, conditions are thus fostered for a generalized solution, which the pragmatist herd can now be drawn to. The movement of the herd further reinforces a de facto set of standards, thereby removing much of the paradigm shock while at the same time delivering significant application breakthrough. This is the perfect circumstance for a market tornado.

As the tornado subsides, late-entering conservatives who are seeking parity with their peers buy into the now-modest application breakthrough with minimal paradigm shock. The market evolves to one in which innovations are of a strictly continuous nature and increasingly directed to specific niche segments. When customers cling too long to the comfort of the status quo, they once again risk paradigm shock as the infrastructure moves on to new standards, thus reducing or eliminating support for what was the tried and true. For example, try finding *new* software applications written to the DOS or VMS operating systems.

Finally, the model posits an impenetrable wall between the lower left and upper left quadrants. If a discontinuous innovation is fielded for the purposes of extending an existing application but causes paradigm shock in so doing, it is essentially unmarketable. Since conservatives and laggards will not tolerate any paradigm shock, any benefits that exact this cost will be ignored. You have reached the end of the cycle.

While there are other forces that can affect where an innovation should be placed on the TALC, considered analysis of both application breakthrough and paradigm shock provides a practical starting point that can be modified as new evidence is gathered or observed. Such analysis also serves as the underpinning for using the next set of tools.

USING THE TOOL

In practice, we begin our investigation by assembling a strategy team of interested parties. We ask each team member to place the category somewhere on the TALC, then discuss the individual answers and search for common ground so that we can decide on a single location.

The object of this exercise is not to arrive at an absolutely correct answer. The tool does not provide for such precision, so resist the temptation to parse or otherwise impart conditions on either the exercise or your answer. The critical success factor for any team performing this analysis is to reach consensus and act on that basis. The point is uniting a team to pursue the same course. The following are some guideposts to keep the team focused:

- Analyze where a product will enter the Technology Adoption Life Cycle when it is brought to market—that is, actually shipped. For example, if you are about to ship a product new to your organization but well understood and accepted by an existing market, it is not a priori an early market product.
- Life Cycle placement is geographically sensitive—that is, the category can be in different places depending on where it is in the world. If you are performing this analysis in a global context, make sure you specify the market under consideration.
- Rapid acceptance and adoption of a product in the early market does not necessarily mean that the product is consequently in a tornado. Quite often, new product categories experience this phenomenon because technology enthusiasts and their visionary sponsors react quickly to the newness of the category. Consider this adoption as early market only, until you're sure that significant numbers of pragmatists—usually found in definable segments—are adopting the category as well.
- A tornado of sorts is also possible in bowling alley markets. These occur when an application is found to be extremely effective in resolving a problem besetting a particular segment. Demand will outstrip supply. This is a good thing! However, don't assume that this local condition can be projected or sustained into other segments until you see evidence of such a move.
- If the transference does not occur, you can go to Main Street without having sustained a tornado. This happens whenever a product is found to be efficacious only in niche markets. A generalized solution and infrastructure never materializes beyond the niche segments served. Eventually, the category becomes commodity-like and the game is played under Main Street rules.
- If your product is failing, it may just be *you,* and thus it is not de facto a chasm category. Product categories can fail anywhere along the

Technology Adoption Life Cycle, though tornado failures are relatively unheard of. Also, emergence from the chasm of one competitor's product—or even several companies' products, for that matter—does not necessarily indicate that the category as a whole is emerging. Each competitor must extract itself from the chasm of its own accord. Here, a rising tide does not lift all boats.

9

Assessing the Sources and Impact of Discontinuity

DISCONTINUITY ANALYSIS TOOL

Continuing the application breakthrough/paradigm shock analysis, it's now useful to place the given product within a grid to assess the levels of both that you—and, more important, your organization—believe currently exist in your market offering. Use the following model to assess your current product offering:

Discontinuity Analysis Tool—Assessing Source and Impact

The benefit to users

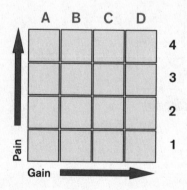

A: Provides modest enhancements
B: Adds substantial new value
C: Gives dramatic productivity gains
D: Changes the competitive field

4: Significant reengineering, new systems
3: Major changes to existing systems
2: Modest changes to existing systems
1: Integrates with existing systems

"Cost" of obtaining the benefit

USING THE TOOL

Ask your team to rank individually where they believe the current product resides. Remember that you're considering both gain and pain as a customer would see and experience it. The exercise will not pay dividends if you engage in wishful thinking rather than a candid assessment of the product. Accordingly, be realistic about what you're actually bringing to market.

After each individual has weighed in on where he/she believes the product to be, and has explained the rationale for such a decision, attempt to reconcile the selections to a final answer representing the team as a whole. Incidentally, it is quite common to see a diverse set of individual answers. This dispersion is indicative of how each individual perceives *what* the product does and *how* it actually does it. Coming to a common view serves once again to unify the team responsible for the product by declaring, if possible, what the product is.

Now, overlay the grid with the following additions. Note the positions of each TALC inflection point. These represent the ideal positions for each.

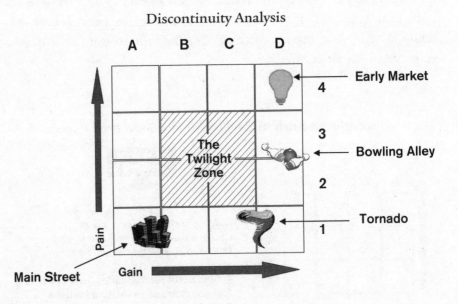

Discontinuity Analysis

DISCUSSION AND IMPLICATIONS

The positions of each icon shown in the grid above are emblematic of where your offers *should* be relative to gain and pain.

But first, let's consider the places we *don't* want to be. The first and most obvious positions occur in column A, row 2 through row 4. Nobody is interested in offers that promise pain with no commensurate gain. Such offers can be considered DOA—dead on arrival.

Of far more significance are offers that fall into what I call the twilight zone.

"You're traveling through a land of both substance and shadow . . ." intoned Rod Serling during the opening of this notable American television show of the 1960s. He could have been referring to products occupying this space in our grid. Offers placed here face an uncertain future. While they may offer gain, they do so at an equivalent level of pain. "Too little gain for too much pain" is how we might colloquially describe them. While far from being DOA, they nonetheless are not very compelling, leaving one equivocal as to their true value. Such offerings do not spur market movement.

In our consulting practice, we see numerous examples of teams rating their products in just this position, particularly when cautioned against either unbridled optimism or outright hype. Clearly, redress is in order. But what should we do?

MOVING FROM WHERE YOU ARE TO WHERE YOU WANT TO BE

The first step is to move the product from the twilight zone by either making it more valuable—that is, causing the offer to provide more gain— or lessening the paradigm shock—the pain—associated with its adoption. *What you are really deciding is whether you should leverage an existing value chain or attempt to create a new one.* The following can help guide you through the decision:

- *Moving to the early market (D4).* This decision entails creating a new value chain and is governed by whether such an offer can actually be significantly improved. In other words, can it deliver order-of-magnitude benefits and create sufficient barriers to entry to all but technology enthusiasts and visionaries as to warrant the development of a new value chain that will eventually challenge an existing chain? This then requires new innovation, new technological breakthroughs—and all the attendant resources necessary to create the new chain.

- *Moving to the bowling alley (D2/D3).* This move requires careful market segmentation in order to complete a compelling whole product solution and value proposition for a given niche segment while at the same time minimizing the pain of adoption, or at least making the pain a more than favorable trade-off.

- *Moving to the tornado (C1/D1).* Going into a tornado assumes that (a) tornado warnings are present and a tornado may be imminent; (b) your product can be generalized and commoditized for widespread adoption; and (c) your business, operational, and go-to-market footing can accommodate the demands of the tornado. For a customer, all this translates to all gain and no pain, at least to the extent that this pain can be managed through an already changing infrastructure or the realization that what I suffer, my competitors will suffer as well.

- *Moving to Main Street (A1/B1).* Moving in this direction requires that you segment your market beginning with your installed base—your most likely customers—and extend the effort to those market segments that may be underserved or have not adopted. Having learned what various segments are looking for in additional benefits and what they're willing to pay to acquire them, you commence the process of mass customization, approaching each segment with an appropriate offer. Bear in mind that many high-tech organizations fail here because they focus on adding too many functions, thereby risking discontinuity and/or higher prices; or they attack their competitors' installed base without a careful examination of the potential infrastructure switching costs that customers might experience.

The key to using this exercise in an effective way is understanding that equivocal, "centered" offerings will be more difficult and confusing to manage than offerings found at the "eastern" and "southern" perimeters of the grid. Using Tool 1 and Tool 2 together provides you with the navigational aids necessary to move to the next phase: strategy development.

10

Building a Market Development Strategy

Pray, on one side of this paper, state how the British navy is being modernised for warfare.

—WINSTON CHURCHILL

This section details our fundamental methodology for expressing a market development strategy using the Market Development Strategy Checklist (or MDSC).

The MDSC consists of a set of assumptions around which a strategy statement can be built. This statement can be likened to a *blueprint* that one would use to build a house or office building. The starting point and underpinning of the statement—the foundation—is a description of the *target customer*. This, like the foundation of any structure, influences significantly how the remaining elements of the structure will be built.

The strategy statement can also be seen as a *declaration of intent.* Such a declaration should direct the development of the go-to-market programs—for example, sales strategy, marketing communications, and the like—so that strategy and execution are directly related and unified.

Market Development Strategy Checklist

Source of money ➡ **1. Target customer**

2. Compelling reason to buy ⬅ Source of demand

To fulfill the compelling
reason to buy ➡ **3. Whole product**

4. Partners and allies ⬅ Needed for whole product

Function of whole product
integration complexity ➡ **5. Distribution**

6. Pricing ⬅ Function of perceived value

For customer's money ➡ **7. Competition**

8. Positioning ⬅ Relative to competition

Next move ➡ **9. Next target**

The MDSC template holds for all stages in the Technology Adoption Life Cycle.

USING THE CHECKLIST

To begin, and to use this model properly, you *must* start with element number one before you address element number two, and so on. Each element or key assumption is based on the assumptions that precede it, although different market development strategies will stress certain elements so the time and energy you devote to considering each element may vary significantly. Thus, when you consider an element—for example, deciding upon channels-based distribution rather than utilizing a direct-to-customer approach such as you had chosen previously—such a strategy modification may render subsequent assumptions—pricing, competition, and so on—irrelevant or invalid. These subsequent elements must also be reconsidered in light of the modification you have made to a preceding element. The model is both hierarchical and recursive. Beginning with or changing one assumption affects all subsequent assumptions.

Using the tool this way keeps your thinking focused and logically arrayed. The process can also be iterative. If you find yourself blocked on a certain element, you can get past it by going back and reexamining earlier choices, changing your thinking as necessary. The model is also designed to combat the tendency of high-tech organizations to *assert* certain elements of strategy—for example, declaring a distribution strategy solely because "that's the way we always do it." And finally, using the MDSC enables, with appropriate editing, an entire strategic statement to be summarized on a single screen, slide, or piece of paper. This is a very effective means of communicating an overview of what you intend to accomplish to a variety of stakeholder organizations.

You begin the exercise by expressing your answers for each element in the checklist. This section describes each element in summary. In the next section, we will examine in detail how each element varies depending on Technology Adoption Life Cycle considerations.

MARKET DEVELOPMENT STRATEGY CHECKLIST DESCRIPTION SUMMARY

1. **Target Customer.** High-tech target customer sets typically comprise an economic buyer, a technical buyer, and an end user. Each group asserts its influence at different points on the TALC. The economic buyer is the key to all phases prior to the tornado. The technical buyer is the focus during the tornado, while the end user dominates on Main Street.

2. **Compelling Reason to Buy.** To build an effective strategy you must understand in detail the target customer's motivation to buy. These motivations change over the course of the Technology Adoption Life Cycle as follows:

  - Technology enthusiasts and visionaries in an early market are *searching for and investigating novel technologies and applications in search of dramatic competitive advantage,* resulting in substantial upside gains versus the status quo.
  - Pragmatists in chasm and bowling alley markets are looking to *solve a significant business problem that is not addressable by current methods, applications, or systems.* If the problem is left to persist, it threatens to cause even more widespread problems across an organization or enterprise.

- Pragmatists in tornado markets are moving to *deploy new, now reliable (and soon-to-be ubiquitous) infrastructures*. Such customers are now moving almost in unison to adopt this new paradigm; as a result, the phase shift tends to be massive and pervasive across market segments.
- Pragmatists and conservatives in Main Street markets are now exercising several different prerogatives, including *cost optimization* through the acquisition of lower-priced versions and *personal preferences* to acquire specific benefits.

These reasons to buy are not easily combinable because the market development strategies required to address them contradict each other. Prioritize one over all others based on your current TALC placement. You should change to the new value proposition during any transition phase even though it may feel that it is too early to do so.

3. **Whole Product.** This comprises the minimum set of products and services needed to fulfill the target customer's compelling reason to buy. The whole product is the critical success factor in chasm-crossing and bowling alley market initiatives leading to segment and market dominance. If any part of the whole product is left unaccounted for, then the entire solution falls apart. As a result, the compelling reason to buy is not addressed satisfactorily and the market does not emerge. During the tornado, whole products should be standardized and commoditized as much as possible to speed deployment. On Main Street, market segmentation once again determines how the product will be differentiated, typically through further commoditization or +1, value-added efforts.

4. **Partners and Allies.** These groups represent anyone outside the chief sponsor of the whole product who can play a potential role in creating, delivering, and/or endorsing the whole product. Beginning in the early market and reaching a zenith during the bowling alley, partner recruitment must be aggressively pursued. Such partners will only be attracted to those opportunities in which they see a clear and obtainable economic rationale that benefits them. During a tornado, partners must be pared back to increase both efficiencies and margin allocations. By Main Street, partners are typically at a minimum and may emerge only on an ad hoc basis.

5. **Distribution.** Two principles govern what distribution method should be chosen to sell, deploy, and support a new product: *solution complexity* and *marketing complexity*. Typically, early market efforts rely on vendor-sponsored, direct distribution. Chasm-crossing and bowling alley markets are segment directed, and thus the nature of the segment often determines additional channels that may serve segment-specific requirements. Tornadoes require dramatically expanded distribution to satisfy customer demand. Main Street markets most often reward low-cost distribution efforts.

6. **Pricing.** Pricing models shift over the Technology Adoption Life Cycle as business models change. Early market pricing is the most fluid, often based on a deal struck between buyer and seller based on anticipated value, discounted for risk, often as part of a specific customer project. Bowling alley pricing is value based, derived from eliminating the costs associated with the problem addressed. Tornado pricing is based on competition and considers one's position within the gorilla/chimp/monkey or king/prince/serf hierarchy. Main Street pricing typically is the most complex, reflecting an offering that is based either on a commodity or on a given level of differentiation.

7. **Competition.** Competitive positions typically reflect two sets: *reference* competition, a set of alternatives that reflect an overall position (benefit and differentiation); and *economic* competition, a set of alternatives that compete for a customer's budget. Offers are *differentiated* from both one's reference competitors and one's economic competitors. In the early market, the reference competition is the status quo, and the economic competition is in the form of alternative discontinuous innovations that also promise significant, competitive advantages. In the bowling alley, the status quo remains the economic competition, necessitating that a crisis be recognized that the status quo can't address. In contrast, reference competition is chosen and highlighted so that customers recognize that there is a choice as to how to address the crisis. These are offers that are not directed to a specific target segment (and a specific problem) and thus cannot provide either an adequate or comparable whole product solution. In the tornado, all competition is biased almost exclusively to economic factors, and thus every competitor is the enemy. On Main Street, economic competitors may be low-cost alternatives that are competed

against through *business models;* or they may be other reference competitors that are competed against through *various forms of differentiation.* Both involve +1 offers. Increasingly, many companies gain competitive positions through the influence and domination of the value chain they occupy. Since new market creation is inherently a cooperative initiative that is very apparent to customers, they choose value propositions after weighing the pros and cons of competing or alternative chains.

8. **Positioning.** This element refers to asserting and occupying an advantageous position within two systems: the first is the system of *buying choices* that the target customer may consider; the second is the system of *partners and allies* that constitute a given value chain in the marketplace. In the early market, the target customers are technology enthusiasts and, more significantly, visionaries; and the buying choice alternatives consist of various discontinuous innovations that might lead to dramatic competitive advantage. The desired position is to be the *best choice.* In chasm-crossing and bowling alley markets, the target customer is a pragmatist searching for a solution to a vexing business problem. Buying choices consist of alternatives that appear promising, albeit somewhat risky. The desired position is to be the first verifiably *complete solution* to the problem, thus mitigating the risk. Partners and allies complete the formation, delivery, and endorsement of the solution. With such compatriots, the desired position here is to be the *leader of the pack*—that is, the one who has sorted out a complete solution that will lead to wealth for all who participate. In the tornado, the target customer continues to be pragmatists and the first conservatives now challenged with implementing infrastructure change. Buying choices consist of all competitors vying to supply such infrastructure, and the desired position is to be the *gorilla,* number one in market share and the de facto standard for the market. *Chimps* opt for the best solution, aiming at retaining and expanding if possible their niche following, while *monkeys* may pursue a best, low-cost alternative. Main Street positioning involves primarily appealing to your installed base, providing offers that reward end users for their continued loyalty.

9. **Next Target.** Literally the next target customer, this element is based on the inflection point and market development model appropriate

to each phase of the Technology Adoption Life Cycle. In the early market, it is either the next visionary customer; or, if chasm crossing, the first niche segment. In the bowling alley, it is the next niche segment selected because it parlays previous efforts in whole product development and/or customer references. In the tornado, the next target is the next set of infrastructure buyers, reached through new geographies, new distribution channels, or new versions of the platform. During the Main Street phase, the next target is the next imaginable end user. Such targets can be described in myriad terms, including geographies, user profiles, or most profitable.

11

Market Development Strategy Checklist: Market Creation Variables

As long as I have a want, I have a reason for living. Satisfaction is death.

—GEORGE BERNARD SHAW

You can see a lot by watching.

—YOGI BERRA

This section details the first three of nine fundamental assumptions that constitute a market development strategy statement and specifies how each element should be considered across the Technology Adoption Life Cycle.

STRATEGY ASSUMPTION 1: THE TARGET CUSTOMER

If the ultimate function of strategy is to create wealth for a company, its shareholders, its employees, and the community, the key to this objective is determining the first of two demand variables: *who are the customers that currently have money and are willing and able to transfer it to you?* Customer selection may be based on rather precise definitions arrived at through various segmentation methods. Or it may simply be an educated or intuitive guess. In either case, a good starting point is to understand thoroughly the customer domain of the value chain model, specifically: technical buyers, end users, and economic buyers. It's useful to consider these customers in the following array:

MARKET
DEVELOPMENT
STRATEGY
CHECKLIST:
MARKET CREATION
VARIABLES

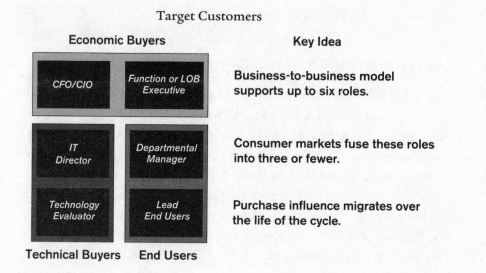

A business-to-business market model, most prevalent in high-technology markets, can support up to six different customer roles (as shown above). While the titles may change depending on specific industry, the roles of these various buyers tend to remain the same. By contrast, most consumer marketing models typically consolidate these roles to a singular one—we as consumers act as all three. To be sure, you will also encounter B2B markets and circumstances where all three roles are consolidated as well. However, when we consider an entire life cycle, the *influence* that any one group or individual exerts during the purchase cycle is likely to change as we move from early to mainstream markets.

Typically, success with a given set of prospects will be predicated on whether or not you have found potential customers who are:

- Identifiable and thus can be accessed through sales and marketing efforts
- Sufficiently well funded as to be able to purchase in a reasonable time frame and under appropriate circumstances
- Have the ability and power to actually make the purchase

Customers who either lack the wherewithal or lack the authority to make purchase decisions are, shall we say, *less attractive* than people who meet such criteria. Ultimately, pursuing a customer who can say yes is our strategic objective. The following describes the three buyers and how their influence waxes and wanes though the TALC.

TARGET CUSTOMERS IN THE EARLY MARKET

Early markets develop when a visionary *economic buyer*—the primary sponsor—supported by a *technical buyer*—the secondary sponsor—searches for and finds a discontinuous innovation that the economic buyer believes can deliver significant competitive advantage, provided that the innovation can be properly harnessed and utilized. Typically, the economic buyer is a senior-level executive who has both the funding to purchase the innovation and the power within the organization to sponsor a potentially risky initiative. Because of these traits, early market economic buyers tend to be the least price sensitive of any group that will be encountered going forward. Intellectually curious, ambitious, and acquisitive, such buyers also serve as bellwethers to other visionary groups, often in different industries. Many of them are only too willing to serve as highly visible references garnering attention from the press and pundits in their own right, but also transferring this attention to start-up or fledgling enterprises.

The secondary sponsor is usually best described as a *technology evaluator.* This description does not indicate where such an individual is in an organizational hierarchy. Rather, this individual (or group) has an affinity for sniffing out the intricacies of a discontinuous innovation to discover (a) what will actually work in practice and what will fall apart; (b) what others in the techie fraternity are saying about this approach; (c) what the various camps are that may now be forming to support or resist the innovation; and (d) the overall likelihood that the innovation will have enough horsepower to really provide the kind of advantage the economic buyer is looking for.

Note, however, that it is insufficient to target just the technology evaluator (though it is vital to build strong relationships with them). In order for the market to spawn, money must be cadged from the economic buyer who is prepared to move past an evaluation and rapidly into deployment. Naturally, the visionary committed to sponsoring your discontinuous innovation will also exact a quid pro quo. He or she will be a highly demanding and vocal customer who will seek to influence significantly your future product and marketing direction and will go directly to senior management to state his or her case or air his or her views, making any number of people's lives miserable in the process.

Just remember the money . . . the money . . . the money.

MARKET
DEVELOPMENT
STRATEGY
CHECKLIST:
MARKET CREATION
VARIABLES

TARGET CUSTOMERS IN THE CHASM AND THE BOWLING ALLEY

The primary sponsor for both these markets is typically a senior-level manager who represents and is part of an *end user* constituency. The secondary sponsor is the executive to whom this end user group ultimately reports. Both sponsors are now likely to be pragmatists, intrigued by a certain level of discontinuity but unwilling to abandon currently working (or barely working) systems until forced of necessity to do so. And, unlike many visionaries, they are unlikely to come looking for you. Instead, you must look for them. Identifying who they might be is an intuitive exercise initially, and it won't be accomplished by poring over reams of statistics concerning total *available markets* or sifting through traditional segmentation data based largely on demographics or *vertical markets*.

In fact, the most difficult challenge in crossing the chasm or working the bowling alley is target customer segment identification, particularly when you have what you believe to be a purely *horizontal* product line—that is, one designed so that everyone can use it. Targeting niche customer segments simply seems wrong. (And when you do quantify the initial segment, it will seem almost impossibly wrong.) Bear in mind, however, that you are going after pragmatists who will first adopt at the fringes or outskirts of the main herd. The only way to accelerate adoption later will be to find these prospects now. The tool we use to search for these initial ideal customers is the application scenario. This is effectively a day-in-the-life summary of a target *end user* describing conditions before—and after—they obtained the new product. The focus of the summary is the change in effectiveness of the end user, postpurchase, particularly as it relates to a critical concern of the *economic buyer*. (See the Appendix for a detailed explanation of how to segment a potential market.)

Identifying the target customer involves a critical understanding. You must learn *not* how the end user benefits from the new system per se, but instead how the economic buyer redresses the economic conditions and consequences currently being endured through end users operating under the status quo. More simply, we are looking for end users whose current way of doing things is breaking or broken, all of which causes great pain to the people they report to.

TARGET CUSTOMERS IN THE TORNADO

In *Inside the Tornado,* Geoff Moore exhorted readers to ignore the customer during the tornado. He went on to state that when market tornadoes occur, the proper response is to focus on the infrastructure or technical buyers—the primary and only sponsors—rather than economic buyers and end users. He did not mean literally *ignore customers!* The issue, you see, is one of appealing to infrastructure buyers in the most relevant and efficient way because these individuals are now tasked with the duty of acquiring the obvious, and doing it quickly. A case can be made that in fact, the economic buyer and end user both will be disrupted, since infrastructure swap-outs are rather pervasive and unsettling (similar perhaps to remodeling your home and living in it at the same time); thus, spending too much time with either of these groups is bound to make you, the vendor, less appealing rather than more. Just ask how many executives would like to revisit their decisions to approve ERP deployments over the past five years. It's not that they don't like the ROI associated with these new systems; they do. It's that the disruption, uncertainty, and cost that they and their companies lived with—for longer periods than promised—are still fresh in their minds. And many now find that all their other systems—indeed, their business—are captive to this new animal.

The point is that spending time identifying in great detail the motivations of economic buyers and end users is *not* time well spent. A highly targeted segmentation effort is, for the most part, not a critical success factor. Most often, any segmentation that is useful has to do with geographies, vertical markets, platforms, and special applications. We don't envision using the scenario methodology noted above except in cases where chimps, having conceded the gorilla position, now must circle back to their original devotees in an attempt to become a "gorilla in the niche."

TARGET CUSTOMERS ON MAIN STREET

MARKET
DEVELOPMENT
STRATEGY
CHECKLIST:
MARKET CREATION
VARIABLES

Of course, those of you who did completely ignore customers, particularly end users, during the tornado now have a lot of work to do. Prior to Main Street, end users have taken a backseat relative to economic and technical/infrastructure buyers. Their concerns, for the most part, have been subordinated to other two groups. However, their influence comes to the fore in Main Street markets. Economic buyers have now turned their attention to other matters since ROI is no longer an issue. And technical buyers are no longer very interested, either, because they view the support of such systems as maintenance. Now you need to reconnect with the end user.

These buyers are looking to acquire additional features based largely on issues that can be lumped into the category of *personal satisfaction*. This motivation now serves as the new, once again fertile ground of competition based on segment selection and differentiated offerings, practiced through the art of mass customization. Since margin pressures are most often felt in Main Street markets, insightful segmentation of these end users offers margin-rich opportunities, or at least margin relief, from the otherwise commodity nature of the typical market at this stage. As such, segmentation efforts can now explore many different avenues, typically through market research, including focus groups, usage and attitude studies, customer satisfaction surveys, and the like. In fact, for the first time, marketers can now drive the differentiation process—indeed, the business itself—since large-scale reengineering efforts are both unnecessary and unwanted by customers. Ceding the process to the marketing department is not always celebrated within high-tech organizations, but it's the first time where it is completely warranted.

STRATEGY ASSUMPTION 2: THE COMPELLING
REASON TO BUY (CRTB)

The target customer's willingness to part with his/her money is dependent on this second demand variable. In business-to-business transactions the motive to purchase invariably is a function of the *economic consequences* of either doing nothing or making an investment to exploit a current opportunity or redress a current problem. This economic motivation can be *overt* and thus very apparent to all involved in the decision, particularly in bowling alley and tornado markets. Or the motivation is more *latent* (early market and Main Street)—that is, the benefit of purchase may not be apparent to all concerned but is understood and appreciated by the person(s) willing to put up the money. This is not to say a compelling reason to buy is always a rational decision. It can be a highly emotional one. Rather, I suggest that unlike many purchase decisions we face as consumers, the criteria by which we analyze whether we will choose to move one way versus another are more objective rather than less, and less emotional rather than more. After all, it's usually not our money! As a general rule, we must justify our thinking and decision process not only to ourselves but also to our colleagues, managers, and shareholders alike. The necessity for such justification has significant implications for your strategy depending, naturally, on where you place your category using the TALC.

"BUT ENOUGH ABOUT YOU. LET'S TALK ABOUT MY PRODUCT."

You have been admonished previously. Permit me to admonish you again. **Do not confuse a customer's compelling reason to buy with your compelling reason to sell.** The answer to the CRTB question is *not* a function of the features and benefits (all twenty of them!) that you and your product purport to offer. To answer this question, you must know who your target customer is and the situation that customer faces. If you don't know your target, you can't know their compelling reason to buy.

Similarly, if your target selection is overly general—for example, "IT directors in Global 2000 companies"—and your understanding of their issues is superficial or misinterpreted—"They want to obtain competitive advantage through a highly reliable, available and scalable customer relationship management application . . ."—you have accomplished little by way of informed, useful, and actionable information. In our experience, by the way, such mistakes are commonplace. They are usually indicative notably of sales and marketing organizations overly preoccupied with their own products—a condition also prevalent throughout high tech in general. Such organizations are prone to squandering valuable resources, notably time, haggling over *what* a customer is supposed to buy rather than *who* such customers are, *why* they would buy, and *how* their situations are improved when they do buy.

COMPELLING REASONS TO BUY IN EARLY MARKETS

MARKET
DEVELOPMENT
STRATEGY
CHECKLIST:
MARKET CREATION
VARIABLES

Technology enthusiasts and visionaries enthralled by discontinuous innovations as a means of achieving technical and/or competitive breakthroughs are like the batter in baseball who hits a grand slam in the bottom of the ninth. Or the forward who drives downfield to score a seemingly impossible goal in the final seconds of a soccer match. Or the point guard who waits, then shoots a three-point basket with one second left on the clock. In the language of sports, we call these *low percentage plays;* they don't happen very often and, chances are, they won't happen at all. Yet we call the players who seem to specialize in them heroes. Figuratively, our visionaries aren't interested in an invigorating dip in the ocean. They want to swim the English Channel. Seeing a new part of the world may not provoke their curiosity. Going to the moon does.

In science and the arts—and certainly in business—these individuals are motivated to break with the status quo and use the discontinuity of any innovation to chart a course previously not taken. Visionaries' motivations literally fuel the existence of many high-technology companies because they provide the first real testing ground, not to mention financing, for those companies to strut their stuff. And your stuff better be pretty damn good. Visionaries' compelling reasons to buy are not based on achieving modest gains or any type of incremental advance. They are looking instead for massive, paradigm-shifting market busters that can rearrange competitive landscapes if successfully mastered. The ability to tame such beasts (the innovation, not the customer!) also must be seen by the visionary and technology enthusiast alike as *nontrivial.* Techies and visionaries, like bodybuilders, seem just as interested in the process as in the result. They know the process itself throws up barriers to entry to all those who cannot abide the pain of developing, structuring, and deploying the discontinuity to achieve such results. Thus, high gain is only achieved with high pain.

COMPELLING REASONS TO BUY IN CHASM AND BOWLING ALLEY MARKETS

All that high-pain, high-gain stuff may sound good to visionaries, but the pragmatist early majority thinks it's all a load of rubbish. Pain is involved, that's for sure. But it's the pragmatist who is suffering it. All because his/her business or operational processes are beginning to break down, and the current systems—the value chain now in place—are just not up to the task of reversing these declines. Here, prospects in the form of departmental managers are trying to cope with the problems that end users are now facing with frightening regularity. Their bosses, the economic buyers, are now thinking of their businesses (not to mention their careers) as in jeopardy. Quite simply, the compelling reason to buy for both groups is get out of this predicament. In practice, we call this situation "bleeding from the neck."

Chasm-crossing failures typically stem from vendors not really finding enough pain out there. Pragmatists are sensible sorts, and they're not going to trade one pain that is at least known for another that is not. Thus, you must be able to quantify (best case) or at least model the results that your innovation will deliver over the pragmatist's current system. The beachhead segment in chasm crossing is identified chiefly on the basis of that segment that is under the most pain and therefore must solve the problem now.

To work the bowling alley, you must continue to identify segments whose problems are similar to the ones labored under by previous segments you have served *and* who believe that your references are valid. Bowling alley efforts can fizzle out because marketers do a poor job of targeting like-minded segments. Or they choose a segment that virtually no one else in the market would reference, like the U.S. Defense Department or the U.K.'s Ministry of Defense. (It's hardly surprising that in this post–Cold War era, many defense contractors who are well versed in taming discontinuity have had to sell off many of their assets due to an inability to really extend their capabilities beyond the world's armed forces and government agencies.)

Thus, the key to ascertaining a compelling reason to buy and acting on it involves identifying and empathizing with the customer's problems, intimately and completely. This is hard work. It's no wonder we dislike doing it.

COMPELLING REASONS TO BUY IN THE TORNADO

The only time during the Technology Adoption Life Cycle when the compelling reason to buy will be glaringly obvious is leading up to and during the tornado. The period just preceding the tornado is when it is apparent that a significant number of customer segments are now adopting the new paradigm. These are the tornado *warnings* that I refer to earlier in this book. At some point, the remainder of the herd, now led by technical or infrastructure buyers, answers affirmatively to the question, "Is it time to move?"

We needn't belabor buyers' motivations at this point, for they are neither profound nor surprising. First, buyers need to stay competitive within their own market spaces. The new paradigm has now demonstrated its ability to reward the haves and penalize the have-nots. No one wants to be left behind. Second, tornadoes are built typically around infrastructure swap-outs that are often necessary because of a larger goal—for example, application servers and e-commerce IT platforms are acquired to enable and support e-business. Therefore, future processes and products will be built around these new infrastructures. Legacy infrastructures will be ignored or expressly left behind. No one wants to be incompatible with future developments.

Those who man the laboring oars within the organization's infrastructure—be it physical plant or IT—see the tornado opportunity as a way of both getting rid of the old stuff that has now outlived its usefulness and embracing the new paradigm as a way of prolonging and extending their own value. New systems require new expertise, and such chances don't come often. Since all these motivations tend to merge as one, and since all the people with such motivations tend to act as one, demand vastly outstrips supply. The compelling reason to buy? I gotta have it.

COMPELLING REASONS TO BUY ON MAIN STREET

On Main Street, the fundamental reasons to buy encountered in earlier markets—untapped opportunities, solving problems, or infrastructure transition—are now largely absent. In fact, the reasons to buy may be largely secondary in nature. The economic buyer cares only that such purchases are within budget and are not otherwise disruptive to the business (and why would they be?). The technical buyer's interests are purely that of compatibility and meeting standards. Thus, Main Street buyers are *end users* who will exercise their own prerogatives, usually emphasizing personal preferences.

But what are these preferences? How do we find out? As noted in the section on target customers on Main Street, the answer is that of "seek

MARKET
DEVELOPMENT
STRATEGY
CHECKLIST:
MARKET CREATION
VARIABLES

and ye shall find." There are many ways to go about this with the Internet now offering exciting new possibilities for almost instant customer feedback. Now that the adoption of an innovation is reaching its zenith, your ability to extend this reach and lengthen the *profitable* duration over which the innovation persists is directly correlated to your ability to segment your customer base. Now you need to find those customers who will be your best customers—that is, customers who will continue to purchase and who may pay premiums to obtain additional benefits highly personal in nature. How do you find them? To paraphrase a line from *The Godfather,* "Make them an offer they can't refuse."

As an example, consider the airline industry. As a frequent traveler, I belong to the frequent-flyer clubs of numerous air carriers, based both in the United States and elsewhere around the globe. I'm told that British Airways is "the world's favourite airline," and I'm aware that American Airlines claims to be the largest. I assume that both claims are made on the basis of numbers of passengers flown, destinations served, number of aircraft in the fleet, or whatever. I assume that both airlines invest some effort understanding something about all the passengers they serve. But judging from the amount of mail I receive every month, I also assume that they invest a great deal of effort trying to find out about me and the small but incredibly lucrative segment of the air travel market I represent: the frequent business traveler. You may hold this somewhat dubious honor as well.

Owing to our schedules, we often must pay full fares for tickets. While we're awarded lots of miles for our efforts, these are a pittance compared to our value as customers. In fact, we account for *over two-thirds* of the profits of the airlines that serve us while accounting for *less than one-third* of their total passengers. (We stay in business-oriented hotels and often rent cars and are as prized by these companies as well.) Is it any wonder, therefore, that my mailbox is stuffed with offers enticing me to fill out one more questionnaire "so that we may better serve your every need"? However, instead of asking me questions about my habits and preferences (something I have little time for anyway), *give me an offer and see what I do.* For example, entreat me to "book your next *business* trip to Europe with us and receive triple mileage credits." But I have lots of miles, you might say. Ah, but what if I'm approaching some mileage credit threshold where I will achieve some new and exalted status, thereby entitling me to be showered with all manner of gifts, booking privileges, onboard meal choices, and the like? And so it goes.

In a world of commodity-like offerings, those who prosper on Main Street will understand who I am, what I want, and what I'm willing to pay for—and be able to compare and contrast such a profile to that of, well, you. More important, we can both be served well.

This is the stuff of business to consumer (B2C) commerce on the Net. Progress to date has not been all that thrilling given that many high-tech organizations are still exploring this most basic marketing discipline: *finding out what the customer wants and giving it to them*. In fairness, the capability was probably not utilized extensively during the tornado, when reasons to buy were obvious. In Main Street, however, reconnecting with the customer, specifically the end user, is virtually mandatory. In fact, if you do not, you risk conceding future purchase to purchasing departments. And if you do not, you can't address the next section—to which we now move.

STRATEGY ASSUMPTION 3: THE WHOLE PRODUCT

A whole product is defined as the complete set of products and services needed for the customer to fulfill the compelling reason to buy, and it is the first of three *fulfillment* variables. The whole product concept is detailed extensively in Theodore Levitt's *The Marketing Imagination*.[1] Levitt postulates a gap between the marketing promise made to customers and the actual ability of the purchased product to deliver on that promise. To eliminate or otherwise bridge the gap, additional products and services are necessary to augment or complement the product so that it becomes a complete solution and thus lives up to its value proposition. Defining and completing the whole product is crucial for crossing the chasm and extending your reach into the bowling alley. Moreover, the completion of a whole product designed to meet a specific compelling reason to buy is fundamental to the creation and propagation of a *killer application* that persists well beyond Main Street. To define a whole product is obviously dependent on your target customer and CRTB assumptions. But you also must consider whether such a solution can be assembled in a timely manner.

---

1. Theodore Levitt, *The Marketing Imagination* (Free Press, 1993).

Whole Product Model

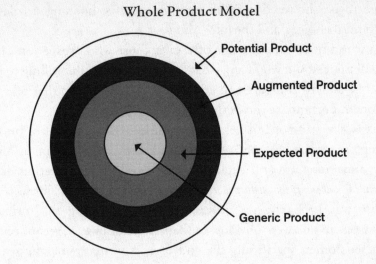

Using Levitt's whole product model shown above, consider whole product in context for each stage of the Technology Adoption Life Cycle.

Generic product indicates what is shipped when a purchase is made. *Expected* product is the product that the customer thinks she is buying when she orders the generic product. For example, if the generic product is a personal computer, the expected product is the CPU, plus a keyboard, a mouse, a monitor, and the appropriate cabling. *Augmented* product is the idealized form of the product so that there is a maximum chance that the buyer will achieve his/her stated buying objective. Using the PC example, this would include software, a printer, Internet connections, and a variety of other services to ensure or improve a favorable user experience. *Potential* product represents the ostensible growth path of the benefits conveyed by the product as it is enhanced and as it is complemented and strengthened by other products and services, thereby extending further the benefits of the product.

Early market products most often resemble *generic* products, though they are often marketed as *potential* products. (In my opinion, most of us are suitably inured to such posturing that we interpret such potential as pie in the sky until proven otherwise.) Going forward, mainstream markets form only through the successful development and deployment of *expected* and, more important, *augmented* products. As the model suggests, these two interim steps are necessary before the real potential of the product unfolds.

We can bring together the whole product model and the TALC in the following diagram:

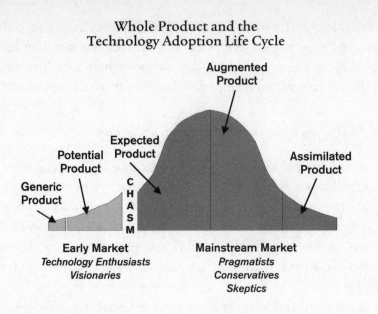

Whole Product and the Technology Adoption Life Cycle

Augmented Product

Expected Product

Potential Product

Assimilated Product

Generic Product

C H A S M

Early Market
Technology Enthusiasts
Visionaries

Mainstream Market
Pragmatists
Conservatives
Skeptics

MARKET
DEVELOPMENT
STRATEGY
CHECKLIST:
MARKET CREATION
VARIABLES

WHOLE PRODUCTS IN THE EARLY MARKET

Technology enthusiasts value and expect the *generic* product. True to form, they will often pull together the necessary bits to make it all work. The *potential* product, measured in terms of its ability to create strategic advantage, whets visionaries' appetites. This explains many vendors' pie-in-the-sky marketing. This is not necessarily a faulty strategy. Yet visionaries know they will need to pull together a whole product to actually exploit such an opportunity. Increasingly, they turn to systems integrators to perform this valuable but expensive process. The growth in systems integration during the previous decade is directly attributable to visionaries who increasingly see high-tech products and systems as potential sources of profound competitive advantage.

Since a complete solution can only be developed from scratch at this stage, the goal in the early market is to demonstrate the validity of your technological approach and the *possibilities* associated with one (or more) of its applications. Visionaries, acting as economic buyers, will be asking themselves whether the potential advantage, in the form of a potential product application, is worth assuming the adoption and solution complexities that will undoubtedly be encountered, versus other high-risk, high-reward opportunities. Technology enthusiasts acting as technical buyers will be investigating the merits of the core product. Can it/will it work? Will it be supportable? Are other techies also enthusiastic? Who/what are the various camps now forming around the product?

WHOLE PRODUCTS IN THE BOWLING ALLEY

Pragmatists demand *expected* products—products that are complete from the outset. Moreover, they will expect that whatever needs to be done to complete the product—that is, transform it from product to solution— will be done prior to or simultaneous with their adoption. Pragmatists hold the vendor responsible for this process rather than themselves. Nowhere else on the TALC is a thorough analysis of the whole product more important.

The following model is the centerpiece of developing effective chasm-crossing and bowling alley strategies built around whole products, the goal of which is to be the first vendor to complete a whole product solution built around a discontinuous innovation to serve a particular and targeted customer segment (or niche market).

Whole Product Analysis

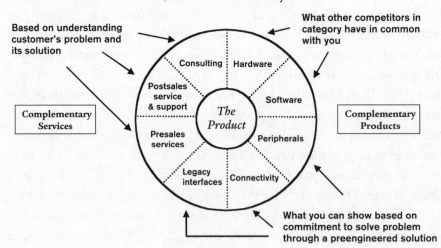

Based on understanding customer's problem and its solution

What other competitors in category have in common with you

Complementary Services

Complementary Products

What you can show based on commitment to solve problem through a preengineered solution

Consulting • Hardware
Postsales service & support • Software
The Product
Presales services • Peripherals
Legacy interfaces • Connectivity

MARKET
DEVELOPMENT
STRATEGY
CHECKLIST:
MARKET CREATION
VARIABLES

To use the model, you place the discontinuous product innovation (you may also think of it as the product being marketed) at the center and, in the surrounding wedges, using as many as necessary, name or outline all the other complementary products and services needed to fulfill the promised value proposition. Remember that the value proposition you are promising to supply is the complete solution necessary to fulfill the compelling reason to buy. Thus, whole product modeling is always defined relative to a particular application or usage scenario, and not just in isolation. Your experiences with early market customers and, perhaps, current prospects can guide your thinking. You may also want to refer back to the value chain model for clues as to where any weak links may be.

KEY INSIGHT ▶ ▶ ▶ ▶ ▶ ▶ ▶ ▶ ▷ ▷

The weakest link almost invariably is between product and application/system. That is, the technology can be "productized," but the product alone lacks one or more key elements necessary to establish itself as a *complete* solution to a problem. Such deficiencies retard the emerging value chain, and thus prevent it from displacing other, more established chains.

Chasm-crossing and bowling alley market development efforts hinge on creating effective whole products. Whole product development during these phases focuses on removing *adoption complexity*. Your success is directly correlated to your ability to field complete product solutions for customer segments laboring under broken processes that you can fix. By working through all the elements, thereby demonstrating your understanding of the segment(s) in question, you overcome the natural resistance of pragmatists to adopting applications that still contain a degree of complexity and risk. *In our consulting practice, clients often report that they find this analysis the most enlightening aspect of the entire engagement!*

WHOLE PRODUCTS IN THE TORNADO

During the tornado, whole product engineering and development shifts again. Demand for the new product, now seen as part of an overall infrastructure shift, vastly exceeds supply. The vendor who can serve this demand most broadly and most efficiently can win the coveted gorilla position in the market. Adoption complexity is no longer the issue; reducing *solution complexity* is. The goal during this phase is to make the product and infrastructure like a commodity. The steps can be diagrammed as follows:

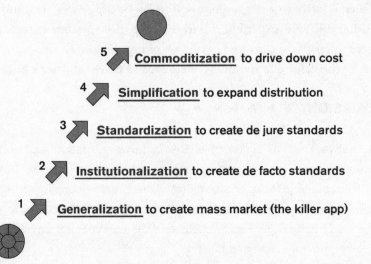

Whole Product Evolution in the Tornado

5 — **Commoditization** to drive down cost

4 — **Simplification** to expand distribution

3 — **Standardization** to create de jure standards

2 — **Institutionalization** to create de facto standards

1 — **Generalization** to create mass market (the killer app)

This activity completely reverses the previous goal of providing a differentiated product for distinct market segments. Such differentiation was indeed the vendor's competitive advantage versus those who did not create a complete solution. Now the *killer application* is becoming apparent to many others outside the segments pursued earlier. The competition now is built around time-to-market considerations—for the vendor and customer—and thus the spoils go to those who can deploy most rapidly.

Moving to commodity status is, however, an evolutionary process. The first step is to generalize what was a niche application into an architecture or platform capable of supporting a mass market. The next step is a race to determine which platform will become the de facto standard. This is a standard born of dominant market share and the point where gorilla power asserts itself. Concurrently, whatever standards that may have existed, typically created through industry-sponsored standards committees, may now fade. These standards emerged from well-meaning efforts by various competitors in an attempt to institutionalize a whole product in the early market and bowling alley. (You may recall such efforts to standardize UNIX in the 1980s, or Java in the '90s.) These early efforts usually result in competing camps, offering further evidence to pragmatists and conservatives that they are well served to wait until a dominant force emerges. Once a dominant standard is in place, the market accelerates as third parties and customers now understand how the value chain is likely to develop. A *de jure* standard may emerge as the value chain becomes codified, though such validation may be effectively irrelevant by now.

Going forward, vendors should seek to *simplify* the solution to expand the potential for widespread distribution, ending with the solution now approaching *commodity* status and thereby lowering the overall cost of supporting, deploying, and acquiring the emerging paradigm. These last two steps were a painful lesson for Netscape. The tornado was still an open competition when Microsoft thwarted Netscape's emerging gorilla status by effectively offering an Internet browser for free.

As a final note, don't be confused by the term *commodity*. The intellectual property represented in discontinuous innovations should not be compared to the commodities—wheat, corn, copper, steel, or whatever—that we typically associate with this term. Rather, the commodity we speak of here represents a new status quo, widely distributed and easily acquired, upon which further enhancements will now be built. The winner of this contest takes huge advantages into Main Street. And the winners are those who move most quickly.

WHOLE PRODUCTS ON MAIN STREET

With the end of the tornado, you must once again focus on creating demand. You pursue this by understanding the personal desires of the end user, focusing on the various demographic and psychographic differences that may stratify a market. Your responses can be manifested in whole product +1 offers, where the +1 factor meets a specific end user desire, or implemented through business processes (a distribution scheme, terms and conditions of acquisition or ownership, etc.) whereby customers obtain their next versions through a model that provides additional value. Both directions provide the basis for differentiation. The +1

MARKET
DEVELOPMENT
STRATEGY
CHECKLIST:
MARKET CREATION
VARIABLES

differentiation also allows for potentially higher prices, thus permitting you to win back some of the margins that, characteristic of Main Street markets, have been eroded.

The +1 offerings can be offshoots of the existing commodity product, engineered and manufactured at relatively low cost and targeted at specific segments. We refer to this discipline as *mass customization*. Such offerings are not—repeat *not*—a reengineering of the whole product solution and/or platform. New solutions are not what the overall market is seeking (though it may be what visionaries are now pleading for). The value chain is now established and well understood. Stability is the order of the day. Reengineering a Main Street product invariably introduces a level of discontinuity that is completely unwelcome at this stage of the market's development. To be successful, you must be able to introduce +1 offers quickly, with little disruption to what has now become an understood and well-oiled value chain, and keep on offering them to sustain revenue growth.

For example, how does a PC manufacturer differentiate its offering? Offer a read/write CD-ROM capability that allows college students to create their own music mix by downloading their favorites via the Internet through Napster (the entreaties of the recording industry or the courts notwithstanding). Occasionally these offers may take on a life of their own because they tap a previously underserved market that will sustain continued investment in increasingly more sophisticated and value-added offerings. And such offerings may become entirely new categories represented by the likes of Palm or Handspring, spawned from laptop computers that morphed to notebooks, which gave rise to the personal digital assistant. This is how conservatives extend the life cycle: by looking for *augmented* products—products that are specifically tailored off the shelf for their particular needs.

What makes +1 marketing possible often hearkens back to whole product strategies pursued during the tornado. On its way to becoming commodity-like, vendors are likely to throw all manner of features into a product—features that do not compromise the overriding goal of simplification but are added as a way of appealing to a technical buyer's evaluation. We usually refer to this as tick-the-box marketing. As the tornado wanes, products are now loaded with possibilities, most of which are ignored by customers as they try to cope with deploying the new paradigm. As such, vendors now have the capability to reinvent the feature(s) and package them as a special offer or under the banner *new and improved*. I suggest that you look at your own products carefully for these possible +1 (or even –1) features before you do any new engineering. If the feature/functionality is already there, your R&D is essentially free.

Finally, referring back to the diagram detailing whole product evolution across the Technology Adoption Life Cycle model, we end product evolution with the *assimilated* product favored by many skeptics. These customers are interested in the benefit provided by the product, but they are not interested in acquiring the actual product themselves. They may seek such benefits through a service-providing vendor.

Summarizing, one of the biggest mistakes made by high-tech organizations is assuming that their whole product solutions will come together through some magical process resembling alchemy. They won't. Use the whole product analysis tool to plan what and how you will develop your product across the life cycle. And, since one company can rarely do everything itself, whole product modeling leads to the next key assumption: Who is going to help us do all this? The next chapter gives us the answer.

MARKET
DEVELOPMENT
STRATEGY
CHECKLIST:
MARKET CREATION
VARIABLES

Market Development Strategy Checklist: Market Attractiveness Variables

This section details the three fundamental market attractiveness assumptions as part of the Market Development Strategy Checklist and specifies how each element should be considered across the Technology Adoption Life Cycle.

STRATEGY ASSUMPTION 4: PARTNERS AND ALLIES

Nowadays, forming so-called *strategic alliances* with everyone for everything seems to be quite de rigueur. Meetings are held. Memos of understanding circulate. Plans are hatched and deal terms haggled. Budgets are set. Venues are decided upon and invitations issued. Press conferences are held. Press releases are released. Hands are shaken. Optimism runs rampant. On the following day life returns pretty much to normal with conditions resembling those that existed prior to this paroxysm of courtship activity. The partnership is memorialized on a piece of paper and in some clippings from various industry journals. And later, like an arranged marriage, it is consummated only under duress.

In fairness, strategic partnerships obviously can and do work. Accenture and SAP, Hewlett-Packard and Oracle, and Microsoft and Intel are all examples of very productive relationships that have resulted in more market power for each partner because of the relationship than each would have enjoyed standing alone. On the other hand, *tactical* alliances among groups of *interested parties* often do the heavy lifting necessary to field a

MARKET
DEVELOPMENT
STRATEGY
CHECKLIST: MARKET
ATTRACTIVENESS
VARIABLES

whole product solution. These relationships may be far more strategic than the kind that are formed for PR purposes, and they are the type we discuss here.

Creating alliances as part of a market development program should be driven by two fundamental motives:

1. Achieving market leadership by *accelerating the formation of whole product solutions* for chasm-crossing and bowling alley efforts
2. Achieving and sustaining market leadership by *differentiating a commodity-type offering* for tornado and Main Street markets through distribution and/or +1 types of efforts.

Practically speaking, partners and allies should be chosen based almost exclusively on these criteria. Since our overarching goal through the strategy process is to increase significantly our time-to-market advantages, alliances based as above are far more important than the more grandiose but potentially far less effective relationships that many high-tech organizations pursue (sometimes without knowing exactly why). As the product evolves through the life cycle, so, too, must your approach to the partner/ally management process. Not surprisingly, your activities going forward will actually reverse your previous efforts to some degree.

The following diagram illustrates how products evolve during the Technology Adoption Life Cycle:

Whole Product Evolution Through the Life Cycle

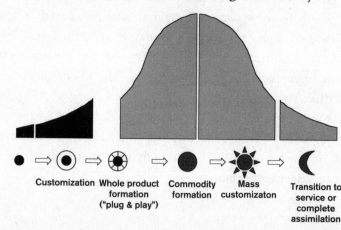

Customization   Whole product formation ("plug & play")   Commodity formation   Mass customizaton   Transition to service or complete assimilation

PARTNERS AND ALLIES IN THE EARLY MARKET

Certainly, all partnerships could be said to have their purpose, but your overriding goal should be to develop partners and allies based on what the demands of the life cycle require relative to complete whole products. In the early market, partners should be brought together ad hoc based on their ability to add value to the fundamental core technology and product such that the product becomes useful in a given application. Often, these pioneering efforts are part of a larger project that a particular visionary customer may be embarking on, and thus your *number one priority* is to ensure that the customer is successful, for this is the only way in which you can create a market. Your efforts to customize or otherwise harness the potential of your discontinuous innovation at this stage set in motion the formation of a new product value chain. Thus, your partners in early markets are often systems integrators adept at taming your innovative but unpredictable technology and product.

You are also well advised to recruit partners in an early market so that your product and proposed solution appears to be—and is—*validated* by others. For start-ups, think of this as bringing in a degree of adult supervision to the activities you have planned. This is a process, incidentally, that is increasingly the basis for many high-tech incubators. And it is also the reason that start-ups and early market companies should recruit *advisory boards* consisting of various experts and other interested parties who can not only add value in strategic decisions, but also carry weight with the outside world. Whatever the process you employ, the overriding goal is to show your potential customers—visionaries at this stage—that you have some degree of gravitational pull based on the novelty or efficacy of your innovation. While you should structure your efforts to derive significant and real benefits from these early partnerships, do not underestimate their perceptual value. Your objective is to look and act like you're real.

Summarizing, partners and allies with real clout in the early market are those who possess advanced technology expertise, systems integration capabilities, business process and change management consulting skills, and project management expertise.

PARTNERS AND ALLIES IN THE BOWLING ALLEY

MARKET
DEVELOPMENT
STRATEGY
CHECKLIST: MARKET
ATTRACTIVENESS
VARIABLES

In order to extend and sustain a new value chain, you must navigate the chasm into the mainstream. Now you need to *recruit* partners and allies to participate with you in developing the market—and participate on a sustainable basis. This effort is crucial to chasm-crossing and bowling alley efforts, and its importance should not be underestimated or minimized. The initial goal is to fulfill the requirements demanded by the niche segments you're pursuing and thus complete the whole product for such niches. The wedges in your whole product analysis model that have been identified but not accounted for may now fall into the domain of the partner.

But the longer-term objective is to create a market *ecosystem* that with proper nurturing will grow and expand to that of a desirable, compelling, and durable value chain. Partner recruitment is based on several assumptions not limited incidentally to outside/third parties; some partners may emerge from your own company. Ask yourself the following questions:

- Who/what will I need to complete the product so that it is a working, repeatable solution that delivers to customers a positive—and quantifiable—return on investment?
- Who will I need to deliver and deploy this solution in a value-added manner into the chosen market segments? What special knowledge do I require of the segments themselves, and who might have such knowledge?
- Who will I need to complement the whole product solution so that it becomes of even greater value to my chosen customer segments?
- Can and how do the chosen partners enjoy a favorable economic return through their participation in the value chain and the market it will address? Can chosen partners form their own value chains and/or bring complementary chains into the mix?

PARTNERS AND ALLIES IN THE TORNADO

As the whole product evolution diagram suggests, partner or ally activities during a tornado should be focused on *rationalizing* the number and type of partners currently comprising your value chain. Since demand will exceed supply during a tornado, vendors who not only can fulfill this demand most completely, but also do so most quickly, stand to win the most customers. This means that vendors must eliminate any impediment that compromises either their efforts to serve the market or their customers' efforts to install and deploy the new value chain. Invariably, some partners simply get in the way of both vendors and customers.

Service partners, for example, who are used to adding significant value by buffering any discontinuities that may be felt by customers now find that they're no longer needed (or wanted). The adverse effect on their revenue streams at this stage is dramatic, so they attempt to invent new processes to keep themselves in the game. Partners who contributed the bits and pieces necessary to complete the value chain now find that the efforts of the sponsoring vendor to commoditize the whole product either reduce their overall margins or eliminate them altogether. In both cases, customers support these rationalization efforts because they streamline their efforts in both vendor selection and solution deployment.

Thus, having worked diligently to design partners into the value chain, you must now work as diligently to *design them out*. Naturally, there is a huge opportunity here for hurt feelings among all the partners that you previously had courted eagerly. Large companies in particular tend to devote significant human and financial resources to managing their stable of partners. Typically, the mandate for such efforts is *maintaining a level playing field* for all partners. As the tornado approaches, this approach, seemingly laudable in spirit, actually becomes an acute liability. All partners are *not* created equal. They do not provide equal value and should not be courted as if they do. You need to solidify your most crucial relationships, keeping your commitments to them and demanding the same from them as well. But you need to free up resources devoted to marginal partnership efforts and redeploy them to programs with partners that can make real impact. This means choosing gorillas, where possible, over chimps and monkeys. It means redirecting service partners to products and markets in earlier stages of the life cycle. The head must prevail over the heart in such matters. The tornado will not wait.

PARTNERS AND ALLIES ON MAIN STREET

MARKET
DEVELOPMENT
STRATEGY
CHECKLIST: MARKET
ATTRACTIVENESS
VARIABLES

By the time markets reach Main Street, margin pressures are such that *eliminating* partners altogether is the optimal strategy because customers now expect solutions that are completely preintegrated. Plug-and-play partners are no longer desirable unless they complement the solution seamlessly; nor are integration/deployment service partners, because this is no longer an issue. Partners who provide +1 types of services—for example, troubleshooting LANs and WANs, installing and configuring new software, or providing tutorials on new features or functionality—still may be welcome, however. On the other hand, you may wish to pursue *virtual partners* who can add +1 differentiation to your product solution through any number of offerings that add value in a noninvasive, nonintrusive manner. Product solutions that previously have had lots of different players associated with them now face an uphill battle because customers will tolerate interoperable systems from multiple vendors if, and only if, they can be obtained as one product. Main Street rules of engagement still apply, however, and no real or perceived discontinuity can be added accidentally or otherwise.

Finally, at the end of the TALC, you may wish to consider another type of virtual partner who delivers the benefit of the product without necessarily delivering the product. Emerging to provide this service are numerous service providers, such as application service providers (ASPs), who will rent you the application, typically hosted on their platforms at their locations. These "apps on tap" are garnering interest among customers who no longer wish to support certain applications internally but must continue to utilize such applications over an extended period, and/or who may no longer possess the talent to reconfigure them on the fly as their fast-moving environments now dictate.

Then there are what we call platform or application *gerontologists*. These vendors and service providers support and extend aging hardware and software applications that continue to be relied on by niche market segments but are considered moribund by the market at large. For example, Client Systems in Colorado specializes in supporting and maintaining the HP 3000 computer system. Companies such as these are prized highly by customers who neither desire nor need the latest and greatest, preferring instead to effectively outsource the care and feeding of their aging but still useful systems.

Finally, we can examine partner and ally selection using another model: that of the overall type and level of *service* they will provide for any given point on the life cycle. Service in this context is defined more broadly than the conventional applications of the term, referring instead to the type and nature of expertise that might be needed to support a complete product.

The following diagram models this concept metaphorically:

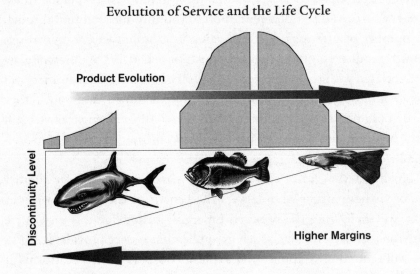

Evolution of Service and the Life Cycle

The fish illustrated in the model are chosen specifically to contrast their relative abilities to survive varying depths of discontinuity and corresponding margins. Each fish can thrive, but only at its appropriate depth. The shark (chosen with tongue firmly planted in cheek) might represent a systems integrator. Such a partner can bring a significant skill set to bear, notably to create the first application for a given discontinuous innovation. In so doing, it will demand—and is worth—a disproportionate level of the customer budget allocated to the solution. By contrast, the guppy on the right might represent a distributor, a superstore, a catalog retailer, or an e-tailer. Between these two swims a value-added reseller (VAR) who brings expertise to the deployment of repeatable whole products.

Organizations inhabiting the left side (or deep end) of this model tend to sustain themselves because of their ability to add a level of service that is based fundamentally on human expertise and intellectual property. Similarly, organizations on the right survive because they, too, provide a singular expertise, often logistical in nature. VARs, however, typically face a less certain future. They enter a market at the bowling alley stage and quickly succeed because of their ability to provide *specific* levels of both expertise and logistical support, most often tailored to the requirements of niche markets whence they may have emerged. Following the market into a tornado, however, sows the seeds of their demise as lower-cost, volume-capable channels quickly outpace them. These VARs fail due to the very event, a tornado, they've been working to bring about. Because tornadoes reward commoditization, the VAR's expertise becomes both unnecessary and unwanted.

The correct response for both VARs and the vendors that partner with them is to see that the VAR remains in bowling alley markets. VARs should venture into tornadoes and Main Street only when they are prepared to reinvent themselves and can create a business model that competes favorably with those who make this part of the market their permanent home.

▶ THE SEVEN DEADLY SINS OF PARTNERING
by Philip Lay, managing director, The Chasm Group LLC

Today partnering of all types—from truly strategic alliances for joint technology or marketing purposes to channel partnering to enhance product distribution—is considered a key ingredient in every high-tech company's go-to-market plan. From traditionally being a field support function, business development has now become a mission-critical function. This is especially so in an Internet-focused world, where every company relies on third parties for key components of the solutions they provide to end customers. So you'd expect most companies to be working hard at getting it right, wouldn't you? Not so fast! There are stiff obstacles preventing good partnering.

Most technology companies are still driven by engineering and sales mind-sets that favor direct, control-oriented approaches to managing partnering relationships, rather than using more indirect means to influence and mobilize partners to good effect. By definition, of course, partners follow

MARKET
DEVELOPMENT
STRATEGY
CHECKLIST: MARKET
ATTRACTIVENESS
VARIABLES

their own corporate agendas, which is not always convenient for a company anxious to achieve immediate market objectives. This, together with several other reasons, causes most partnering initiatives to produce disappointing, and sometimes disastrous, results.

It is perhaps easy to forget that partnering is not a noble cause per se. It is only remotely interesting when companies need help to gain access to desirable and suitable target markets by (a) understanding critical customer problems, (b) providing a complete solution to those problems, or (c) finding the most effective way of attracting and serving customers. Thus, partnering should be treated in a businesslike manner, with objectivity and seriousness of purpose. In many instances, however, it is still addressed frivolously and without much thought to the consequences—intended or otherwise.

Below is a list of the "seven deadly sins" we have encountered in our consulting experience that explain why many partnerships don't work out. As a diagnostic, if a partnership you contemplate or are engaged actively in suffers from just one of the following symptoms, you should start asking questions. If you suffer from one to three of these symptoms, you need to review why you are in this relationship. And if you suffer from more than three symptoms, you are almost certainly in a no-win situation—best to get out as gracefully as possible, and find a different way to accomplish your goals.

The First Deadly Sin: *Lack of Trust Going In*

Accustomed more to adversarial rather than collaborative thinking in their market development activities, most technology companies still approach partnering initiatives from a base of (a) mistrust, (b) insecurity, (c) impatience for results, (d) hidden agendas or deviousness, or (e) all of the above. This being the rule, partners don't invest energy in building a joint strategy, because this would require a level of intimacy they are unwilling to commit to.

The Second Deadly Sin: *Failure to Understand the Other Party's Goal*

Company executives demonstrate a lack of understanding of (or interest in) how to adopt a *win/win* approach. Perhaps they should heed Stephen Covey's mandate: "Seek first to understand before seeking to be understood." In other words, find out literally and specifically what the other company's agenda is, respect what they are trying to accomplish, and then pursue your own goals *through* them.

MARKET
DEVELOPMENT
STRATEGY
CHECKLIST: MARKET
ATTRACTIVENESS
VARIABLES

The Third Deadly Sin: *Attitudes Worthy of Machiavelli*

Impatient to achieve their own objectives, companies use (or misuse) language in order to get what they want, with little or no regard for what their partner wants. For example, executives on both sides throw around terms such as *strategic alliance* when all they're really after is access to the other company's customers or deal flow without necessarily contributing anything of value in return. Therefore, this term should be used sparingly. *Strategic* and *alliance* are loaded words that imply a special kind of synergy and commitment among the parties. When these terms are used inappropriately, partners are misled into promoting the wrong programs, with one side committing more resources than the other, leading to both failure and opprobrium.

The Fourth Deadly Sin: *Unchecked Executive Egos*

My personal favorite. When executives from two or more high-tech companies get together to negotiate an alliance, it may not take long for them to start tossing promises and challenges back and forth, while their colleagues—tasked with doing the real work—cringe, dreading the commitments they will have to implement—usually without sufficient resources or authorization to do so (see the Seventh Deadly Sin).

The Fifth Deadly Sin: *Losing Sight of the Real Customer*

Perhaps the most insidious sin is this one. Vendor A, needing to develop a mainstream market for its product and having little success doing so, engages with vendor B, who has demonstrated success in attracting this market. Vendor A's only goal is to use such a partnership to cause its product to "leap across the chasm." Vendor A's legitimate goal of engaging partners to penetrate a target market—pitched as "let's you and I partner so we can both sell something"—degenerates into "let's you and I partner so you can sell our product for us." The result? Disappointment and disillusionment for both. Vendor A sees vendor B as a distribution channel only and works to *sell in* rather than help to *sell through.* Vendor B comes to find that it is doing all the heavy lifting without any commensurate support or compensation. This merry dance is exacerbated when executive management teams are involved because corporate pride and individual egos (not to mention compensation plans) prohibit either side from admitting the truth: "We need your help!"

The Sixth Deadly Sin: *In the Absence of a Strategy, Shoot from the Hip*

This loops back to the First Deadly Sin. Because there is no basis of trust or commitment on which to build a feasible joint market development strategy, partners default to extremely tactical approaches leading to a frequent default strategy—the notorious *bundle*—more often than not a collection of difficult-to-sell products and services lumped into a package and marketed at a discount price. As a corollary, go-to-market strategy in these cases usually consists of no more than joint press releases, appearances in each other's exhibits at trade shows, and other completely conventional and unimaginative programs.

The Seventh Deadly Sin: *Resource Commitments Don't Materialize*

Disillusionment runs rampant. Executives on both sides have made commitments to many partners simultaneously, without necessarily gauging how each partnership could succeed and without sufficient care in allocating resources. As a result, business development and alliance managers are now strapped for resources, and are only partially authorized to make things happen.

Now, how do your efforts match up?

◀

STRATEGY ASSUMPTION 5: DISTRIBUTION

Retail trade is justly censured because the gain which results is not naturally made but is made at the expense of other men.

—ARISTOTLE

Selecting an effective distribution channel is a strategic exercise, for indeed it is part of your strategy. This is to say that choosing an appropriate form of distribution is also based on some key assumptions. Sadly, as noted previously, an organization's choice of distribution model is often a function of what it has always done or how it is currently organized. Such an approach is extremely shortsighted.

The primary objective in selecting a distribution channel is to ensure that you can create and sustain a relationship with the most influential customer—the economic buyer, the technical buyer, or the end user—as the product moves through the life cycle. Very simply, if an effective channel to reach this customer can't be established, nothing further is possible. You can optimize your choice based on two criteria that will also change over time. They are:

- How complex is the product to install, deploy, and use? This is an expression of *solution complexity*.
- How difficult is the product to source, buy, and/or support? This is an expression of *marketing complexity*.

The following model illustrates this relationship trade-off:

MARKET
DEVELOPMENT
STRATEGY
CHECKLIST: MARKET
ATTRACTIVENESS
VARIABLES

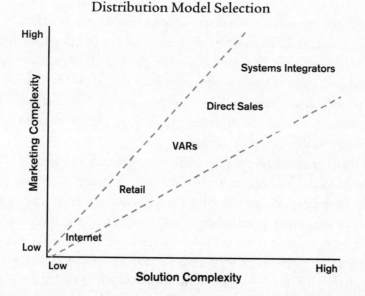

Distribution Model Selection

The linearity of various distribution options shown above illustrates the natural allegiance of channel and product when a constant solution complexity to marketing complexity ratio is maintained. The dashed lines further demarcate the range of the ratio showing the relative flexibility of each channel. When a product is out of sync with the ratio—that is, when it is significantly outside the range shown—structural problems will occur in the marketplace, typically as follows:

- *High marketing complexity/low solution complexity.* In this upper-left quadrant, products reside in higher priced channels that cannot add enough value to warrant their margins. This imbalance creates either a bad deal for the customer, a bad deal for the originating vendor, or both, since one or both is now paying for something that really isn't needed. For example, you would not sell personal computers or Handspring Visors through a direct-sales force (would you?).
- *High solution complexity/low marketing complexity.* By contrast, products in this lower-right quadrant now require a level of services to field a whole product solution that can't be supported by the relatively low price point. Now the distribution channel is suffering. You would not, for example, try to sell a complex supply chain management soft-ware application through the average computer reseller.

In both instances, such distribution maladies retard efficient market development. Product vendors with products in the upper-left quadrant will need to change channels. Increasingly, e-commerce is the choice of enlightened sales executives who recognize that their human resources—that is, their direct-sales force—no longer can add the value they once did, and no longer need to. Products residing in the lower-right quadrant require, typically, a change in pricing.

Finally, if tornadoes are to develop for product categories, marketing and solution complexity must ultimately be reduced significantly or vir-tually eliminated altogether. This fundamental explains why direct-sales organizations must ultimately give way to alternate channels that provide much more modest value added, at a trade-off of far greater scope and efficiency. Organizations expecting, or at least hoping for, a tornado will find their progress impeded significantly when they fail to shift their channels of distribution. To assess your organization's willingness and propensity to tailor distribution programs based on market development strategy, consider your organization's response to the following question:

"How will you distribute the product?"

Your initial answer may be along the lines of "Most likely through [choose your answer based on your company's history]." Now, ask the question "Why?" If the answer is similar or identical to "because we have [that current channel]," you may be headed for trouble later. Your distribution strategy is no longer a function of solution or marketing complexity. Rather, it is based on historical context, which now drives the strategy and much of what it will become. Strategy should drive business processes, not the other way around.

MARKET
DEVELOPMENT
STRATEGY
CHECKLIST: MARKET
ATTRACTIVENESS
VARIABLES

STRATEGY ASSUMPTION 6: PRICING

There are numerous books, articles, and other references on this subject. I have found most to be unfathomable. They are either too complicated or theoretical to be practical, or they are based on premises that don't necessarily translate well to the world of high tech. I believe that the most useful way of considering your pricing strategy is to think of it as a reflection of the *value* of your product—something rarely thought about in practice. Instead, organizations try to adhere rigidly to pricing based, for example, on cost-plus-profit models projected (or dictated) as part of a spreadsheet analysis.

Then, of course, there is the typical price book that many sales forces cling to, as do their finance departments. Typically, only a handful of people within the company can explain the indecipherable calculus that comprises all the possible pricing configurations based variously and ambiguously on numbers of seats, users, processors, nodes, sites, previous versions, and the like. These wizards are guaranteed lifetime employment for their ability to divine such pricing runes, particularly in the software industry. Yet their efforts go for naught at the end of every month, certainly at the end of every quarter, as the customer gleefully tells the salesperson to "put that silly book away" and instead explain how much the product will be discounted if the sale is to be consummated today.

All of these exercises may be standard operating procedure for many organizations—and some actually may be somewhat valuable. But they also obscure some fundamental and underlying strategic aspects of pricing in developing markets—namely, that pricing must reflect, sooner or later, the *perceived* and *actual value* of the product and the prevailing *business* model associated with delivering this value.

How customers perceive product value—and the actual value they receive—can be considered in terms of the following questions:

- Who are the target customers? Do they have the budget to buy? Do they have the ability to buy—that is, can they actually make the decision?

- What objectives are they trying to meet in purchasing the product—that is, what is their willingness to buy? How persuasive is the opportunity, or how grave is the risk of doing nothing?

- How is the product assembled to meet such objectives?

- How is the product delivered, supported, and complemented within a value chain? Will partners and allies get a fair return for their efforts? (If they don't, they are likely to resist partnership efforts or secede from any alliance, thereby retarding or collapsing market growth.)

Pricing, thus, is a reflection of the first five assumptions or elements in the Market Development Strategy Checklist. And since business models change over the course of the life cycle, so, too, will your pricing models and assumptions.

Thinking ahead on our checklist, we may also consider pricing relative to the value of the new solution compared to *competitive offerings,* in addition to considering the *inherent value* of the new solution compared to the *status quo.* Such offerings are not strictly limited to alternatives within a given category but may reflect any potential alternative likely to compete for a target customer's compelling reason to buy. Prior to the tornado, product value propositions are based either on a visionary dream or a novel solution to a niche market problem. Value-based pricing—that is, the upside return versus the status quo, or the minimization or elimination of downside losses as a result of switching to the new paradigm—is the norm in early, chasm-crossing, and bowling alley markets. These markets can be characterized as relatively price inelastic. Pricing decisions should reflect the goal of margin creation in order to fund successfully the demands placed on creating necessary infrastructures.

Tornado markets exhibit price elasticity because the product infra-

MARKET
DEVELOPMENT
STRATEGY
CHECKLIST: MARKET
ATTRACTIVENESS
VARIABLES

structure is now in place, facilitating the commoditization of the product, and because there are likely to be many new market entrants. Gorilla,
chimp, and monkey status now largely determine the reference price from
which competitors can either command a premium—in the case of the
gorilla—or offer a discount—in the case of a monkey. Making the transition to competition- or business model–based pricing is absolutely critical to capture market share during tornadoes. Upon reaching Main
Street, pricing will once again favor some degree of value creation, but
this time the value premium can only be reflected in the +1 value being
added. The price level of a given product category on Main Street may be
lower by an order of magnitude or more compared to its early market-
entry price. And once again, your market status will affect your price relative to that of your competitors.

The following model depicts pricing considerations relative to TALC
inflection points:

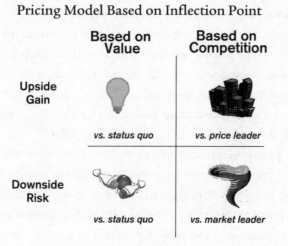

Pricing Model Based on Inflection Point

	Based on Value	Based on Competition
Upside Gain	*vs. status quo*	*vs. price leader*
Downside Risk	*vs. status quo*	*vs. market leader*

Now let's consider some more specifics.

PRICING IN AN EARLY MARKET

As a practical matter, setting a price in the early market will likely include
some guesswork because the value of the product at this stage is largely

unproved, or is theoretical at best. You can assign a price to the new product, but your efforts can be guided further by answers to the following questions:

- What is the *expected* return on investment (ROI) associated with the new paradigm in general, and your new product specifically, when compared to the current way of doing things?
- How much money does the customer have and is willing to part with?
- What, if any, referential price could be utilized as a proxy for the new product?

As a rule of thumb, discontinuous innovations should provide an order of magnitude (10×) return versus the status quo. Such superior returns provide inducements to visionaries both to invest in the new paradigm and to override the pain associated in coping with the problems inherent in discontinuous innovation adoption.

The second point refers to a customer's *willingness to pay* for certain benefits. Visionaries, in addition to assessing the overall value of a new paradigm, may also be willing to pay a high premium to be the first adopter and/or obtain some period of exclusivity. However, vendors will have to provide some degree of *risk discount* as well, since the efficacy of the new approach is relatively untested. Thus, if a 10× return is possible, will customers pay a reasonable fraction of this anticipated return in order to get it first, and get it tailored to their needs?

The last point—reference pricing—often is problematic with many discontinuous innovations; the reason is that either comparisons are difficult because the product category is just being conceptualized, or we do not wish to compare ourselves with the very status quo we are attempting to overhaul. One solution to this dilemma is to price the new product as part of an overall project now contemplated by visionaries as part of their hunt for competitive advantage. Since early market development efforts are inherently deal oriented—that is, we search for a deal and, having closed one, we now search for another—we can price our product relative to the size of the overall deal. Transactions of this kind are often part of large-scale systems integration projects. The new product can be tucked into the overall budget for the project and thus appear relatively minor in the overall scheme of things. Or, when faced with closer scrutiny, you can compare the cost of the new product favorably to the cost of developing the same product from scratch as part of a systems integration effort. Putting it all together, an early market pricing effort for a new enterprise-class software installation (for example) might posit a price of 10 percent of the customer's expected gain, priced for the entire project, divided into staged payments that would include up-front licensing and setup fees, service and maintenance fees, milestone achievements, and completed implementation.

MARKET
DEVELOPMENT
STRATEGY
CHECKLIST: MARKET
ATTRACTIVENESS
VARIABLES

PRICING IN THE CHASM AND THE BOWLING ALLEY

To cross the chasm, and later in the bowling alley, pricing must be based on *value,* derived fundamentally from redressing or eliminating altogether the costs associated with the critical problem being addressed. The questions to ask are as follows:

· How much money is the customer now losing due to problems associated with current modes of operation?
· What will be the expected ROI associated with the new whole product solution (and value chain) when compared to the current way of doing things (the existing value chain)? When will such returns be realized?
· What ROI could be derived from using new, alternative solutions to solve the problem?

Recall that to cross the chasm you must identify a seemingly intractable problem or condition under which an identifiable group of pragmatists now labor. In order to steer these pragmatists to your better solution, you must be able to hypothesize and prove as possible that your new way will, in effect, staunch the financial hemorrhaging now being suffered. Thus, understanding the financial consequences of the customer's problem—and, by extrapolation, the problems of the segment—is the first step in developing a price based on value.

The return on investment associated with your new approach must also be realizable in a timely manner, typically within eighteen months at the maximum, and under twelve months at the optimum. Remember the bleeding-from-the-neck metaphor. Solutions that deliver positive ROI but do so indeterminately are not attractive to our poor customer specifically, or the segment as a whole.

PRICING IN THE TORNADO

As and when a tornado ensues, market focus shifts to migrating to a new infrastructure. This task is delegated typically to the technical buyer who, although funded by the economic buyer, acquires and exercises enormous purchasing influence, if not outright control. A buyer's key issue in adopting infrastructure is that it be based on stable, common standards that can be built upon over a long period. The buyer's *natural* inclination is to defer to market-leading vendors based on their ability to set de facto market standards. The primate positions—gorillas, chimps, and monkeys—reflect buyers' choices.

For these infrastructure buyers, return on investment is not the driving issue. Indeed, ROI may be very late in coming. During the enterprise resource planning software tornado of the mid to late 1990s, it was clear that ROI would not be realized until the business process reengineering phase, prior to installation and deployment of the software. This process took most Fortune 500 companies a minimum of two years, on average, to complete. ROI was *not* the galvanizing motive to adopt ERP software. Fear was. The move to this new paradigm was driven by the fear of being left behind (and, for many companies, to ensure Y2K compliance).

Thus, during the tornado, our cleverly constructed ROI pricing models based either on upside gain or downside risk become even more decidedly based on downside risk—the risk of not adopting a soon-to-be prevailing standard. The value of adopting the new paradigm is now well understood by customers. Now the key question for buyers is not "Should we buy?" but "From whom shall we buy?" Pricing strategy assumptions shift, therefore, from being formerly based on value to now being based on *competition*.

Even though demand peaks during a tornado, markets show signs of price elasticity as numerous competitors, typically monkeys, rush into the market to ride the tornado. Many of these late-to-the-party competitors are only too willing to discount their offerings in the hopes of garnering market share at the expense of larger, better-known players. Your first and fundamental pricing decision must be to shift to a competitive, commodity-based price platform in order to compete in—and not surrender—the market share battle now ensuing. Future pricing decisions will be based on where you are in the competitive pecking order.

MARKET
DEVELOPMENT
STRATEGY
CHECKLIST: MARKET
ATTRACTIVENESS
VARIABLES

THE PRICING GORILLA GAME

If you're a gorilla, congratulations. You can set the reference price for the category. This represents the minimum ante for customers desirous of acquiring the market-leading solution, and also represents a pricing *fulcrum point* from which other competitors will either discount (in most cases) or charge a premium for special features or benefits not available from the gorilla. Gorillas can easily become greedy, because they represent not only safety but also stability. "We should charge for this," you might assert. Be careful. Your overriding concern is to win the market share competition. Price too high and you provide ample reasons for turning customers elsewhere, not to mention inviting even more competition from low-price entrants.

Instead, gorillas should use their market leadership to further commoditize not only their product, but also the category as a whole. "What?" you cry. "Doesn't that just accelerate the margin declines that you say will happen on Main Street?" Probably. Let's repeat the mantra of the tornado: market share . . . market share . . . market share. Not margins. The goal is to draw new sources of customers by constantly searching for and hitting the next lower price point so that a new flurry of buying activity is unleashed— all directed, we hope, to you. This is particularly important in retail markets, but it also applies in industrial markets as well. Hewlett-Packard has employed such a pricing strategy for years in the printer market. Here, HP is a king rather than a gorilla, since there is really no architectural control. Tempting as it might be to charge a premium for the *leading brand*, HP opted for big money over easy money, first through market share gains at the expense of such competitors as Lexmark, Epson, and Xerox; then through the consumables aftermarket—ink-jet and toner cartridges— where there *is* architectural control. Buy an HP ink-jet printer and you become devoted (read "locked in") to HP ink cartridges. Incidentally, the profit margin on these products is breathtaking. This strategy continues to pay off like a broken slot machine as personal computer manufacturers, eager to penetrate the so-called *home* market on the back of the Internet, have chopped their prices significantly to reach this previously reticent, price-sensitive segment.

The point is a simple one. The vendor who can keep hitting the next lower, *strategic* price point can keep attracting new customer bases that were reluctant to adopt before due to price. In addition to the immediate revenues created by this pent-up demand, such good fortune is extended through expanded market share and larger installed base. Once again, greed and the conventional wisdom of premium pricing for market leaders will not hold. Someone is going to aim for that lower price point.

Which brings us to the only real pricing strategy open to the monkey and the serf: offering a discount. Monkeys must discount down from the gorilla, and serfs must discount off the king to account (perhaps atone) for their status. If this is your lot in life, at least for a given category, you probably understand why such discounting is not only inevitable but will be demanded by customers. Quite simply, monkeys and serfs have little else to offer. They can win a sale but never win a market. While customers may view monkeys and serfs as interesting alternatives, they do so with two notable caveats:

- *Monkeys and serfs represent technical risk.* Is their product really as good as that of the gorilla or king? Is it engineered to the same standards? Will the same application vendors support it? What is their technical heritage and track record?
- *Monkeys and serfs represent market risk.* Will they be around a year from now? What about five years from now? Will others (in the value chain) widely distribute, support, and service them? Are they strong enough to go the distance?

Invariably, these two concerns cause buyers to reduce such risks through the only option available to them: offer or bid less money for the monkey/serf. Monkeys and serfs can thrive under these conditions, particularly since their up-front R&D investments are low. But playing a *me too* game carries its own set of risks. Successful monkeys and serfs play this game living by their wits, reading and reacting to the market more quickly than their larger competitors. However, their market position and long-term viability will always be tenuous and inherently unstable.

By far the most difficult pricing decisions are faced by chimps and, to a lesser degree, princes. Princes are viewed as being relatively equivalent to kings. There is little downside risk associated with choosing a prince over a king. Princes may need to discount off a king in certain markets, but this decision is probably one based solely on situational criteria and intuition. The prince may have further latitude in pricing the offering through *soft* discounts such as extended warranties, more favorable terms and conditions associated with the sale, more favorable service and support, and the like. Princes, for the most part, represent virtually no technical or market risk.

Chimps, on the other hand, face more difficult decisions. The gorilla/chimp/monkey hierarchy emerges as a result of a significant number of customers voting with their wallets for the gorilla. Choosing the gorilla means choosing a value chain in which the gorilla is dominant. All others in the chain who support the gorilla are also subordinate to it. Chimps represent viable alternatives to the gorilla but, in most cases, must compete for the same value chain partners. Unlike monkeys, chimps have invested sizable sums into creating their own product architecture; one that they, too, hoped would be dominant. Since events have turned out otherwise, the chimp faces a dilemma. Can it expand its customer base more broadly by discounting off the gorilla, yet maintain a sizable enough margin to provide for future investments in its product architecture, thus sustaining its own viability and customer trust?

Historically, such decisions and others that we'll discuss in the next chapter have not been kind to chimps. The chimps' first inclination will be to price at, or even above, the level of the gorilla, arguing that its product is superior to that of the gorilla. Customers, ever sensitive to the technical and market risks associated with any vendor that is not the gorilla, effectively knock the price down to below that of the gorilla. The usual discount offered by the chimp to close the deal now becomes a de facto discount, necessary to even begin closing negotiations. If the chimp can justify or otherwise show that customers' trust is warranted—particularly if the chimp provides a complete solution tailored for specific customer segments—the chimp's pricing is probably safe from future erosion. It can achieve local gorilla status within its customer niche and benefit from barriers both to competitive entry and customer exit.

On the other hand, if the chimp still believes that it can become a gorilla, and thus achieve a status its management and board still crave, it

MARKET
DEVELOPMENT
STRATEGY
CHECKLIST: MARKET
ATTRACTIVENESS
VARIABLES

will increasingly see "buying the business" through competitive discounting as a viable strategy versus the gorilla. This preoccupation sows the seeds of the chimp's eventual destruction.

The scenario typically plays out like this.

Initially, buying the business—in other words, providing significant discounts to customers to win the deal—benefits the chimp. Its market share increases, and its market stature rises as it signs up customers intrigued by the chimp's approach to the market and won over by its economic arguments. Management is enthused with the progress, and the sales force, feeling rather successful with this apparent (though rather transparent) silver bullet, presses for even more latitude in pricing flexibility. Often, this success will reignite or further reinforce a view held among many in high tech that focusing on specific target customer segments is, well, for chumps. "Not only can we compete against the gorilla, we can beat the gorilla!" becomes the rallying cry.

The chimp now goes after every deal, good or bad. Its justification, quite correctly, is increasing market share. Its weapon of choice, pricing, will not be fatal to the gorilla, but it will be to the chimp. The chimp's own organization is now rushing to keep up with all the so-called deals the sales force has found. Product specs and release dates are changed to satisfy certain deals. Terms and conditions, customer support, and other post-sales activities are modified to satisfy others. At the same time, the gorilla is probably beginning to react. From meeting the chimp's price on a deal-by-deal basis to pre-announcing the next set of features in its upcoming release, the gorilla acts to further demonstrate its overall commitment to leading the market—for the benefit of both customers and everyone else in the value chain.

At about this time, life being what it is, the chimp is about to miss its numbers. Either due to the tornado waning, or prospects pausing to understand more about what the gorilla is doing—remember, its story is fundamentally more compelling purely owing to its market status—or because the chimp's profits are not meeting previously set expectations, the quarterly announcement disappoints. And Wall Street pounces on the stock like a lion on a limping gazelle. One only has to recall the travails of both Baan and PeopleSoft as they challenged the hegemony of SAP during the waning days of the ERP tornado.

Now, suddenly, it appears that the chimp in question has lost market

MARKET
DEVELOPMENT
STRATEGY
CHECKLIST: MARKET
ATTRACTIVENESS
VARIABLES

power. *Market risk* suddenly reappears because the chimp is in the equivalent of the financial markets' *penalty box*. It can only reemerge through resuscitating its sagging numbers. At the same time, others in the value chain—service providers, application vendors, distribution partners, and the like—begin a quiet reevaluation of the chimp to determine if it is really worth standing by in its time of trouble. Market risk now translates to *technical risk*. And skittish prospects, knowing they must move with the herd, take notice. They either snub the chimp or ask for even more concessions to mitigate risk. Unabated, this commences a steady erosion of the chimp's power and prestige.

"All this just because the chimp discounts?" you may ask skeptically. To be fair, I have illustrated a worst-case scenario of the chimp's travails to demonstrate what can and does happen when a chimp attacks the gorilla directly, based solely on price. As we shall see, chimps must play the most complicated of games. Their pricing strategies must both reflect market realities—they are not the leader—and also account for the fundamental value that their customers have seen fit to acquire. Thus, a chimp's best destiny in tornado markets is to build market share, ideally aiming for the number two market position overall, taking care that such a position is augmented by clusters of customer segments in which it is number one. This niche market power allows the chimp to establish—and charge for—its own architectural standards, its power in the value chain, and, overall, its extrinsic and intrinsic value, amid a customer base that truly values them as well.

PRICING ON MAIN STREET

Upon reaching Main Street, continued profitable growth no longer will come from selling commodity-oriented products to all the new customers flooding into the market. The demand/supply imbalances characteristic of the tornado have subsided, and supply is now plentiful. New customers are not flooding into the market as they once were. Accordingly, growth can only come from once again selling differentiated products—what we call whole products +1—to specific *existing* customer segments that value the +1 element—and are *willing to pay* for it. This does not mean that selling commodity products is no longer a viable business. But power has shifted back to the buyer, and vendors will once again need to compete for follow-on business (notwithstanding the degree of control that goril-las can exercise over such future transactions). What it does mean is that your pricing models must change once again to reflect how you will attract and satisfy the various segments that will likely view +1 elements in different ways.

The following model illustrates how to consider pricing strategy as a function of four distinct domains. *Price*, *value*, *premium*, and *convenience* were chosen as exemplars, but they are also viable options. These domains will influence significantly the competitive rules of engagement as the market matures further.

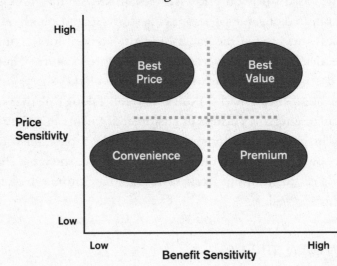

Pricing on Main Street

As is often the case in Main Street markets, customers are looking to buy the *next* version of the product they acquired in earlier market phases, either because they want or need more of the item, desire additional or different functionality, or any combination thereof. From the model, we can hypothesize that certain segments—conservative economic buyers and purchasing agents, for example—may be extremely sensitive to the cost of their next purchase. These two constituencies may lead the forces behind a *commodity-based* market. Marching to a different beat, however,

MARKET
DEVELOPMENT
STRATEGY
CHECKLIST: MARKET
ATTRACTIVENESS
VARIABLES

end users also may exert significant control over the same category, willing to pay a premium to acquire additional benefits or alternative capabilities. These groups create the basis for attractive and profitable niche market segments built around *added value*.

Thus, developing a Main Street pricing strategy will be a function of, once again, the preceding elements in the Market Development Strategy Checklist, with a particular view to resolving these questions:

- Who is the major influencer and "owner" of subsequent purchases?
- What is their compelling motivation or reason to purchase again?
- What is the resulting product offering? Is it +1 based? Commodity-based? Both?

Answers to these questions should facilitate the creation of one or several product offerings, each predicated on occupying one—and only one—quadrant of the model. Thus, an offering that provides all the proverbial bells and whistles should be optimized and marketed to customer segments that value substantially the added benefits attendant with such features, and who are willing to pay a pricing premium to acquire them. Conversely, a price-led offer should be just that.

Importantly, you need to resist the temptation to blend quadrant-targeted offers. They are difficult to market because they invariably resemble all things to all people, and they create operational nightmares for other organizations within the company, notably engineering, manufacturing, and support, since such blended offerings exact too many trade-offs in their development.

Perhaps the most overlooked quadrant in the model is the one based on *convenience*. As many of us struggle under burdensome time pressures, there are emerging across many different product categories value propositions that are based not on a product itself, but rather on how we acquire the benefits of such a product. One only has to think of Amazon to understand this concept applied to the publishing industry. Or Kinko's for printing. The idea of convenience can also take many different forms. As a matter of financial convenience, I may wish to rent rather than own. As a matter of operational convenience, I may wish to buy a product but not to service it. Better yet, I want the product itself to tell the service people when it needs service. Or I might want a product only when I want what it does—a sort of just-in-time delivery system that is now applicable to many different product categories.

All the quadrants represent whole product +1 pricing offers (with perhaps the best price space representing a –1). Each leverages an existing, commodity-based infrastructure. And each is differentiated based on the specific requirements of a target segment. Your goal is to win one or more of these segments and thus justify as possible your higher price based not on higher cost but on higher value, both perceived and received.

Want more context? Go visit your local grocery store or supermarket. There, on the shelves, you will see these strategies in action. They are part of the modern-day consumer packaged goods business, and have been for most of the twentieth century. Will the twenty-first be different? Not likely.

Market Development Strategy Checklist: Market Penetration Variables

Cry havoc, and let slip the dogs of war.

—WILLIAM SHAKESPEARE

This section details the three fundamental market penetration assumptions as part of the Market Development Strategy Checklist, and specifies how each element should be considered across the Technology Adoption Life Cycle.

STRATEGY ASSUMPTION 7: COMPETITION

As this is a field book, please note that this section is not intended as a seminal treatise on the sources and nature of competitive advantage, the wielding of core competencies, effective competitive analysis, and so on. This is fertile ground to be sure, but it has been plowed many times in many different ways, by professors, authors, and other assorted gurus, each with their own thought-provoking set of theorems and *best practices*. Michael Porter's works, *Competitive Strategy* and *Competitive Advantage,* have always been influential to my thinking. I would also commend readers to the recent work of Harvard professor Clayton Christensen, who has provided numerous important insights specifically relevant to high tech in his book *The Innovator's Dilemma*. Both these scholars have contributed much to our current thinking, including models from which countless managers have framed and focused their competitive responses. My intent here is to once again provide a simple, efficient framework for your strategic assumptions, so that they are posed *not* in response to what the other guy is doing, but rather as an outgrowth of your TALC placement and your preceding strategy assumptions.

At the same time, it's also clear that thinking about the competitive dynamics of the high-tech industry must be considered not in isolation—one company's competitive posture or response relative to its market and other competitors—but rather in more, dare I say, *holistic* terms. Our feeling at The Chasm Group is that a company's competitive position, even its competitiveness, now has far more to do with its posture and behavior within the various *ecosystems* in which it lives. If we substitute the term *value chain* for ecosystem, we can understand more deeply how companies can compete against one another—their strengths and vulnerabilities at each point in the chain. More important, we can understand how *value chains themselves* compete for supremacy among the market's alternatives. For example, will the market favor one value chain whose members resemble a *coalition* of vendors who have come together opportunistically, quickly, but temporarily to serve a particular market? Or will the market seek the value chain solution composed of members who have an abiding interest in the longevity of the chain and will work together to perpetuate the chain as long as possible? Companies that understand these dynamics—both competing within a chain, and being a dominant part of a chain competing with alternative chains—can thus wield power not only over the chain, but also *through* the chain to assert and sustain advantage.

The market typically considers competition in two ways: *reference* competition, the set of alternatives within a category; and *economic* competition, the set of alternatives competing for the same budget. You *differentiate* your offering from those of your reference competition; and you *fight for supremacy* against your economic competition. (It is also why you should think about competitive considerations subsequent to thinking specifically about whole product definition and pricing respectively.)

The following model depicts summarily where the competitive battle is joined for each point in the life cycle.

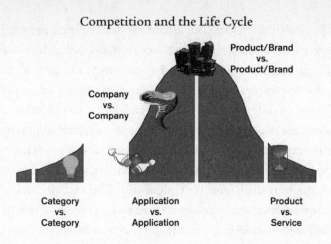

Competition and the Life Cycle

Product/Brand
vs.
Product/Brand

Company
vs.
Company

Category
vs.
Category

Application
vs.
Application

Product
vs.
Service

MARKET
DEVELOPMENT
STRATEGY
CHECKLIST:
MARKET
PENETRATION
VARIABLES

COMPETITION IN THE EARLY MARKET

In the early market, competition is biased significantly to one's *economic* competition, manifested in the form of alternative discontinuous innovations that may also be sources of competitive advantage to the visionaries who can wield them effectively. While such alternatives may appear to be reference competitors, the real competition here is the status quo or inertia now present in a given market. To illustrate briefly the difference, I might choose to buy a sales-force automation application to make my sales force more efficient; or I may invest in sell-side e-commerce systems to broaden my distribution and/or eliminate an element of my sales organization altogether. The visionary's quest remains the same: Where will I get the biggest bang for the buck?

This orientation may be completely at odds with the pragmatist agenda within the same company. Pragmatists are looking for solutions that are more narrowly defined as those which solve immediate problems associated with business as usual. This is a dynamic that as a practical matter makes it virtually impossible for early market technologies, and the strategies that are associated with them, to win over pragmatist customers. The pragmatist orientation during this market phase is to compare products and vendors within known or associated categories. Rational competitive alternatives are in fact a prerequisite for pragmatist sponsorship of new initiatives, and as such it is a loser for marketers in the early market. The point: Don't bother with the pragmatist-led mainstream at this early market stage. Instead, you must *create your own competition*.

To do this, you must focus your efforts on developing a persuasive argument and credibility within the domain of *technical specialists* who focus on new technologies and products and are therefore preternaturally disposed to seeking the "new, new thing." This is a competition based in *product-centric* attributes of the new paradigm. (At last we get to talk about *product!*) It is the fastest, the most easy to use, the most functional, the most elegant in design, the cheapest to use, and is destined to replace wholesale that which is not. Java, for example, was marketed as all the things existing development languages (read C and C++) were not. The fact that relatively few applications or multivendor standards existed at its inception mattered not. Java was marketed, correctly so, as the next *big idea* in application development languages with capabilities spanning a wide spectrum of potential uses that could not be duplicated fundamentally with status quo approaches. Think applets downloaded via the Internet; or rapid application development regardless of platform; or enabling applications for small-footprint home devices. In other words, do not compare what Java is to that which came before it. Rather, consider the potential of rethinking fundamentally what could be accomplished with its use. There is no *product* alternative. There may be a *market* alternative. Let the games begin.

COMPETITION IN CHASM-CROSSING AND BOWLING ALLEY MARKETS

I have combined these two inflection points as in earlier sections because the considerations and techniques surrounding competition at both points are similar if not identical. Crossing the chasm into a mainstream market is based on achieving market leadership within a well-defined niche market that can serve as a jumping-off point into adjacent niches. Providing a whole product solution that directly and distinctly answers the niche's compelling reason to buy is the pacing factor for adoption. When a whole product is fielded, pragmatists begin to rally behind this new solution, perceiving it to be not only equivalent to existing paradigms but also superior to them. Incidentally, until such a solution is brought forward, competition remains open to anyone.

In a practical sense, then, your competitive efforts will consist of *fighting against the economic competition* because this is the status quo; and *differentiating from other product alternatives* that have not been created to address

MARKET
DEVELOPMENT
STRATEGY
CHECKLIST:
MARKET
PENETRATION
VARIABLES

the problems of the niche, and thus are not whole products. You will see later in this chapter, in the section concerning positioning, how this is accomplished through the selection of a *differentiated benefit*.

As noted, success in the bowling alley is driven through creation of whole products. In order to do this, the competitive advantages that may have been won in the early market, built around one's ability to develop and project *product leadership*, now must be complemented with another critical ability: understanding deeply the realm of the target customer. We call this discipline *customer intimacy*.[1] The former enables a new whole product solution to be differentiated from the existing, status quo solution; while the latter enables compelling differentiation from other, similar new offerings that are not focused on the particular requirements of the niche.

Unlike the early market, there is no need to create competition. There is, however, a need to *choose* one's competition—and do it thoughtfully. Niche markets are often populated with status quo vendors with whom customers remain, sometimes grudgingly so, because such vendors previously demonstrated their abilities to serve these customers. As you and other new paradigm competitors attempt to displace them, it *appears* that the most these incumbents (or dinosaurs) are guilty of is, perhaps, complacency. High-tech organizations' typical responses to such conditions assume that the customer is in search of a new option, and thus individual vendors' competitive efforts will be directed against their fellow travelers—the other *new wave* vendors currently vying for the same mainstream customer. Such conventional wisdom is usually counterproductive.

The hyperbole and breathless claims made by the new market entrants can actually alienate the customers of the *old wave* if they're not using a new high-tech solution. Claims and counterclaims are heralding signs that such new approaches are still risky. "Better to stay with who I know, than go with who I don't" is the customer's sentiment. Even if customers are persuaded to the new way, the reference focus is now typically product based, subject to price-based competitive efforts. When this happens, mar-

---

1. Michael Treacy and Fred Wiersema detailed what they called the three value disciplines of competitive advantage—product leadership, customer intimacy, and operational excellence—in their book *The Discipline of Market Leaders,* first published in 1995.

gins inevitably go south, thereby straining further the economics of creating whole product value chains marshaled through partnering efforts.

Yet the seeds of the dinosaurs' demise are present. As in nature, they are unable to adapt to new surroundings. In this case, it is the gradual yet inevitable breakdown of the niche's current systems—systems built on the incumbents. They are and should be the focus of your competitive assumptions. Your objective is to focus on the nexus of product leadership—the ability to do it better—and customer intimacy—the ability to do it predictably and appropriately for that segment. The incumbent now appears as part of the problem, not part of the solution. Indeed, all incumbents associated with the old paradigm take on this dubious distinction. Your ability to win over the beachhead segment when crossing the chasm thus is underpinned by your ability to shift from an early-market *product* focus to that of an application-led *market* focus—the market now consisting of the initial segment, and later those segments that will reference it. And since pragmatist customers are naturally drawn to market leaders, winning this competition stands you in good stead for the next battle—an all-out assault on winning mass-market supremacy.

COMPETITION IN THE TORNADO

Shakespeare's quote at the beginning of this chapter could be the rallying cry for tornado competition. Of course, we'll need to change the species. In the tornado, all competition represents *economic* competition, and thus every competitor is your enemy. The reference competitor for every vendor but one is the *gorilla*. The gorilla's reference competitors are all the other competitors considered as a group. Competition is thus vendor versus vendor, company versus company. Your competitive strategy in the tornado should be based on your role—gorilla, chimp, or monkey—within the market hierarchy. Kings, princes, and serfs are noted corresponding to their primate counterparts. A thorough review of tornado competition is found in chapter 6.

The vendor who is winning the bowling alley competition becomes the odds-on favorite to achieve gorilla status when the market explodes. The immediate reward is typically a dramatic spike in market capitalization. The gorilla becomes the oddsmakers' favorite, and the bets are placed accordingly. Companies like i2 in supply chain software, Siebel in customer relationship management software, and BEA Systems in e-commerce infrastructure software have enjoyed during the past three years significant growth in their market capitalization as an acknowledgment and reward for their market share leadership. Though the race is far from over in each company's respective category, the pundits (who have been wrong before!) have tipped these competitors as front-runners. And as we have seen so often in tornadoes, strength begets more strength.

MARKET
DEVELOPMENT
STRATEGY
CHECKLIST:
MARKET
PENETRATION
VARIABLES

Competing as a Gorilla

The gorilla's tornado imperatives should be as follows:

1. *Maximize market share by winning as many sales as possible without resorting (yet) to rampant price discounting.*

   Both strategically and tactically, this is accomplished by aggressively pursuing as many deals as possible. In order to do this, gorillas and kings need to expand distribution wherever possible to include new territories and geographies and new channels of distribution. This means rethinking current go-to-market plans and programs built around the channel(s) originally employed in the early market and bowling alley. Sales force expertise is no longer the primary issue. Sales force coverage is. To illustrate the point, the distributed computing (or client/server) tornado of the early 1990s benefited Hewlett-Packard significantly at the expense of companies like Digital, Unisys, and, to a lesser extent, IBM. HP expanded significantly the availability of their products through supplementing their own sales forces with numerous third-party value-added resellers. HP offered attractive incentives to partner and "win with HP." Sun, employing VARs as well (and as a matter of course), managed to legitimize itself as an enterprise player during this same time. On the other hand, DEC, in a corporate state of denial that a tornado could actually spawn around UNIX, proceeded to hunker down, focusing instead on *not losing* its existing customer base. Unisys, meanwhile, influenced by its direct-sales force and their fealty to a purported but illusory account-control customer orientation, would fail repeatedly to mount a credible third-party effort, fearing its possible success more than it feared the possibility of failure (see chapter 6, the sidebar titled "A Change Will Do You Good"). Both Digital and Unisys possessed a reputation for fielding excellent technologies and products. But both cemented their own fates by a lack of aggressive strategy and a devotion to "doing things this way because that's the way we do them." For Digital, this period of denial was the second in a decade, the company having also dithered over the advent of PCs. And so it was that we witnessed a once formidable force in computing go quietly into the night at the hands of an acquisitive Compaq. Unisys, a would-be and legitimate challenger owing to its well-honed expertise in enterprise computing, maintained its independence but, unable to resolve its own internal divisiveness, receded into relative obscurity, choosing instead to refocus its corporate strategy on systems integration.

2. *Foster the further development of a category value chain built around the gorilla's architecture so that additional partners and allies are drawn into the chain, strengthening it further. The endgame is the market's recognition that the gorilla now has the most powerful and prevalent solution. The gorilla's product has become the platform upon which other products and applications can now be built.*

This is both a science and an art. A science because the gorilla must typically be prepared to forgo *actual* technology leadership in favor of standardizing its products so that other partners—application providers, service providers, complementary product vendors, and the like—can be assured of a relatively unchanging standard upon which to design their own value-added innovations. The risks of technology innovation at this stage actually augur better for chimps, because they have fewer customers and, frankly, less to worry about. A chimp's strategy is never about being all things to all people. But the gorilla's is. The gorilla is attempting to build a standard, and not necessarily build the best. Too much innovation can actually retard this process as partners can't keep up, or find that their most recent efforts now run counter to the most recent efforts of the gorilla. The downside here is that eventually gorillas earn the enmity of their original acolytes, the technology enthusiasts and visionaries. This is a regrettable but worthwhile trade-off requiring some necessary handholding, and thus . . . science becomes art, as the gorilla still should maintain the mantle of technology leadership for as long as it can be legitimately supported. As such, the gorilla's correct response when challenged on a technology/feature/functionality question is to point to the *next release*.

A king's ability to influence and fashion the value chain directly to its benefit cannot be employed under king/prince/serf market conditions since the king is *not* sponsoring a *proprietary, open architecture*. Instead, kings must utilize their leadership to build a *virtual* center of gravity for partners and allies, consisting of adherence to standards, market share, marketing activities in which partners can share, and, most important, *a superior partners and allies program*. The king should not expect perpetual fealty or even loyalty from his partners in the absence of some compelling reason for partners to pledge allegiance. There are no inherent switching barriers for partners, thus they will only stay with the king because they want to, not because they (eventually) have to.

3. *Be declared the winner of the tornado competition as early as feasible by technical, financial, and third-party analysts, as well as other industry watchers.*

This outcome requires a *reference competitor* that can be vanquished. The gorilla's foe is dependent on the relative life of the tornado. When the tornado first appears, gorillas should reference the old paradigm, and the corresponding technologies and products it is displacing. Other new paradigm vendors who desire to quash the old guard aid the gorilla's efforts. These allied efforts are possible at this stage because other primates and the market do not yet acknowledge that the gorilla is the gorilla.

Once the old guard is in retreat, the gorilla can now reference (and dismiss) all competitors as a pack. If there is a particularly threatening challenger, the gorilla then focuses its efforts at singling out and defeating this challenger. The game is similar when three or four competitors all make leadership claims (usually supported by rather dubious evidence), in an attempt to *assert* gorilla status. The relevant and *only* metric is market share. The gorilla should once again direct the market's attention to it and the most threatening chimp, referring to any false gorillas either by name or by dismissing them as part of the group ("other competitors") battling for the number two, three, or four position in the hierarchy.

Finally, once the gorilla's leadership is assured, the reference competitor can actually be the gorilla's other products—for example, HP positioned its laser printers against its own ink-jets—or other product

MARKET
DEVELOPMENT
STRATEGY
CHECKLIST:
MARKET
PENETRATION
VARIABLES

categories that may threaten the gorilla from its flank—for example, Intel's program to co-opt other vendors' ASIC, graphics, audio, or low-power consumption efforts as part of Intel's overall microprocessor strategy.

4. *As an organization, a gorilla should be seeking ways to streamline its operations in order to put maximum resources to the key activities required to support its market goals and to eliminate any bottlenecks that now have appeared under hypergrowth circumstances.*

Beware the slow, intransigent, or bloated gorilla. Gorilla power is advanced when the gorilla can compete effectively on price with the monkey, thereby forcing the monkey to be even more price competitive, possibly driving it into the land of negative margins; and when the gorilla can generate sufficient margins to outspend its chimp competitors via R&D, marketing, or both. Gorillas who fail to make themselves as lean and mean as possible give back these significant strategic degrees of freedom, and then some. This plays out when monkeys or chimps, unable to wrest control of the overall market from the gorilla, nevertheless set upon the gorilla in a coalition, forcing it to maintain high margins to pay for its sloth or gluttony. The gorilla may find itself forced into a corner strategically; eventually, it pays the price when the market transitions to Main Street and margin pressures now favor the low-cost provider (monkey) or the segment's value-added leader (chimp). This is what finally brought IBM down in the personal computer market in the early 1990s (a market now operating under king/prince/serf dynamics) as its commitment to manufacturing multiple dozens of SKUs (stock keeping units) proved to be completely out of sync with the evolving market and margin realities that now favored the efficient manufacturing processes of Compaq, and Dell's marketing and distribution model.

Competing as a Chimp

The most difficult position to occupy during the tornado is that of the chimp. Chimps, facing a seemingly invincible gorilla tide, must reorient themselves quickly to consolidate their position and set their sights on competing effectively over the long haul. Thus, the chimp's imperatives should include the following:

1. *Maximize market share by winning as many sales as possible without resorting (yet) to rampant price discounting.*

    That's right. This is the same objective as the gorillas. While a demand/supply imbalance remains, chimps should strive to win their fair share of deals. The mainstream market still *wants* alternatives to the gorilla. But from the market's point of view, this is a hedge. Do not misconstrue this intention as a desire to overthrow prematurely the market-favored gorilla. Value chains have been constructed around the gorilla/king *standard,* and chimps can't be easily accommodated in such chains. Chimps must aggressively construct their own chains while the opportunity still exists. And while the market may permit chimps to acquire market share—perhaps significantly so—the market will not permit the gorilla/king to be dethroned. There is simply too much riding on returning a rollicking market to one of equilibrium. Bear this in mind: *Customers don't like tornadoes.* The sooner they're resolved, with clear leaders, followers, and "all others," the better. Thus, for chimps, the battle is not for the number one position, it's for number two; for being number two is better than being number three. And so on.

2. *Once market share is minimized, target specific customer segments that are either not served or not well served by the gorilla, and build complete value chain solutions around these segments.*

    This is both an offensive as well as defensive move. Chimps should not fight gorillas directly. This is not only the wrong strategy; it is also foolhardy. Gorillas simply have too much going for them, and the market has voted with its feet. Thus, while attempting to win as many sales as possible, practically speaking the chimp is best served doing this where the playing field is more level—that is, where the market is not overly predisposed to the gorilla. The chimp can and should *overserve* specific customer segments and innovate within these segments to establish itself as a *gorilla in the niche.* Effectively, this strategy is an extension of the chimp's bowling alley efforts, expanded to the limits of the chimp's focus and value chain. The goal is to create segment-specific whole product solutions augmented with other complementary products, services, or business models that are valued by the segments, so that defensible barriers to entry can be established and sustained. Now the chimp's reference competitors are those who have not chosen to add such value. Lawson Software effectively pursued this strategy against a more powerful set of competitors in the ERP category by focusing on the healthcare services niche, a large and, for many vendors, somewhat scary segment due to its perceived heterogeneity and complexity. And we expect to see similar strategies played out in e-commerce software as well.

Defensively, this strategy offers a safe haven after the tornado has receded. But for some, it will appear as if the chimp is caving in too early to the gorilla's hegemony. You must resist these feelings. You have not lost. Instead, you have declared the territory that you will defend and create future innovation for. This is potentially very attractive to customers who are alienated by the gorilla's approach or not well served by it; and it's attractive as well to partners and allies who have not been included or are not dominant in the gorilla's value chain. It is also attractive to the investment community. While members of this group will continue to love the gorilla during the tornado, they will also hedge their positions, placing bets on a chimp or two who appear well positioned to maintain their market share, margins, and competitive posture when the tornado subsides.

COMPETING ON MAIN STREET

When the tornado subsides—all good things must come to an end—competitors must again shift their focus to now reaping what they have sown. Main Street shifts market dynamics back to equilibrium. Demand and supply are once again in balance. The market's insatiable thirst for tornado products has now been slaked. While there are still more customers to win, most have already declared their allegiance to a vendor, or they have signaled their intentions to sit this one out, betting that they can survive without the new infrastructure or obtain it in some other way, perhaps through a service. For many competitors, it now appears that the fun is all over. No more big deals (and big commissions). No more event-style marketing and marketing budgets. No more waking up each day and noticing that the share price has gone up another five points.

Get over it. The market welcomes this return to sanity. Now it can get down to the business of actually using this new infrastructure efficiently—*and building upon it*. And that means that people are going to buy more of the same, and buy complementary things that are used with or consumed by the new infrastructure. The people buying will be acting largely on their own initiative. No more lengthy purchase cycles and cumbersome approvals, as occurred in the bowling alley. End users drive the market, proclaiming, "Now I can get what I want, when I want it!" Most often, such follow-on purchasing follows two distinct paths by two different customer groups: those who are *price sensitive,* and those who are seeking *additional features and/or benefits.*

Price-sensitive customers are looking for products (offerings really) that are differentiated almost exclusively by their lower cost relative to previous purchases. Pursuing such a strategy can unlock entirely new markets, as we saw during the late 1990s when the price of personal computers dropped dramatically, along with peripheral devices such as printers and storage products. The nascent home market—sought by PC vendors for years with decidedly mixed results—suddenly blossomed into a sizable market of its own, the Internet now serving as the killer application. In North America, HP, Dell, and Gateway all benefited handsomely from this development. HP expanded its distribution model to warehouse stores like Best Buy and Costco, and Dell and Gateway pursued their direct-to-consumer model with stepped-up direct marketing campaigns.

Meanwhile, Apple resuscitated itself by returning to its developmental and marketing roots after years of unfocused and clumsy attempts to be something that the market did not want, and Apple could not deliver. Steve Jobs has never forgotten that great products—"insanely great," as I remember his entreaties—can attract a market that not only treasures such things but will pay more than the market rate to get them. Apple's iMac was just such a product. Its refreshing, cutting-edge design, priced reasonably (though higher than comparably equipped Wintel boxes), and marketed intelligently with the kind of style that Apple pioneered in the early 1980s, was a smash hit in the home and education markets. Similar forays into the laptop and professional graphics markets with high-end notebooks and workstations also proved successful, as Mac enthusiasts and those who relied on the Macintosh platform for their very livelihoods rallied around Apple's new products and renewed focus.

Apple's efforts exemplify +1 marketing and mass customization at its most sophisticated. Their efforts were not confined simply to tangible product features. Apple also reintroduced its brand through a reinvigorated marketing effort, most apparent in the company's advertising. The

MARKET
DEVELOPMENT
STRATEGY
CHECKLIST:
MARKET
PENETRATION
VARIABLES

net result was that Apple reconnected itself with the Apple *faithful*—a user base famed for both its loyalty to all things Apple and its willingness to share such enthusiasm with any and all who will listen. When the time came for computer novices to buy a home PC, Apple seized the day. From product design to the tone of voice of the advertising, Apple added +1 value to it all. And the market responded by embracing an old and newly welcomed friend. Of course, Main Street markets always raise the question, "What have you done lately?" Apple, once again, must answer.

Main Street competition extends some of the competitive dynamics of the tornado, chiefly the search for new price points and the addition of new features. But it will not tolerate further adoption or solution complexity. Therefore, competitors must *quickly—and without fail*—adopt a Main Street market development posture that serves Main Street realities. Once again, your status should influence your strategic and tactical decisions. And once again, market segmentation plays a key role in a successful outcome.

For monkeys and serfs, the best way forward is becoming the *low-cost provider*, delivering commodity products with minimal overhead, perhaps using differentiated or novel business models. The market segment to search for and find is the *price-sensitive buyer* who wants or is directed to lower the operating costs associated with running the newly adopted infrastructure. Serving these segments conveys a certain power to the monkey/serf because it is now the reference competitor based on price. If your product is now falling under the aegis of a purchasing department, you become quite attractive, particularly if no other competitor responds. Do not be misled that such attraction will fundamentally alter the primate or royal family pecking order any time soon. It will not. Your margins must also be able to sustain the strategy because investment will be required at the supply chain level. You must look to become maximally operationally efficient. The strategy can only be based on this capability, and if you don't have it, you can't play this game.

Chimps and princes face a different challenge. You must *avoid* the purchasing department and make sure that you've won the hearts and affection of your end users with whom you now seek to engage directly in the buying process. Your strategy should continue to be the value-added provider who serves up offerings that are differentiated based on specific end user requirements. Purchasing departments often ignore such requests, or press vendors to provide these additional benefits for free. When feasible, run—don't walk—away from this group. Reconnect with your installed base and segment it carefully, including those remaining customers who have not bought. Give them what they want. But give it to them in ways that allow you to avoid the state of profitless prosperity that often characterizes those who stray too far in their quest to seek out new customers, or attempt to woo those who are already betrothed. Chimps (and princes) can pursue the price-sensitive buyer with new, lower price points, but they must realize that any advantage won will be temporary. Both gorillas and monkeys can emulate this same strategy—something the market actually looks forward to as lower prices for the entire category are sure to follow.

Chimp/prince strategies should be built around +1 offerings that can be fielded often and in novel ways. Nimbleness is the key here. And marketing budgets should be allocated to this effort, not just R&D. The idea is to keep providing a stream of new offerings—*without any discontinuity*—aimed squarely at the segments that the chimp/prince already has an advantage with, and keep 'em coming. Slower moving competitors typically will be forced to respond, but the secret is not in *outfeaturing* the competition, it's *outoffering* them, utilizing a combination of tangible and intangible +1s that draw further allegiance from the installed base and *curiosity* from those who may not have yet adopted or who may be tempted to switch. In markets that are characterized by very high switching costs, where it's unreasonable to expect customers to switch vendors, the strategy nevertheless serves to further extend the vendor's influence with its installed base, rendering it impenetrable by others. Finally, the strategy may also be a sign indicating a safe haven to customers who have reason to suspect that their current vendor may, at some point, no longer be viable. Here, gorillas in the niche can be just as attractive as the overall gorilla.

All of which brings us to the most satisfying competitive position: that of the gorilla. Not surprisingly, *gorillas* (and to a lesser extent *kings*) have the most strategic freedom. Gorillas can attack both the low end of the market and the premium market with a number of +1 offerings.

At the low end, the gorilla's goal is to keep monkeys (serfs) off balance by continuing to cost-reduce the base price of any entry-level offering to the maximum extent possible. The net effect of this strategy serves to co-opt and undermine the monkey's ability to execute on its primary strategy as the low-cost provider. Lowering the cost of base products is not restricted to the product itself. The strategy can be executed via the overall business model through, for example, alternative low-cost distribution models, favorable terms and conditions associated with acquiring the product (e.g., leasing versus buying), and so on. Perhaps the most powerful efforts are those that combine new benefits based on insightful segmentation with significant and visible marketing efforts, including increased efforts in demand creation—for example, advertising with distribution optimization built again around careful segmentation.

An alternative strategy, though more risky, involves altering subtly the underlying or de facto standards associated with the product and its infrastructure. This strategy forces any monkey who clones the gorilla into new rounds of reengineering. The effect is felt on the monkey's bottom line as the marginal profit now resulting from the category must be reinvested into new engineering efforts. But be careful. The strategy is not without its risks. If the gorilla attempts to introduce too much of a change, the effect is likely to be felt more acutely at the market level in the form of discontinuity—an unwelcome and unintended consequence— that now forces customers to spend as well. This is precisely the sin committed by IBM in 1987 when it introduced, in effect, a proprietary version of its next models of PCs through changes in its external connection or bus architecture (called MicroChannel). IBM, at this time a market gorilla, went directly contrary to the clone industry it helped to foster— and the market wasn't buying. Compaq and others, emerging princes as the market destabilized, announced that they would continue the current bus architecture—the previous IBM standard—and would continue to provide new feature/functionality around this architecture, forcing no changes from anyone in the value chain. IBM, which had to reverse itself, began the long slide from gorilla power to its current position today.

Summarizing, gorillas have three significant strategic degrees of freedom:

1. *They can cost-reduce their products through supply-chain optimization, reduced manufacturing costs, and the like to force new lower price points without corresponding margin erosion.*
2. *They can continually provide new offers to the market, combined with aggressive and targeted marketing activities.*
3. *They can shift de facto standards slightly to force competitive reengineering.*

Or they can pursue any of these basic directions in concert with each other.

Finally, gorillas should also pursue strategies that will ensure their continuing domination through the acquisition of fledglings who might be developing the next set of discontinuities that could overhaul the market at large, given time, and thus disrupt any and all related value chains and the power structures they represent. Cisco Systems has elevated this strategy to high art, effectively buying its way into new markets (why spend your own money on R&D when you can acquire the fruits of someone else's?), while at the same time protecting its flanks from nascent technologies, products, and companies that would threaten the company's main business.

It's good to be the king. And better to be the gorilla.

STRATEGY ASSUMPTION 8: POSITIONING

What we have here . . . is failure to communicate.

—STROTHER MARTIN, IN THE MOVIE *COOL HAND LUKE*

"Is it position or positioning?" (Does it really matter?) "We need to reposition the company for growth." (What were your prior efforts devoted to?) "The product's positioning is unclear." (See previous question.) "We need to reposition the entire product line by next year." (How much money do you have?) "We've filed our S1, so it's now time to position the company." (Really. What did you tell the SEC?)[2]

The above are verbatim statements or requests put to me over the past twelve months. They are indicative of the confusion that surrounds this most mysterious of all the elements that make up a strategy. Positioning may start with an idea, a product, or a company, but as Al Ries and Jack

---

2. Prior to offering shares in the U.S. public market through an initial public offering (IPO), companies must file a detailed and comprehensive document with the Securities and Exchange Commission disclosing virtually all aspects of the company's business: its current ownership; the category in which it competes; and all the risks associated with investing in the company.

MARKET
DEVELOPMENT
STRATEGY
CHECKLIST:
MARKET
PENETRATION
VARIABLES

Trout note in their landmark book on positioning, *"positioning is not what you do to a product. Positioning is what you do to the mind of the prospect."*[3]

To begin, let's dispel some commonly held myths about positioning by summarizing some fundamentals first detailed in *Crossing the Chasm*:

1. *Positioning is first a noun, not a verb.* It is best understood as an attribute or condition associated with a company or product, and not as the marketing and communications gymnastics that marketers engage in to build such associations.

2. *Positioning is the single largest influence on the buying decision.* Customers evaluate market alternatives based on their own mental map of the market. Each individual's map is different based on his/her own view of reality and his/her own prejudices, beliefs, and point of view.

3. It follows that *positioning exists in people's heads and not in positioning statements.* You cannot be the superior choice if you are not the *relevant* one first. Therefore, the first goal of positioning is demonstrating your relevance, using supportable, credible, and factual terms. Positioning statements are *not* hyperbole, fluff, or supercilious. In other words, they are not advertising copy.

4. Contrary to conventional wisdom, *people do not easily or willingly change their minds concerning a company or product's positioning.* The most durable positioning is that which is rooted in simple and fundamental truths.

5. To change a company's or product's positioning in the market requires significant investment in marketing communications. In marketing, it wise to remember an old adage from the advertising business: "People only know what they're told."

In packaged goods marketing, companies such as Colgate-Palmolive, Unilever, and Kellogg's battle for physical shelf space within a grocery store or supermarket. Products that occupy the most favored positions on the shelf—typically the space between the buyer's eye and his or her waist—enjoy some natural advantages because they are physically the most *easy to buy*. In high tech, the battle is for *mental* shelf space. Unlike the supermarket, the choices may not be that apparent. Consistent with

---

3. Al Ries and Jack Trout, *Positioning: The Battle for Your Mind* (New York: McGraw-Hill, 1981), p. 2.

the prior assumption, both reference competitors—the set of alternatives within the category—and economic competitors—the set of alternatives competing for the customer's money—need to be pointed out in order to frame minimally the parameters by which the market can evaluate the offering. The advantageous mental shelf placement conjures in the customer's mind the opinion that "for this situation, this product is the best choice." In other words, making the product easy to buy through effective positioning makes the product easy to sell. There is nothing mysterious about this admittedly difficult goal.

MARKET
DEVELOPMENT
STRATEGY
CHECKLIST:
MARKET
PENETRATION
VARIABLES

Naturally, positioning goals and positioning efforts should reflect where the product/category is on the Technology Adoption Life Cycle. The positioning focus and emphasis should also take into consideration the competitive framework shown earlier in this chapter ("Competition and the Life Cycle"). A company's positioning goal—its desired place in the mind of the market—can be summarized for each inflection point as follows:

- *The early market.* The first task is to *define the market* and our place within it. The intended net impression (or take-away) we need to create among visionary economic and technical buyers is that the company appears to be a leader within an emerging and highly promising category, *and* that this new category shows the promise for providing dramatic competitive advantage to those who can harness it.

- *The chasm and the bowling alley.* Next, positioning effort must now *build a market.* The net impression to establish among economic buyers and end users should be that the product and the application are the most complete and therefore most appropriate for the needs of a given segment. As a result, the company sponsoring this whole product is now seen as dominating the segment.

- *The tornado.* Positioning now seeks to establish *dominance* within a burgeoning market. The net impression to be established with infrastructure and economic buyers is that the company is the market leader (aka *gorilla* or *king*) in a hypergrowth category.

- *Main Street.* The final goal is to *extend the market* and our place within it. The net impression to be established with end users is that the company now provides the best *offers* on a regular basis, *and/or* the brand values represented by either the company or the product are the most appealing.

What follows are some basic tools to use for most high-tech positioning exercises. The first are designed to help you map the market from which to identify and stake out the most relevant territory. The second is a positioning template that you should use to articulate further the placement based on the identification of the target customer, the fundamental value proposition or promise based on the compelling reason to buy, and the reason why such a choice is most relevant.

The mapping tool reflects our view that positioning involves rigging the system in your favor as a function of two elements: (1) the value proposition choices or products available to customers; and (2) the companies that sponsor these choices. This does not imply that such efforts are based on subterfuge, clever "wordsmithing," or other marketing sleights of hand. It is instead about establishing—and controlling, if possible—the benefit and differentiation axis by which the market thinks about the product category in general, and you specifically. Positioning is an exercise of fitting yourself favorably into the market using variations of the following mapping tool, shown here detailing the dynamics of an early market offering:

Basic Positioning Map: Early Market

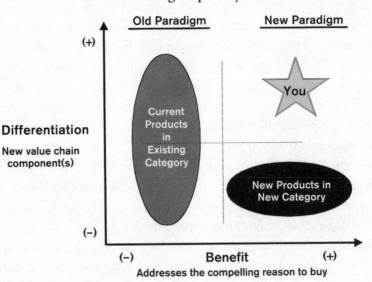

The **benefit** is the advantage conveyed by the product to the target customer and is based on the target customer's *compelling reason to buy*. **Differentiation** is an expression of one element within the vendor domain of the new value chain, for example, technology, product, application, or distribution, that (a) makes the benefit possible, (b) is itself relevant to the *target customer,* and (c) is unique relative to the market alternatives.

The second tool is a proven positioning template that allows you to express precisely the fundamental value proposition or promise that the product provides to a target customer and by proxy, the market:

MARKET
DEVELOPMENT
STRATEGY
CHECKLIST:
MARKET
PENETRATION
VARIABLES

- *For* (target customer or market) . . .
- *Who* (have a compelling reason to buy) . . .
- *Our product is a* (new/existing product category) . . .
- *That provides* (key benefit that addresses directly the compelling reason to buy) . . .
- *Unlike* (the reference or economic competitive alternatives) . . .
- *Our product* (reflects a meaningful differentiation specifically related to an attribute(s) associated with the target customer) . . .

This template corresponds directly to the positioning map shown on page 182, and works as follows:

The first two lines identify the segment for which this positioning statement is intended, using the technique of focusing on the ideal target customer, one that passes the key qualifying test of line two.

The third line places the product or service in a category, in effect telling the prospect where to go looking for the product, and what the competitive set is likely to consist of.

Line four states the key benefit, the same thing that is expressed by the *X* axis.

Line five identifies the primary alternative source of the same benefit.

Line six states the key difference or point of differentiation that is expressed by the *Y* axis.

Taken all together, this template expresses the essence of any product or service position. You can think of this as the minimum amount of information that you need to establish (a) who you are, (b) what you are offering, (c) whom it is for, and (d) why it is important and compelling. It is the platform upon which all further marketing claims will stand. And in noisy markets, this is all you should try to communicate.

Finally, the positioning statement must satisfy several key criteria if it is to be of maximum utility:

1. *The target customer (or target segment) must be identified effectively, and the situation they face or labor under must be unambiguous and understandable.* Positioning statements that identify customers in general terms—for example, "IT directors in Fortune 500 companies"—or that cite conditions that strain credulity and reasonableness, or that don't reflect reality, or are simply the marketer's wishful thinking—for example, "who want best-of-breed networking solutions in order to achieve competitive advantage"—are virtually useless. The disciplined marketer realizes once again that you simply can't be all things to all people.

2. *The claim—that which you are offering and the benefit it provides—must be concise, singular, compelling, and supported by credible evidence.* Weak claims weaken the positioning because:

   - The claim won't be transmitted by word of mouth—the most important medium in high tech—because the claim is too long, too complicated, or not true.
   - Marketing communications based on deficient claims typically are imprecise, equivocal, or banal.
   - The positioning can't be used effectively to recruit partners because they're unsure of what they would be supporting.
   - The claim can't withstand the scrutiny of other market makers, including your competition, who will attempt to disprove or displace it.
   - The positioning can't be used to secure funding from experienced sources due to all of the above.

3. *Differentiation attributes used to support the benefit must also be concise, singular, compelling, and supportable. They must also reflect the attributes of the target customer and his or her environment.* The most common mistake made here is assigning a differentiation that may be interesting or otherwise unique, but is insignificant when considered in light of the customer and the environment. In practice, we note this gaffe particu-

MARKET
DEVELOPMENT
STRATEGY
CHECKLIST:
MARKET
PENETRATION
VARIABLES

larly when engineering, marketing, and sales can't agree on the real promise made by the product, or wish to cover all bets by basing both benefit and differentiation on multiple elements. Such equivocation leads to confusion rather than clarity because resulting marketing communications will reflect a "claims du jour" orientation.

4. *The positioning must pass the "elevator test."* Can you explain your product (or your company) in the time it takes to ride up in an elevator (and we're not talking here about going to the top floor of the Sears or Petronas Towers!)? In Silicon Valley parlance, this is known as the company's "elevator speech." Consistent with the above, resist the urge to blurt out all your product's features and benefits, numerous as they undoubtedly are. Your audience has so little time—and potentially even less interest. Recall that you are trying to create and occupy a place figuratively *inside someone's head!* For most of us, there is not a lot of excess room.

Finally, positioning is a dynamic process, not a onetime event. As we shall see, it must change according to Technology Adoption Life Cycle priorities, but there must also be room for adjustment as the positioning takes hold (or fails to) in the marketplace.

POSITIONING IN THE EARLY MARKET

The target customer in the early market is the technology enthusiast and the visionary who are evaluating a range of discontinuous innovations to ascertain what might provide them with dramatic advantages over the market in the shortest period of time. Referring to the positioning mapping model shown earlier, your positioning chore in the early market is to *name and frame* the product category and the benefit it delivers or advantage it conveys versus a chosen status quo. This is the minimum amount of information necessary to communicate with the *technology enthusiast*.

This is not as easy as it seems. Discontinuous innovations often are not easily pigeonholed using conventional terminology. On the other hand, marketers often will create categories with coined terms that are intended to convey something entirely new—*middleware* and *personal digital assistant* (PDA) come to mind—only to succeed in muddying already turbulent waters by category names that either are ambiguous catchalls for any number of subcategories (e.g., middleware, which became widely derided as "muddleware") or that conjure up many different potential products or applications, all of which require further explanation—e.g., the PDA, something that Apple called its ill-fated Newton, instead of the more conventional and understandable *personal information manager* (PIM) or *electronic organizer*—chosen by Sharp, Palm, Psion, and others. Both of these descriptors name and frame the space by defining these products in terms we can readily identify with or ascribe characteristics to (personal information; organizer) that we all commonly understand. Whatever you choose, the category will live or die based on its ultimate technological efficacy, and whether it gets traction with the technical community, and the pundits and cognoscenti who follow and prognosticate (pontificate?) on all things new and discontinuous.

Going forward, the goal is to add to the positioning in order to highlight and clarify the offering to *visionaries*. To do this, you must specify in greater detail for whom the product is targeted, its purpose, and the overwhelming advantage it conveys to those who can harness its power. Once again, the most common mistake is stating in overly general terms who the product is for and making claims that are either bombastic or unsupportable in theory or in practice. The software category known as data warehousing labored under such conditions in the early 1990s. Sponsoring software vendors promised that data warehousing would be a boon for everyone virtually regardless of industry. The promise was that by using such software, managers would obtain significant insights into, for example, customer buying behaviors by collating numerous data points and analyzing them through sophisticated data algorithms that could "slice and dice" the data in every imaginable way to enable further analysis and decision making. The category was marketed, correctly so, to senior executives, notably CFOs, marketing and merchandising VPs, manufacturing and logistics managers, and the like. However, it was also marketed to such people regardless of industry, and those efforts virtually ignored or vastly understated the amount of hard work necessary for IT managers to deploy the applications. In order to really take advantage of the capabilities promised, organizations had to reengineer many of their business processes in order to make active and timely decisions based on the data. Absent such moves, data warehouses were characterized by many as nothing more than another database, or even spreadsheet, with sophisticated analytical capabilities of dubious practical value. Of course, no one could agree on what constituted a real data warehouse. An acronym war broke out (OLAP, ROLAP, DOLAP, etc.) among competing vendors trying to describe their approach and trump the competition at the same time. Data warehousing seemed destined to be a textbook case of opportunities squandered and promises unmet. Visionaries turned their attention to the next "next big thing," that of enterprise resource planning (ERP) applications.

To be fair, data warehouses and their cousins, data marts, were breakthrough applications. The problem lay in clarifying exactly who was going to buy them and for what specific and strategic reasons—reasons that could not be easily translated across multiple industries and multiple applications. Later in the life cycle of the category it became clear that such applications were not panaceas for every industry, but they were increasingly necessary to support industries such as retailing, distribution, logistics, and telecommunications. Overall, the category failed to secure sufficient support in the early market and thus wilted there prematurely. The category did manage to cross the chasm, but it continues today as a niche solution to niche problems.

The lesson here is that early market efforts often require new entrants to, in effect, *create a crisis* in order to justify their arrival and validate early demand. The technology itself has to be sufficiently unique and compelling, and be explainable in its differentiation from existing categories or simply the status quo. To do this requires a degree of complicity among the new entrants to position primarily—and quickly—the category first, *before* they can position themselves as credible sponsors of the category. Increasingly, marketers are learning (or maybe relearning) that you are only as powerful as your category, and never more so. Simply put, if the category fails to achieve a level of *gravitational pull* that attracts early adopters, other value chain members, the usual pundits and gurus, and so on, further efforts to position a specific company within this new system will likely disappoint those involved. Moreover, the time window to position the category is shortening. There are simply too many new "new things" screeching for attention in an environment where there is, increasingly, an attention deficit due to all these new things.

Marketers are thus faced with developing a preliminary positioning in order to influence and preordain, if possible, how a *powerful value chain* will grow up around a discontinuous innovation. These efforts presage the future power of the category relative to the industry as a whole. When this case is made, or is at least generating interest, only then can individual companies begin to jockey for position within the category, with the

MARKET
DEVELOPMENT
STRATEGY
CHECKLIST:
MARKET
PENETRATION
VARIABLES

goal of obtaining the top slot in a suggested new pecking order. Most often, doing this requires substantiating the initial positioning through a *proof of concept*—otherwise known as demonstrating that the thing actually works—evangelized by a "spokescustomer(s)" who is willing and able to serve as a credible reference among visionaries.

POSITIONING FOR CHASM AND BOWLING ALLEY MARKETS

Extending our positioning model, marketers must now increasingly focus their message to the wary pragmatists who are intrigued by the promise of the innovation yet repelled by the risks that it entails. The challenge here is to articulate your place within the set of purchase alternatives relative to both the status quo (and old paradigm) and the set of reference competitors that have now emerged in the new paradigm. One statement must serve to do both. You must also consider another crucial element: that of building a value chain in concert with partners and allies who will contribute to this effort. You will then have to deal with the numerous third parties—the press, analysts, and industry associations, among others—who are institutionally disposed to critique your efforts.

Within the customer domain of the value chain, the critical audience is the *economic buyer,* for they are the only ones empowered to act in advance of wide-scale adoption. Your positioning therefore must be grounded by a significant and compelling reason to buy that will move this group to action. The partners and allies that you're attempting to recruit must understand and appreciate the wealth generation that is possible through their participation in your coalition. Business development activities therefore must also be directed to the economic stakeholder within the partner company, rather than the technical organization, so that the economic rewards can be recognized and acted upon. The press and analyst community must also be impressed so that they can influence the target customer economic buyer, while the technical press and analysts will weigh in with the partner coalition.

However, the most significant audience, if they can be called that, is your competition—both old guard and new. Convincing the old guard that your intentions to dominate a niche are modest while at the same time using their positioning as a foil for your own is practically an art form. Simultaneously staking out turf against the new competitors so that they must acknowledge, tacitly or otherwise, the legitimacy of your claim requires focus, commitment, and a certain of amount of hubris based on facts.

Using the positioning map once again, we modify its axis slightly, to reflect the basic tenet of chasm-crossing positioning. The desired position represents the intersection of a new benefit previously not available. The benefit answers specifically the compelling reason to buy. The differentiation is based on specific customer attributes associated with the target segment that show how the benefit is uniquely suited for this group.

MARKET
DEVELOPMENT
STRATEGY
CHECKLIST:
MARKET
PENETRATION
VARIABLES

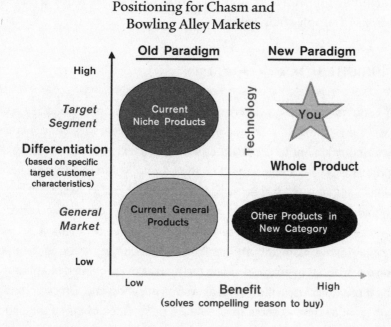

Positioning for Chasm and
Bowling Alley Markets

Successful chasm-crossing and bowling alley positioning involves occupying a space that is defined—and can be defended—by two barriers: *product innovation* or leadership, and *segment focus* (born of customer intimacy). The technology represented in the discontinuous innovation (the new paradigm) forms the chasm that you have now bridged. This allows you to separate yourself from the status quo, that part of the existing value chain that is now breaking down for one or more segments in the market. At the same time, you are differentiating yourself from other new paradigm alternatives by an unflagging commitment to a specific target customer segment. This creates a whole product barrier distancing you from other new players.

Consider the following example:

- *For* corporate planners in large manufacturing companies,
- *Who* must redesign their supply chains in order to minimize delivered cost of goods,
- SynQuest DE is a supply chain planning application that enables the rapid analysis of various supply chain possibilities.
- *Unlike* competitive alternatives that provide only for optimal logistics,
- SynQuest DE analyzes virtually all manufacturing planning variables, including logistics as they affect profit and loss, to deliver a *financially optimized* supply chain solution.

KEY INSIGHT ▶ ▶ ▶ ▶ ▶ ▶ ▶ ▶ ▶ ▶

You do *not* have to provide necessarily more or superior benefits than your new paradigm competitors! Your competitive advantage lies in your commitment to providing a complete solution to the segment's problems. The battle is waged on the basis of your providing a differentiation that is at least equivalent to the status quo (which can't provide equivalent benefits), and is more relevant than other new product entries that have not been tailored for the target segment. It is the sophisticated marketer who realizes that specifying the axis for the new market, in effect persuading the market to judge market entrants on these qualities, is the grand, as well as the endgame. Chasm crossing must also be speedy. To accelerate penetration of the target segment, a successful strategy is to compete against other new entrants based on time to benefit. You can have your solution up and running, and thus solving the problem, long before your competitors. Why? You understand the market segment and its problem better, and you've created a complete solution that can be deployed quickly based on your knowledge. If you were bleeding from the neck, wouldn't you want the problem to be corrected rapidly?

POSITIONING IN THE TORNADO

The target customer priority in the tornado shifts to that of pragmatist *technical or infrastructure buyers*—the individuals or groups responsible for acquiring the next generation of stuff and disposing of the old. The buying choices consist of all vendors in the new product category. The desired position is the gorilla's—number one in market share and the de facto market standard. If you are a chimp, a desired position is to be seen as the best product moving toward niche market leadership (the so-called gorilla in the niche). For monkeys, a desired position is reliable low-cost alternatives, or derivations thereof. Monkeys really compete with other monkeys to achieve a presence, possibly even a dominance of sorts, among other monkeys chiefly within a distribution channel. Thus, how you position your product and company becomes a function of what primate or member of the royal family you now represent in the overall market. Put another way, tornado positioning must reflect a composite of an organization's hoped-for position, its ability to support such a goal, and the market realities that now form the basis for the competition going forward. Your positioning efforts accordingly may now range far and wide from a singular *product* benefit and differentiation to one of financials, company future and outlook, and value chain support. All of these are potential benefits and points of differentiation—context that is very meaningful to pragmatists and also *conservatives* who are now beginning to invest in the product category.

Finally, if you don't provide a meaningful positioning for the market during the tornado, one will be assigned to you! That is, as customers, value chain partners, analysts and pundits, and the press all try to discern meaningful signals from all the marketplace noise, you have but few chances to make a lasting impact. Failure results in either outright marketplace dismissal—"Since we can't hear or understand you, you must not be important"—or being assigned to that dreaded category known as *all others,* a kind of market Siberia where few would venture willingly, and of those sent, few are heard from again.

Gorilla Positioning

The easiest position to stake out is that of the gorilla. Since competition in the tornado now shifts from a product-and-application focus to a company-versus-company focus, customers are now looking to pick the right company, particularly if switching costs are significant. Since the gorilla is the *safe buy* absent any information to the contrary, making the gorilla's products easy to buy is really about making the gorilla itself easy to buy. Benefits

MARKET
DEVELOPMENT
STRATEGY
CHECKLIST:
MARKET
PENETRATION
VARIABLES

in this case can be built around several dimensions—company viability (revenues and profits), demand fulfillment ability, ability to set market standards, strategic partners, and so on—with a single benefit chosen on the basis of specific market conditions. Differentiation is reflective of the gorilla's past success—namely, its market share, or number of *satisfied* customers. The intent here is to convey implicitly that *chimps,* as niche players and incompatible with the gorilla, represent some degree of *market risk. Monkeys,* while possibly compatible, represent potential *quality risks* primarily associated with their complete lack of influence on the overall value chain.

That's it. There is not a lot of finesse required. Kings should remember, however, that their position is directly assailable by princes who do not represent market risks because a market standard exists across the category. But serfs still represent quality risks due to their relative insignificance.

Chimp Positioning

The chimp's goal is to assert dominance and therefore garner continuing loyalty among as many market segments as can be sustained. *You do **not** do this by positioning yourself directly against the gorilla!* Such efforts are not credible, and they can be near fatal as Informix (versus Oracle) and Novell (versus Microsoft) have demonstrated. Instead, the chimp must, like a savvy politician, shore up and play to its base—the customers who elected the chimp through their investments and who also hope they made the correct choice. Chimps need to instill three ideas within their constituency specifically and the market at large:

1. The chimp will continue to serve—in fact, overserve—the segments where it now has dominance or at least a respectable market share.
2. The chimp will defend this turf vigorously.
3. In markets where the chimp and gorilla overlap, the chimp's approach, point of view, and future direction are in marked contrast to those of the gorilla. The point here is to acknowledge the gorilla's approach rather than criticize it, in an effort to show that while the gorilla may be a safe choice, the chimp is the *smart choice.* You may be accorded *grand master* strategist status if you can further cause the gorilla and other chimps to engage with each other directly. We call this the "let's you and him fight" game.

Longer term, the chimp uses its differences to show that it, unlike other chimps and monkeys, is not in the grip of the gorilla, but is instead pursuing a different vision, one that may portend an eventual new category or direction not pursued by the gorilla.

In contrast, the *prince* can position against the king or against other princes. Bear in mind that your positioning can be easily challenged, co-opted, or negated outright by market forces or sentiment, or by significant competitive investments in marketing communications, channel programs, and the like. Positioning efforts thus are likely to more closely represent those engaged on Main Street.

Monkey Positioning

While it is not all that much fun, there are two alternative value propositions for monkeys to pursue:

1. The monkey is the low-cost alternative to the gorilla/king and can provide everything they can (except, perhaps, peace of mind).
2. The monkey provides what the gorilla/king provides and is the easiest to do business with (the differentiator is the business model).

Of these, I prefer the second option. The target customer for the first example is really the distribution channel and purchasing agents, neither of whom typically demonstrates any loyalty. Thus, you are only as good as your last offer. Marketing communications activities therefore tend to be wasted efforts. Your role is consigned to staying one step ahead of virtually any competitor who is able to take you on—and deal you out. Alternatively, option two supports the construction of a competitive advantage that is specifically *not* product oriented. The clever monkey thus negates its own disadvantages, seen by the customer as technology and product risk, for a promise that may be as compelling, if not more so, over the longer term. This is exactly how the formerly humble Dell Computer conquered the realm of the personal computer.

Of course, this direction does not lock out other competitors. But for organizations carrying business processes once designed to serve the customer that are now outmoded or otherwise in place solely to maintain some status quo, this strategy can succeed, perhaps even prevail. The e-commerce Internet wave, albeit waning for the time being, is nevertheless a heralding sign that new business models wielded by the determined can overturn less nimble competitors or those who choose to look the other way.

MAIN STREET POSITIONING

On Main Street, the target customer is the *end user*. Often, they are already part of your installed base. Your own product line now represents the buying alternatives *if* significant switching costs are inherent with the category. However, if switching costs are only modest or nonexistent, then the system of buying alternatives correspondingly is greatly expanded. Let's consider each case.

In markets where product adoption implies a significant commitment by both customers and market makers to a proprietary architecture—a value chain that is not easily replicated or exchangeable by other competitors—positioning is largely an extension of efforts undertaken during the tornado, if one occurred, or the Bowling Alley, if the category did not enjoy widespread adoption. The end game is establishing *customers for life*. These are markets in which your relative position, now assigned if not earned, reflects your primate status.

Gorillas should build on their lofty position with statements concerning both their market successes and, accordingly, their financial ability to invest further in the product category, as well as systematically divulging their future directions in technology and product development as a result of such investments. Such statements are the final ones necessary to win over any lingering conservatives and to preserve to the greatest extent possible the gorilla's legitimacy and influence with its installed base. Cisco, for example, knows well that it does not have to compete directly with the likes of Lucent, Ericsson, or Nortel purely on a "best technology/best product" basis. Its financial clout, industry influence, and the remarkable ability of its charismatic leader, John Chambers, to acquire and integrate other companies to rapidly field new products is a powerful competitive and positioning advantage. Cisco, perhaps like no other technology company on Earth, virtually embodies the oft-mentioned eight-hundred-pound gorilla. Lest we forget, customers have now pledged their loyalty to the gorilla as well, but will evidence this allegiance by grousing that the gorilla has now become "arrogant."

Chimps can follow this advice as well, with a few caveats. Chimps also have erected some barriers to entry from competitors, due to their particular architecture, which in turn erects barriers to exit for the chimp's customers. Like the gorilla, the chimp's primary goal on Main Street is customers for life, retaining its customer base and growing it opportunistically when feasible. Unfortunately, the first instinct is to reverse the order of things: get new customers, then serve the base. The problem with this thinking is that if the category has gone through a tornado and is thus pervasive, there are *very few customers left to get!* The chimp now believes that it can win customers by attacking the gorilla directly, usually a fatal mistake. Instead, the chimp should be concerned with prolonging its power within its own customer base, and then expanding that power, to influence in turn (a) customers who may be dissatisfied or disillusioned with their current vendor and are thus willing to make a move, and (b) value chain participants who by now have dwindled but will continue to build into the chimp's value chain so long as the chimp maintains its status. The point to keep in mind is that customer abandonment in architecturally defined markets virtually ensures that other participants in the value chain will jump ship as well. The combined effect is usually devastating to the vendor who suffers such a fate.

How can you translate these ideas to positioning? Consider the following positioning map.

MARKET
DEVELOPMENT
STRATEGY
CHECKLIST:
MARKET
PENETRATION
VARIABLES

Positioning on Main Street

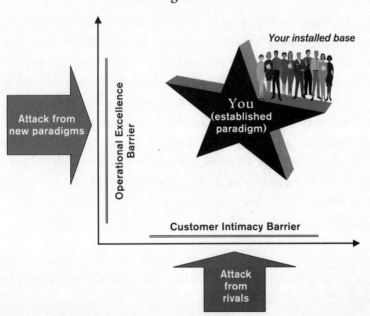

Chimps must build two ramparts against the incursions of (1) new paradigms—new technologies that threaten the new status quo (that's you)—and (2) rival chimps and monkeys that may covet your installed base and attempt to plunder it with rival products that represent a similar but different product infrastructure, application, or value chain.

Defending against new paradigms involves building business models, processes, or ways of doing business that are uniquely suited to your existing customers and are thus attractive to them, in a manner that will forestall new technologies from overhauling the paradigm now established. *Operational excellence* is a way of defining this orientation; it may consist of deploying externally specialized sales or technical resources, new levels of customer support or relationship management, new transaction and/or financial models, and making sure that the entire organization can serve the customer under a new, more rigorous margin model internally.

The second barrier to entry forestalls the attacks from rival companies. The goal here is to continually field a series of +1 offers that are maximally attractive to the *end user* constituency. Here, creating and delivering product offerings that reflect a deep understanding of various end user subsegments—that is, *customer intimacy*—creates additional demand that can be highly profitable and further cement the end users' loyalty to their vendor of choice.

Erecting both these barriers creates the need for a series of ongoing positioning exercises for the sponsoring company built on defining operational excellence and customer intimacy imperatives. However, such efforts should not usurp or otherwise undermine the *overriding positioning goal, that of instilling an abiding conviction among end users that yours is the company they wish to do business with now and well into the future.*

Summarizing, we can turn once again to the counsel of Trout and Ries: *"To win the battle for the mind, you can't compete head-on against a company that has a strong, established position. You can go around, under or over, but never head to head."*[4]

---

4. Al Ries and Jack Trout, *Positioning: The Battle for Your Mind* (New York: McGraw-Hill, 1981), p. 210.

Certainly. But maybe *you* can.

If you're a king, prince, or serf, you face a different challenge. Markets that feature no inherent architectural lock-ins remain fertile ground for battles that can seem like they're straight out of the War of the Roses. Princes can attack kings directly. Even daring serfs can challenge the entire market structure through both operational excellence and customer intimacy. As such, Main Street positioning challenges inherently are based around creating specific benefits, buttressed by differentiation, that last as long as both remain meaningful to the end user community, admittedly a fickle bunch in some markets. Here, the positioning map drawn for bowling alley markets remains in play well into Main Street. Use it.

Once again, winning strategies are built around +1 offers that are maximally attractive to end users regardless of their immediate loyalties. But also consider that such efforts need not always be drawn from short-term feature/benefit distinctions. Intangibles such as brand, the amount of advertising and its tone of voice, accolades from third parties, and so on may be just as meaningful as more tangible benefits such as ease of use, product design, application extensibility, and the like.

Main Street market competitive advantage—and the positioning that reflects it—requires a deep understanding of and connection with the end user. Such markets are like a marathon that is never ending. Absent this connection, vendors are relegated to the whims or clutches of purchasing departments that are only too eager to reduce a vendor's position to that of the commodities found in a farmer's market or merchants' bazaar. May the best price win.

Smart players recognize that the sum total of superior *offers* built around operational excellence initiatives or customer intimacy can and do result in a cumulative positioning for the company that achieves the same goal as noted above: *This is the company I like and will do business with, and all the competitive noise . . . is just that.*

STRATEGY ASSUMPTION 9: THE NEXT TARGET

Now what? The next target is based on the market development model appropriate to each phase of the Technology Adoption Life Cycle. We can model each phase as follows:

Next Target Customer or Market

Main Street

Tornado

Bowling Alley

Early Market

First customers

Start market
development—
validate technology
and product

Niche penetration

Dominate first niche
—then adjacent niches

Mass market growth

Grow horizontally—
new channels and geographies

Niche expansion

Grow profitable revenue
from installed base
through
1-to-1 marketing and
mass customization

In the early market, the goal is to get a customer . . . then get another customer . . . and another. And so on. Ideally, this involves acquiring as many customers in as many segments as possible. You are validating your new technology or discontinuous innovation with as many people as you can persuade, even if only as a *pilot project*. The more customers, the better. Segment focus is not highly prized. Breadth of customer base is. You can stay in the early market if your product is not complete; but when the process of acquiring new customers seems to be grinding to a halt, it is time to cross the chasm. You should also consider the responses of the existing paradigm—the status quo. If they're now beginning to win back the hearts and minds of the undecided, it's time to cross the chasm.

In fact, after a decade of practice, I believe that *when in doubt, you should cross the chasm*. Despite the rage over the past several years to "go ugly early," sooner or later you need to get "ugly" over with. The way to do this is adopt a customer-centric application focus in place of the product-centric perspective that is appropriate for getting to market initially. The inability to do this, by the way, tends to characterize the organization well into the later stages of market development, and eventually will destabilize it. By looking ahead to where you want to go, you take the first steps in understanding what you will need to do to get there and, metaphorically, what you will need to leave behind.

In the bowling alley, your task is to grow beyond the initial beachhead segment by continuing to identify customer segments that can be addressed and won over through either *whole product leverage*—the same or similar whole product application can be utilized by a new segment—or *word-of-mouth leverage*—finding new applications for the whole product within the same segment utilizing customer references. We can diagram this as follows:

Bowling Alley Next Targets

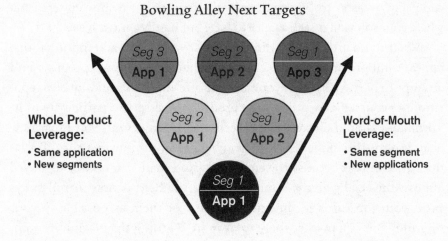

Whole Product Leverage:
• Same application
• New segments

Word-of-Mouth Leverage:
• Same segment
• New applications

Continued success becomes a function of whether there are sufficient niches from which to build dominant segment share, and your ability to dominate those niches. A common strategy flaw at this stage is to go after segments that are massive. Recall my admonitions from the earlier chapters: The issue is total *addressable* market, not total available market. Going after large segments that may on closer inspection be very heterogeneous makes it extremely difficult to dominate. Do the math. The larger the segment, the more customers you'll have to win to demonstrate segment leadership. Ideally, you should pursue segments that are neither so small as to be insignificant to your business plan or of little influence as a reference, but not so big as to make dominance impossible. Paraphrasing Goldilocks, you want segments that are "just right." As well, you must not stretch your own resources too thin. Tailoring whole product solutions for niche segments will prove to be hard work. Trust me. You do not want to be lured into developing new solutions for new segments, however attractive they may seem superficially. Metaphorically, you are trying to knock the pins down in your lane, not the lanes adjacent to yours. Don't bowl diagonally!

Finally, also remember that in the bowling alley, niche adoption happens prior to any standard or pervasive infrastructure support. The value chain is not fully developed or deployed. Only niches that have a strong argument for adopting the new paradigm can justify the expense and possible disruption to their current systems. Thus, you must find segments that have a truly compelling reason to buy, and resist the temptation to pursue segments where your solution is seen as nice to have but hardly a must-have.

What to do after the bowling alley? Move to a tornado footing if one appears imminent. Or find a tornado that is already in progress and attempt to participate with your current offerings. This may involve repositioning yourself or acquiring the products necessary to participate fully. Tornadoes should always take precedence. In any event, you must now abandon the disciplined strategy you held to in the bowling alley. Tornadoes arise in part because the emerging value chain can now be deployed almost universally across a market. Since the herd is now in full stampede, your job turns to directing as many of them as possible to your offering. This is a market share *battle royal*. Winning the maximum number of new customers during this phase is the key to your future going into the Main Street phase, where success will be governed increasingly by the size and nature of your installed base.

Your subsequent target in the tornado is the next set of infrastructure buyers that can be acquired through expansion into other geographies, other distribution channels, and possibly other applications that your product can serve. You stay with the tornado for as long as possible, indicated by your continued ability to derive revenues from new customers. The heralding signs that the tornado is waning include:

- Revenues from new customers and markets are now declining.
- Existing customers are now providing increasing revenues through repurchases, license expansion, service upgrades, and the like.
- Price competition has now seriously eroded margins for the entire category.

At this stage, you are faced with moving to a Main Street posture, increasing accordingly the operational efficiencies discussed in the posi-

MARKET
DEVELOPMENT
STRATEGY
CHECKLIST:
MARKET
PENETRATION
VARIABLES

tioning section while planning and fielding +1 offers to bolster margins and grow segment business as possible. Or you can adopt a bowling alley orientation, particularly if you are a chimp who is losing out to a gorilla, and thus need to secure your base.

The following diagram illustrates three basic options in developing further a Main Street market.

Main Street Next Targets

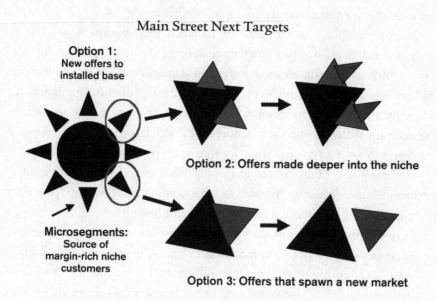

Option 1:
New offers to installed base

Option 2: Offers made deeper into the niche

Microsegments:
Source of margin-rich niche customers

Option 3: Offers that spawn a new market

You may consider option 1 as any +1 offering that enhances the standard product. These offers need to be generated at relatively low costs and should be targeted at various sub- or microsegments that exist as part of the overall market. These offers are likely to have a relatively short half-life because, if successful, they will quickly be imitated by competitors, and thus will represent a new standard. The key to fielding these offers successfully is the ability to bring them to market quickly, with very targeted demand creating communications, through existing supply chains, without adversely disrupting current customer systems. Packaged goods marketers have perfected the linking of customer intimacy with operational excellence to field numerous products of incremental benefit, as well as so-called *line extension* and *flanker* products. High-tech organizations are still perfecting this art as we tend to overengineer products or not be able to field them efficiently and in a rapid fashion.

Occasionally, a microsegment represents a series of related segments within the microsegment itself. Each of these subsegments also represents opportunities that can be exploited through additional, more narrowly defined and perhaps more sophisticated offerings, as represented by option 2. Scientific and medical instrumentation and semiconductor manufacturing equipment are examples of this model.

Option 3 represents the case in which a microsegment adopts +1 products and that adoption spawns a wave of demand, previously dormant, which grows the segment into a new market. Witness the various product mutations within the PC market, with handheld organizers and extremely small, fully functional laptop computers as prime examples. The exciting thing about such occurrences is that they often generate a new tornado with all the possibilities that such phenomena present.

The previous Main Street examples have been predicated on the occurrence of a tornado period as the original innovation proceeds through the TALC. What if a tornado does not occur?

As noted, many bowling alley markets move to Main Street without a tornado having taken place. A transition to Main Street is warranted when you and your competitors face saturation in the segments that have adopted and it seems apparent that there is resistance from other segments. In effect, such segments see no reason to adopt the category to any significant degree. In a practical sense, this is now the de facto size of the category, and you should focus on serving your installed base, acquiring new customers only on an opportunistic basis. If you or your organization finds it difficult to cope with this segment resistance—in getting over the rejection, as it were—you may wish to reexamine how much complexity—adoption, solution, or marketing—still remains with your product. These complexities may explain the general market resistance you're now experiencing. This is an exercise in understanding both reality and perception.

Main Street markets are about renewing and sustaining significant streams of profitable revenue; in other words, getting more and better business from your existing customer base. Profitability is a function of selling up from a commoditized product or application through the identification of subsegments of the market hungry for more, value-added solutions. This activity can continue as long as new paradigms that may threaten you are not significant or simply not present. However, all things must come to an end at some point; therefore, Main Street is also about *renewal*.

To renew into a tornado is most desirable. Once again, consider the massive PC business as an example. Every three years or so, the personal computer industry seems to go through a small but significant tornado as faster processors, new industrial designs, and, to a lesser extent, new applications emerge. The challenge facing PC vendors is to anticipate these changes and lead them if possible, but they do so under extremely unfavorable margin conditions.

When tornado renewal is not possible, and the Main Street market is dwindling, renewal into the bowling alley is possible by locating within your installed base newly broken processes or unfulfilled initiatives that are now hampering customers, and altering your products to address such needs. Currently, the ERP vendors are doing just this by modifying their product offerings to take advantage of the Internet in general, and e-commerce specifically.

Last, there is the fundamental process of renewal into the early market, something many vendors—or at least their R&D and engineering departments—wish would happen sooner rather than later. What organizations fail to realize, however, is that any problems associated with current markets will still be there. Early market renewal is a long-term option that will not resolve any short-term issues. How could it? Early market initiatives by definition begin the journey through the life cycle all over again.

STRATEGIC PRIORITIES OVER THE LIFE CYCLE

You have now completed the Market Development Strategy Checklist. There is not a tenth assumption to be made. Congratulations! But remember, for any modification you make to one item in the list, be sure to reconsider the effect of such a change on the remaining items.

And finally, for each phase of the TALC, various assumptions will be more or less important relative to other assumptions as indicated in the following table:

MARKET
DEVELOPMENT
STRATEGY
CHECKLIST:
MARKET
PENETRATION
VARIABLES

STRATEGIC PRIORITIES ACROSS THE LIFE CYCLE

	EARLY MARKET	CHASM/ BOWLING ALLEY	TORNADO	MAIN STREET
Target customer	✓	✓		✓
Compelling reasons to buy	✓	✓		
Whole products		✓		
Partners and allies		✓	✓	
Distribution			✓	
Pricing			✓	✓
Competition			✓	
Positioning	✓	✓		✓
Market development		✓		✓

The check marks indicate that particular diligence should be exercised in determining the assumption and its underlying rationale, as these assumptions are effectively the strategy *linchpins* for each inflection point. Do not assume that the other assumptions are not important. They are.

In the early market, particular attention should be paid to the target customer, the compelling reason to buy, whole product, and positioning. The emphasis on the *compelling reason to buy* should be on the notion *compelling*. Naturally, this is a function of your understanding of the target customer. However, the challenge is more acute because we are postulating customers by their visionary yearnings to obtain competitive advantages that may be vastly different for each customer. Choosing a particular customer profile will allow for a corresponding CRTB that at least becomes an exemplar for initial strategy development. In turn, this should guide your thinking as to the magnitude of benefit asserted under the *whole product* heading. The product will be far from whole at this stage, and it may be necessary for you to "create a crisis" through *positioning,* the next critical assumption, to move the early market to action.

The chasm / bowling alley column is combined because of similarities between the two phases. The challenge here is to focus on a *specific segment,* understand in detail its unique circumstances and thus its compelling reason to buy (particularly in economic terms), and from this define a whole product solution specific to the segment and its needs, recruiting partners and allies as needed to build the value chain. Those crossing the chasm will need to emphasize positioning with the beachhead segment to specify the value in taking a risk. Once into the market, critical thinking must be applied to discerning and targeting adjacent segments that can leverage the whole product solution and word-of-mouth referencing (as a result of your effective positioning).

In the tornado, there is no need to worry about target customers, compelling reasons to buy, or whole products because the entire market is migrating to the new infrastructure or paradigm. Rather, *partners and allies,* primarily in the form of additional or alternative *distribution channels,* are key. Since *competition* is likely to be ferocious, your critical thinking is required here. And you must be concerned with *pricing,* a key competitive weapon during the tornado.

Once you're on Main Street, the goal is to reconnect with customers, discerning attractive *target customer subsets* that are primarily within your installed base. Understanding the nuances of various segments' *compelling reasons to buy* leads to *whole product +1* offerings that can be tailored and *priced* for each subsegment. The battle for the customers' affections on a sustainable basis requires recurring discussions around *positioning* to entice further demand and loyalty within each group going forward.

Now that you've done all this, it's time to get ready for something new: taking the strategy to market.

MARKET
DEVELOPMENT
STRATEGY
CHECKLIST:
MARKET
PENETRATION
VARIABLES

Part Three

Taking the Market Development Strategy to Market

This section specifies four initiatives that must be planned for and executed as part of fielding the proposed market development strategy.

Introduction

We should not only master questions, but also act upon them, and act definitely.

—WOODROW WILSON

There are essentially four go-to-market programs that can spell the difference between success and failure of a market development strategy in the marketplace. They are:

1. *Strategy validation.* This involves the appropriate use of research techniques designed to test whether the key assumptions made in the nine-point strategy statement are indeed valid and can withstand market pressures.
2. *Whole product management.* This refers to the task and process required to ensure that a sponsoring vendor is doing everything necessary either to create a new value chain for the purpose of displacing the status quo or to extend an existing value chain for the purpose of extending the current paradigm.
3. *Marketing communications planning.* Marketing communications programs should address two fundamental objectives:

   - Creating and sustaining demand for the product
   - Shortening the sales cycle

The former is a *strategic* exercise that focuses on market making and market relations. The latter consists of a set of *tactical* programs that focus on sales promotion.

4. *Field engagement strategy.* The goal here is to specify and achieve alignment between the target customer's buying process and the sponsoring vendor's intended selling process, guided by the market development strategy.

The following diagram illustrates how each element in the MDSC affects programs that will initiate or influence strategy changes.

Programs to Implement Strategy

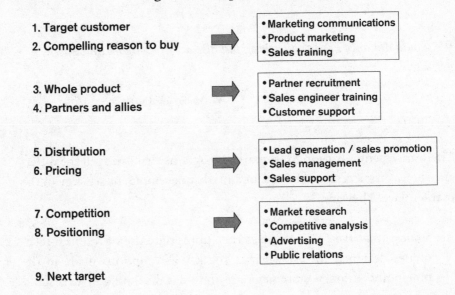

1. Target customer
2. Compelling reason to buy
   → • Marketing communications
     • Product marketing
     • Sales training

3. Whole product
4. Partners and allies
   → • Partner recruitment
     • Sales engineer training
     • Customer support

5. Distribution
6. Pricing
   → • Lead generation / sales promotion
     • Sales management
     • Sales support

7. Competition
8. Positioning
   → • Market research
     • Competitive analysis
     • Advertising
     • Public relations

9. Next target

Each of these topics needs to be considered explicitly in terms of the market development strategy now under consideration and should accurately reflect the assumptions made in the strategy. And while all can be pursued in a parallel fashion to yield results, assuming that each is cross-referenced with the other, there is a certain logic and elegance in pursuing them serially as listed above. I shall detail them in the following chapters accordingly.

14

Strategy Validation

The ways to knowledge are multitudinous—the way to understanding is devious.

—Charles B. Rogers

Basic research is what I am doing when I don't know what I am doing.

—Wernher von Braun

As noted in chapter 11, the appropriate use of market research is necessary to validate the nine-point market development strategy statement. Up to this point, we have built the strategy based variously on observations, insights, anecdotal and empirical evidence, previous experience, input from colleagues and committees, the opinions of consultants, and assorted musings from other interested parties. All of which is fine. And all of which probably contains one or more fundamental flaws that lurk like some hidden gremlin, waiting to spoil our efforts. It is imperative, therefore, that the strategy be explored as to its relevance and validity before it is fielded.

However, an extremely important caveat is now in order.

▶ *No research technique that we know of will guarantee that your strategy and programs are correct and therefore will be successful!*

In fact, you would be surprised (or maybe you wouldn't) by how many high-tech companies base an entire new product launch or major corporate repositioning on the strength of the insights delivered by six groups of IT managers, recruited in three U.S. cities, who've been paid $200 each, fed sandwiches of quite dubious quality, and then invited to share their hopes, dreams, wishes, and fears with a focus group moderator who may be struggling not to confuse this week's new product with the one he presented last week. All the while, the managers who have sponsored this exercise variously snicker, scribble notes, and munch on M&M's behind the two-way mirror, sure in their belief that what they're hearing is true, relevant, projectable, even intelligent.

To avoid such a fate, you need to have some realistic expectations as to what you can accomplish, and what you can't, when you engage in a validation exercise. Ask yourself:

- *What do we want to find out?* Validating activities can be as simple and direct as talking with customers at a user group meeting, or as complex as surveying a projectable sample of customers and prospects as part of a conjoint analysis. You may or may not get better information with the latter, but you will get more. The time and cost to do this will be just as significant.
- *Who can tell us what we would like to know?* The above-mentioned IT managers may have little or no influence over their organizations' decisions to purchase a risky, highly visionary, and highly complex new system. On the other hand, your average VP of manufacturing may have little interest in and little clue about the finer points of your highly available, highly scalable distributed computing application aimed at the manufacturing sector. (He may just be there for the $200 and the free meal!) Maybe your time is better spent talking with your salespeople, who make their living by selling such stuff.
- *What will you do with the information if it can be secured?* Are you using research techniques to *aid* your thinking, or are you using them to *do your thinking for you?* If you plan to stride into your CEO's office and advise him or her that new guidance should be given to the investment community based on the very favorable outcome of the validation, you may have more confidence than sense. Research is not a guarantee of anything, and it should never be relied on as such.

Having said that, we at The Chasm Group respect research and researchers for what they can tell us about things that we would have overlooked, guessed at, or ignored, possibly at our peril. Good market researchers are a curious, intelligent, and naturally skeptical lot who, in my experience, will find or interpret information and offer insights that my clients and I might miss. And we most often use *qualitative* research, mindful of all its shortcomings. Quantitative research can also be employed as appropriate, but, in my opinion, it is far less useful for our strategy validation purposes, particularly under early market or chasm-crossing conditions.

Here's why.

Quantitative research, which is in fact statistically significant aggregated measures of customer activities and/or responses to a given set of questions, results in quite valid data that offers insights as to *what has happened*, but it often yields little in terms of what *will* happen or *can* happen given a new set of conditions. Remember that we are trying to validate (even cautiously predict) what customers, partners, distribution channels, and even the competition will do when presented with a new set of variables—the stuff of our market development strategy. In order to take advantage of such potential insights, our preference is to ask the relevant constituencies directly rather than rely on answers previously given.

To be sure, predicting the future can be full of surprises. Just ask any meteorologist. It is difficult, possibly even dangerous, to interpret the past and extrapolate it to the future. The danger of interpreting the past and extrapolating it to the future is just that. Market research is a tool that can be used appropriately or rather foolishly, depending on one's orientation to its use and its outcome. And like many things in life, considering the time and the place to mount one's efforts is paramount. The question is not only one of intent—what do we think will happen?—but, more important, what do we think will happen as a result of what we intend to do, in the time frame that we will do it? Therefore, your goal is to avoid predicting what will happen in the next three years, but rather concentrate on what the likely outcome will be in the *next six months* if you do what you propose, based on the assumptions you have made. We believe that life cycle forces will impose new conditions on any organization and its strategy as it encounters each inflection point. Therefore, if we can accurately pin down where we are in the current life cycle, we should be in a position to discern which of the many immediate implications are going forward, recognizing that our assumptions and approach will necessarily and quite naturally need to be modified for each life cycle phase. All of which means that our level of precision, confidence, and ability to divine the future relative to our strategy will be a function of where we are on the TALC.

VALIDATING EARLY MARKET STRATEGIES

The early market presents strategists with the most uncertainty. Traditional research is best at assessing the past. New ideas, concepts, and innovations seem almost impossible to measure. Frames of reference are tentative, confusing, and the many proffered solutions seem like pie in the sky. Most of us don't know what we will do until faced with an actual decision. Traditionally, research methodologies at this stage take on the flavor of problem detection. But problems are not what technology enthusiasts and visionaries are responding to. Opportunity is. So we alter the methodology to present, in effect, a rosy hypothesis or assertion of what could be.

"Wouldn't you like to buy something that has numerous new benefits and virtually unlimited upside potential for those that have the foresight to adopt the new solution?" is the approach that typifies and summarizes our validation quest. The obvious answer is "Of course." Electric cars, satellite telephones, wireless personal digital assistants offering collaborative workflow, and the convenience of buying virtually everything through the Internet using an all-purpose Internet "appliance" all seem like sure bets. The total available market seems limitless, bearing in mind, of course, that our venture capitalist reminded us in an earlier chapter that markets are best assessed from the bottom up.

Things get a bit more muddled, however, when we ask such questions in light of what actually must happen, and what the costs may be to avail ourselves of such benefits. Often, we do not have the answers to the first question, and we may be afraid to ask the second. You may argue that no truly brilliant innovation came as a result of market research, and correctly so. It's hard to imagine Thomas Alva Edison seeking the advice of focus groups to proceed with any of his groundbreaking inventions. Therefore, research and validation in the early market must be of an *assertive* nature, but with some important caveats. You must present the strategy in terms of what it delivers and also in term of what, initially, it does not.

Since the value chain is nascent at this stage, the issue becomes one of incorporating trend analysis. If the world looks like this, you could posit, what might be the longer-term implication to organizations (or to the world) if the status quo continues (assuming the status quo will deteriorate)? The expected response might be exactly what you had hoped for—a metaphorical "four horsemen of the Apocalypse" is clearly the consequence of a failing, persistent existing paradigm, or so it seems to those being asked. Taking such a response forward, however, requires sharing with your validation subjects a legitimate discussion of what the initial trade-offs will be. Technology enthusiasts and visionaries naturally warm to a discussion of the former—that is, what could be. But your intent should be to discern what these groups are prepared to trade off to acquire such magic. If you're unable to share the minuses along with the pluses, you run the risk of a validation equivalent of "garbage in, garbage out." You're now using research not to validate a *true* response, but to validate a *desired* response. Later, as the tears flow, you may recall the words of the cartoon character Pogo, who declared, "We have met the enemy, and he is us."

VALIDATING CHASM-CROSSING STRATEGIES

"Why, oh why, would somebody change what they're now doing, in order to do something else?" This effectively is the brief to your research associates in order to learn what mainstream pragmatists are currently thinking and doing. Since pragmatists may look askance at what visionaries are up to, the answers to your questions posed during early market validation must now be questioned. The quest now must be discerning answers to "What is keeping you up at night?" and "What if we proposed the following?"

This is the essence of the questions posed in chapter 11. Now you must identify the target customer posed in the strategy statement and ask specifically:

- Do you have this problem? And if so, what is the nature, magnitude, and consequences of allowing it to continue?
- Is the proposed remedy attractive, specific, actionable, and warranted?
- Who would provide such a remedy? Would you consider such a solution from us?

Ascertaining the answers to these questions might lead you to investigate further via proposed partners and allies the answers to:

- Which collaborators (partners and allies) can and would be willing to contribute to solving the problem?
- Is the proposed solution attractive in terms of their objectives? Is there real value in joining in the crusade?

These answers lead back to questioning the target customer:

- Are there others who purport (or would purport) to offer a solution? If so, who else would you (the target customer) consider?
- Would such a solution be acceptable or attractive coming from us (the sponsors of the proposed solution)?
- Who else could use such a solution in similar circumstances?

Note that this kind of research and validation is *not* of the *problem detection* variety. Such research is perfectly reasonable on Main Street as a way of determining +1 offers, but it is insufficient in determining what will cause someone to move away from the applications and systems they are currently using—exactly what we're asking them to do as we search for an entry into a mainstream market. This is why, having discerned the answers to the questions above, you must now actually discuss the intended strategy as a potential solution (or market-making opportunity as appropriate) with the respondents you have recruited.

The way to do this involves overweighting your investigation to the critical elements of the strategy—that is, the essential points within the nine-point checklist that serve effectively as the foundation of the strategy. These critical assumptions underpin the entire effort, so it's essential that you understand if you are on or off course.

VALIDATION BEYOND THE BOWLING ALLEY

Time spent in strategy validation activities with prospects and customers during a tornado may not be time well spent. Remember, the market wants *what* you are selling, although that may be no guarantee that they specifically want *you*. Then again, if you're losing out in the tornado, it might behoove you to inquire why. More practically, research done during the tornado probably has its greatest value in anticipating when the tornado is likely to die out. At this point, TAM (total available market) and TAD (total addressable market) forecasting exercises may be extremely worthwhile in helping you to anticipate when the forecast is likely to slide lower, not just for you but for the category as a whole. The goal is to understand when you should begin an orderly transition to a Main Street footing, thus avoiding the inevitable shock that accompanies a missed or otherwise disappointing quarter as a result of a tornado that has now dissipated.

On Main Street, validation can take on two flavors: research that seeks to find new segments, or those who have not been previously considered, and understand their desires and motivations; or the more timely (and possibly risky) research in the crucible of the marketplace, that of specific offers made to segments already present or in play. Both approaches are common in consumer marketing, and they are well known and dutifully practiced by most professional researchers and research organizations. Refer to chapter 7, "Main Street," for more guidance.

Summarizing, "Know before you go" is the operative phrase. In our practical experience, organizations that have diligently pursued a strategy development exercise as previously outlined—using objective thinking that is free of wishful thinking, management fiats, and uninformed opinions—are likely to be significantly correct in their outcomes. Not 100 percent mind you. But probably more right than wrong. Life being what it is, however, perhaps President Ronald Reagan, the last cold warrior of the 1980s, had it right when he said, "Trust, but verify."

15

Whole Product Management

If you build a better mousetrap, the world will beat a path to your door.

—RALPH WALDO EMERSON

Marketing is the whole business seen from the point of view of the final result, that is from the customer's point of view.

—PETER DRUCKER

Emerson was undoubtedly a better poet than he was a marketer. Yet for many high-tech organizations, his adage seems like a mantra for engineering, marketing, sales—indeed, the whole company. Peter Drucker, perhaps the most influential management guru or business academician during the last fifty years, knows that creating demand through marketing ultimately will fail if the products and services offered and touted fail to live up to customer expectations. Can we not only apply the wisdom contained in each quote, but also reconcile their divergent implications?

The very essence of the high-technology business is dreaming about and creating breathtakingly compelling technology and product visions. Realizing the dream means that we must add much to the vision, including creating the various organizations—sales, manufacturing, marketing, finance, and so on—that must cope with and add value to the efforts of the scientists and engineers. Indeed, the entire process of creating a high-tech company can be seen as linear, starting always with the product vision. Is it surprising, therefore, that as an industry we are so fixated on the product as the center of our universe?

Problems mount, however, when we have to stop dreaming about visions and building products. That occurs when the first customers, convinced of the vision, start buying the product. As a result, we leave forever the world of the lab, the bench, or the simulation and are forced to serve these customers in ways that we had not previously anticipated. Some retreat from this task, preferring instead to concoct new science, preferring the "R" rather than the "D." Those of us who remain committed to the task of creating not only products but companies must instead increasingly take our cues from the marketplace: from the customers, partners, competitors, and others within the *market infrastructure* (more about this in chapter 16) we are attempting to build and serve at the same time. And as we move through the Technology Adoption Life Cycle, product R&D must give way to *whole product* R&D. Enter the product management organization.

Reconciling the need for building the best stuff while considering the customer's viewpoint involves examining closely but practically the implications of the *high-tech value chain* and managing for each market development inflection point along the life cycle. Consider this chain, now detailed further to show various subcomponents within the vendor and customer domains.

The High-Tech Value Chain

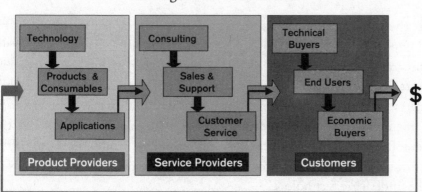

Value chain analysis is highly useful in order to determine the best path to ROI. Product-based organizations must coordinate the internal components of the product with those providers who provide specific services. Recall that for many high-tech products, the whole product solution often consists of both the product and a set of services. Both component and service providers may either be part of the sponsoring vendor or consist of third parties recruited for the task. Whatever the case, each part of the value chain must be accounted for and sponsored. Now consider the value chain pathway for each point on the TALC.

WHOLE PRODUCT MANAGEMENT IN THE EARLY MARKET

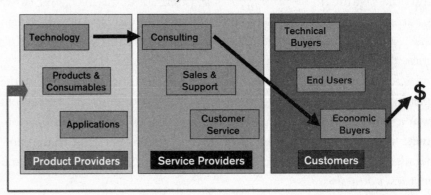

The Early Market Value Chain

In the early market, the coordination effort is rather straightforward. Complex products, notably software, often need a significant systems integration effort not only to install the product within the customer's system, but also to buffer the customer from the discontinuities associated with early market efforts. The goal is to establish the rudiments of a value chain that can be successfully built out going forward. While the first release of the product has been arguably productized, it's often unstable owing largely to the unknowns or unintended consequences of the underlying technology.

On the customer's side, the economic buyer holds sway, risking his or her budget on this largely untested but promising innovation. The good news here is that the whole product does not have to be built yet. Indeed, it is probably impossible to build it at this stage since each visionary's requirements are likely to be different. Recruiting the proper consulting organizations provides the first test of whether a sustainable early market chain is possible in the sense that these consultants must understand the opportunities and limitations associated with the new innovation, and they must reasonably be able to recommend the innovation to their early adopter clients. In a sense, the technology vendor is selling the idea of the technology, and the consulting organization is selling its promise. The economic buyer must believe that both are realizable. Thus, the whole product may not be possible, but the *whole presentation*—that is, the road map for the product and its supporting cast—must be as complete as feasible.

WHOLE PRODUCT MANAGEMENT IN THE BOWLING ALLEY

It is for this stage in the life cycle that the very discipline of whole product management was created. Crossing-the-chasm and bowling-alley efforts require meeting a different and difficult challenge: recruiting the needed partners and allies necessary to truly build out the first incarnation of a whole product solution. Creative technology development must now meet up with creative market segmentation efforts.

Your segmentation results, which should identify the ideal target cus-

The Bowling Alley Value Chain

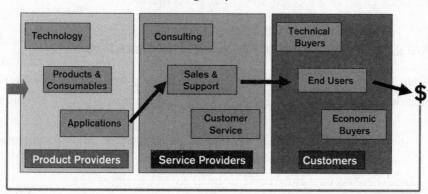

tomer and his or her compelling reason to buy (based on the troubling situation faced by end users, and thus the trouble it causes for the economic buyer) lead you to the whole product solution—the application—required to redress this situation. Creating the solution invariably requires partners and allies. Recruiting them requires putting together a business case and gaining the attention of the economic decision maker with each partner necessary. Once a commitment is made, the focus then switches to whole product *orchestration,* specifically coordinating the timing of the whole product launch, an event in which each partner must show up with their part of the solution set and declare their commitment to the niche market and the sponsor's whole product architecture.

As should be clear by now, the move from product (or project in many cases) to whole product, like everything else associated with the move from an early market to that of the mainstream market, is the most difficult of any transition faced across the Technology Adoption Life Cycle. Not only must you serve completely your niches of customers, you may also be vying for leadership within the new value chain, now developing hopefully as a result of your efforts and those of your competitors. Product management organizations must resist mightily the temptation to keep building features and functionality desired by the few visionaries that the sales force may find, and instead direct *all* efforts to creating a killer application, albeit on a limited basis—the limits driven by the targeted market development efforts suggested by segmentation. Creating the killer app for the target segments sets the stage for asking a most intriguing question: Can the value chain develop into a tornado mass market?

WHOLE PRODUCT MANAGEMENT IN THE TORNADO

If the answer to the preceding question is yes, then managers must quickly determine the answers to some related questions:

- If the value chain can develop into a mass market, what conditions are currently holding it back?
- Are these constraining conditions likely to be removed?
- If so, when is the last remaining constraint likely to be removed, and by whom?

Assuming the answers to these questions can be found, anticipating a tornado requires that whole product management shift its focus from completeness to *commoditization*. Now managers must balance two contradictory forces—the need to simplify for broad distribution versus the need to win or stay even in the features war that always accompanies tornado market competitions. Regardless, complex partner relationships requiring integration expertise in the channel must be forgone, and this requires diplomacy in order to keep the company-to-company relationship viable for future use.

The Tornado Value Chain

Finally, tornado whole product management requires an explicit and final consideration of two sources of complexity: *adoption* complexity and *solution* complexity. Removing these will determine the dynamics of the last complexity, that of marketing. Recall that adoption complexity is reduced through the creation of a killer application that can be readily adopted by many if not all segments of a market. Solution complexity, on the other hand, is managed through the creation of a scalable and replicable whole product that is easily deployable.

What's the point? *The less adoption and solution complexity, the easier the product can be acquired. Easy acquisition implies broad distribution channels, the exact requirement for satisfying tornado demand, and possibly winning the competition outright.*

WHOLE PRODUCT MANAGEMENT ON MAIN STREET

On Main Street, the focus is on whole product +1, and the biggest challenge is for the high-tech company to cede whole product direction-setting power to consumer-style marketing. Partnerships are at a minimum, and the biggest skill is negotiation of price commitments, because typically only one of the two partners can make money on a bundle.

The Main Street Value Chain

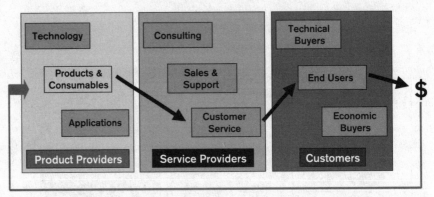

Whole product management now requires an amalgam of high-tech marketing efforts—building in convenience-engineered features without adding discontinuities (read complexity)—based on the well-honed disciplines of consumer marketing; for example, research-based segmentation, packaging, merchandising and advertising, and so on. All these tools, considered in light of the segmentation possibilities afforded by a substantial installed base, serve to extend and augment an existing product line to serve the special needs of newly identified customer groups.

Effective whole product management also means not getting carried away! Organizations can take the lessons of the tornado—win
the competition any way possible—into Main Street with potentially
disastrous consequences. We call this condition *hypercompetitive-
ness.* As you shall see, it can be manifested in different groups
within an organization, and it can be manifested anywhere along the
life cycle. The hypercompetitive engineering organization insists that
the way to win is to outdo the accomplishments of the competition
regardless of whether additional capabilities are valued by the market. The expense associated with this behavior notwithstanding, the
consequences are a raft of product features all of which must be
supported, and many of which are in fact unnecessary and unjustifi-
able. If the goal of Main Street market development is the perpetua-
tion of satisfied customers, then understanding exactly what will
satisfy them must be Job 1. Such efforts may result in necessary but
perhaps rather tedious chores, similar to weeding your garden. And
who likes to do that?

To avoid such a fate, the hypercompetitive engineering organization will seek out its counterparts in the sales force, who may be
complaining loudly that the reason sales are down—or the reason
gorilla status was not attained during the tornado—is or was a function of not having the same features as competition. To be fair, there
may be some merit to this logic. But when these laments result in
wave after wave of costly engineering and product releases, you've
got trouble. And on whom will the blame be laid? The marketing
department, naturally, which obviously has failed to present such
engineering prowess in the proper context and with compelling customer appeals.

To guard against such tendencies, Main Street product management efforts should be of a cross-functional nature. There must
be shared consensus as to what customers want and why. Sit these
overachievers down behind the two-way mirror looking over a focus
group. They'll appreciate the insights, and possibly even the food.

16

Marketing Communications Planning

You do not want to be considered just the best of the best. You want to be considered the only ones who do what you do.

—JERRY GARCIA, THE GRATEFUL DEAD

Advertising is absentee salesmanship and is a meretricious endeavour in which psychological appeals to fear and shame are developed to bamboozle the public into purchasing essentially worthless package goods at bloated prices.

—THORSTEIN VEBLEN, ECONOMIST

Whoa, Thorstein. . . . Lighten up! Marketing communication is for all practical purposes the penultimate weapon, both strategically and tactically, for most consumer marketing organizations, notably packaged goods marketers. In a business where products ranging from laundry detergents, window and floor cleaners, and motor oil to deodorants, shampoos, and toothpaste are for the most part identical, effective marketing organizations create demand and preference for their products through their communication efforts, in many cases imbuing their products with intangible values and a personality of sorts, summarily referred to as a *brand*.

Yet most high-tech organizations seem like relative amateurs in their efforts by comparison. My colleagues and I have witnessed too often an organization's painstaking deliberations over its corporate and market development strategy, later to watch dumbfounded as the planners then toss the project to the "marcom people"—a group highly undervalued in most high-tech companies—to look after the details of communicating all this to virtually everyone in the most time-honored and mundane ways possible, working with other undervalued service providers ("vendors" in the minds of some), chiefly the PR and ad agency, and the design firm or department that will produce the brochures and requisite webpages.

This situation repeats itself over and over again. Why? I believe that unlike consumer marketers, many high-tech companies don't seem to understand or value the process and, as a result, they are not very good at it. Naturally, however, they think they are. A pity really, when you consider how much organizations budget for marketing communication efforts.

So let's examine this process of communicating and understand it for what it is, what it can and can't do, and some of the myths or misconceptions that surround it.

PUTTING FIRST THINGS FIRST

At the outset, let's set a context for developing marketing communication programs. They should address two fundamental objectives: shortening the sales cycle, and creating and sustaining demand for the product being marketed. These are overlapping goals, to be sure, but they are not always addressed in the same way.

As a practical matter, the more expensive and complex a product category is—for example, enterprise-class software like supply chain management software, or mainframe-class computers—the more likely a direct-sales force will be employed to sell the product to customers (see "Strategy Assumption 5: Distribution" in chapter 12). Since these sales cycles tend to be long, marketers must devote their time to—and salespeople will demand—efforts that will shorten this cycle as much as possible. This may include developing a number of tactical programs that employ a variety of different techniques outlined later in the chapter. Whatever the case, marketers should heed carefully the following advice:

▶ *Rarely is there sustainable "permission" to develop strategic communications unless you provide tactical programs that demonstrate an understanding of market conditions on the ground. All programs must affect positively a salesperson's ability to find, engage, and deliver a customer.*

If sales organizations have one gripe about marketing departments (and they usually have several), it's that many marketing people do not understand "what it's like out there." (This sentiment was illustrated to me perfectly by a technical sales representative who, at a company gathering, sported a T-shirt that read: "I'm from the field. Ask me about reality!") Many product marketing and marketing communications professionals have never "carried a bag." Their selling experience has been confined to pushing cookies or magazine subscriptions on their relatives and neighbors.

Unfortunately, when marketing people lack this experience and the resulting empathy for the selling process, tactical sales promotion efforts typically get short shrift. The advertising may be witty and the website may be breathtaking, but if they're not designed or combined with programs to close the gap between prospect interest and the final close, you and your sales team are going to be at cross-purposes. This does not mean that every program must be designed first to accomplish tactical goals, nor does it mean that the marketing outlook and imagination should be paced by the short-term agenda (and attentions spans) of the sales force. Rather, demand creation activities must be developed not only to predispose a prospect to your product, but also to build and support their desire, latent or otherwise, to part with their hard-earned money.

With that key proviso to marketers now stated, let's examine how to accomplish both objectives efficiently.

How many times have you heard the following from your spouse, girlfriend, boyfriend, colleagues, therapist, or even your mother?

▶ *It's not only what you say, it's how you say it.*

Speaking for my gender, it seems that men may lag behind women in our ability to combine message with tone and deliver it in an appropriate fashion. Perhaps our *antennae* aren't as sensitive as those of our female partners, colleagues, or counterparts. Perhaps it's a genetic deficiency. Or perhaps, as I've been reminded, part of our brain has now been given over to the advanced use of a television remote control, or the ability to catalog and recite statistics regarding various sporting activities. Whatever the case, we tend to pay tremendous attention and ascribe tremendous value to the *what* of communication, and disregard or ignore the *how*—the context, the subtext, the message between the lines. In what most would agree is still (regrettably) the male-dominated world of high tech, is it any wonder that many of our communication efforts seem marginally effective? What's going on? (Before I'm deluged with indignant e-mails, please read on!)

Relax, everybody. This assertion certainly has not yet been verified given our knowledge of the human genome. Genetic differences? Maybe. Your profession? Definitely. We in high tech are typically focused on *telling everyone* what our products and services can do—what *we* think is important—rather than reflecting honestly on what our audience might want to *hear*, and thus what *they* might think is important. Both sexes fall prey to this malady. Finding out what to say is the beginning of the communication process. How you say it makes people look and listen. If you're not successful at that, all the work that went into discovering what to say is wasted.

PLANNING THE MESSAGE

To redress this situation, I suggest starting with a model first detailed in *Crossing the Chasm* and known as the Competitive-Positioning Compass. This model suggests how communication strategies evolve relative to TALC market development. We can extend this model further to help

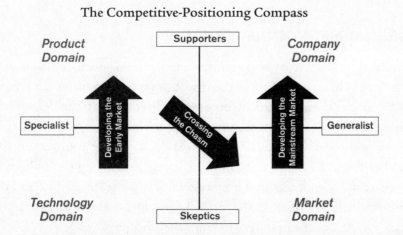

The Competitive-Positioning Compass

determine the specific messages and media required to execute a market development strategy at each TALC inflection point.

Essentially, the purpose of communications is either to move the audience from a state of *skepticism* about a value proposition or marketing claim to one of *support;* or, if they are already supporters, to validate and reinforce this condition. In this effort, audiences for high-tech value propositions include both *specialists* and *generalists.* Specialists primarily care about and focus on technologies and products. Generalists are interested in markets and companies. Few people care about all four. Applying life cycle discipline to our communication objectives, the interests of our audiences can be thought of as *value domains* related, not surprisingly, to the four customer groups we are attempting to win over: technology enthusiasts, visionaries, pragmatists, and conservatives (we shall leave the laggards to their own worldviews and appropriate devices).

As innovations move through the life cycle, the value domains change, and thus communications must change to shape, reflect, and reinforce such values. The vertical axis in the diagram indicates where a buyer might be relative to a proposed value proposition, ranging from complete skepticism to complete support. We begin with the notion that until proven otherwise, all potential target audiences are *skeptics,* virtually devoid of affiliation or allegiance to the innovation now under the market microscope. Restating an earlier point, it is the goal of communications to influence these skeptics, changing their orientation to that of a *supporter.* And we must do this at least twice through the life cycle of any innovation.

EARLY MARKET COMMUNICATION

In the early market, technology enthusiasts are the skeptical reviewers of the *underlying technology* residing in the discontinuous innovation. The market will develop as these skeptics become persuaded that the technology is solid. Visionaries are the next target and are now focused on the *product* issues surrounding the innovation. The market development communication strategy therefore calls for demonstrating a strong underlying technology and the potential advantages that it represents versus the status quo, and then conveying this advantage in the form of a product that visionaries can now include as part of their plans to leverage the advantage.

The horizontal axis in the diagram indicates the range of buyer interests and the understanding and appreciation for the issues associated with high technology. This may be industry, category, product, or even technology specific. What the model indicates relative to early market adoption is that communications advocating market or company issues are *not* warranted at the expense of credible, persuasive arguments focused on technology and product issues. Visionaries care most about product. They are counting on the product to be a key ingredient in realizing their vision. They do not care about the technology per se, except as it explains why the product will perform the miraculous effects they are expecting. They do not care about markets, either, because they are in advance of them. And they may be willing to overlook weakness in the company because they often feel that true innovation can only be sourced quickly and unequivocally from start-ups or "skunk works," and not established concerns.

Thus, until you can demonstrate *product validity* (assuming technical validity) you are simply not real to early adopting generalists. Summarizing, early market communication planning focuses on winning skeptical technology-oriented specialists in order to influence, and later win over, visionaries now enthusiastic about the product.

CHASM-CROSSING AND BOWLING ALLEY COMMUNICATIONS

Just when we thought we were making headway by engendering a level of support among visionaries that is quite favorable, it's time to move to the mainstream market where we will encounter a new level and type of skepticism, this time manifested in pragmatists who are acting in characteristic fashion.

"Don't tell me about the damn product," they complain, "tell me who it's for and how it supposed to help companies facing situations like ours." And so we move from the comfort zone of techies and visionaries who appreciate our vision and our grasp of product-oriented issues to the relatively unknown domain of *market-focused generalists* who remain essentially uninterested, and certainly unconvinced until you persuade them otherwise. Not surprisingly, the skeptical pragmatist begins to take interest in your product when you demonstrate a level of credibility at solving problems unique to the pragmatist's situation or market segment, and when you can show a level of commitment through product positioning and marketing efforts that is worthy of pragmatist support. The issues at hand are business issues, not technical ones, and mastering them both in real and perceptual terms sows the seeds of customer allegiance that result in segment leadership.

TORNADO AND MAIN STREET COMMUNICATION

Should the category proliferate, the goal is to win over the support of the entire market, and thus you must now prove your sustainable leadership qualities to a conservative generalist audience wary of risk and naturally predisposed to de facto leaders. By now, a competitive hierarchy—gorillas or kings, chimps or princes, monkeys or serfs—is now in place. Communication efforts now must reflect the realities of your place within the hierarchy. (Refer to chapter 13 for a description of the strategic alternatives available under Strategy Assumption 7.)

MATCHING THE EVIDENCE

As you navigate your way using the Competitive-Positioning Compass as your guide, you can identify the evolution of the evidence you must pro-

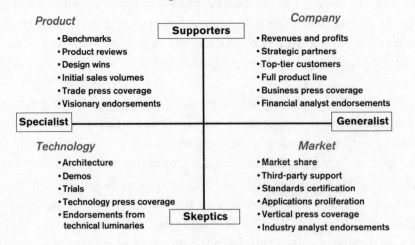

Matching Evidence to Media

Product
- Benchmarks
- Product reviews
- Design wins
- Initial sales volumes
- Trade press coverage
- Visionary endorsements

Supporters

Company
- Revenues and profits
- Strategic partners
- Top-tier customers
- Full product line
- Business press coverage
- Financial analyst endorsements

Specialist

Generalist

Technology
- Architecture
- Demos
- Trials
- Technology press coverage
- Endorsements from technical luminaries

Skeptics

Market
- Market share
- Third-party support
- Standards certification
- Applications proliferation
- Vertical press coverage
- Industry analyst endorsements

vide to your audience and the media by which to deliver it. Modifying the diagram provides these guidelines, as shown in the figure on page 232.

Once you understand the basic interests of each constituency, it is relatively a straightforward process to seek out or create the kind of evidence that will most appeal to each audience.

CHOOSE THE RIGHT TOOLS FOR THE JOB

How should all this be communicated? There are numerous ways to communicate, from smoke signals to satellites. In 1967 the Canadian futurist Marshall McLuhan opined that "the medium is the message." Today, politicians of various persuasions complain that *the media*—an unnamed collection of journalists, columnists, and TV talking heads—unfairly portray or otherwise bias the political message du jour. Yet, these same politicians assiduously covet the attentions of this "chattering class" in order to spin their own particular points of view in the most personally advantageous way. You and I are barraged by communications ranging from the radio alarm clock waking us to the wailings of the local car dealer and his latest "blowout sale" to the last banner ad that intrusively floats across our customized webpage as we finally finish checking our e-mail or lament the performance of our "can't-miss" stocks prior to turning out the light to sleep. For a few blessed hours we are at last free of this media assault. And yet . . . and yet . . .

Intrusive as commercial communication can be, we are all accustomed to looking for and receiving messages, and we all seem to prefer them delivered or packaged in specific ways. How can we utilize all the tools available to us in the most efficient manner? And how can we reconcile these choices to the strategic imperatives of each phase of market development?

Once again, altering the diagram to detail more completely how the evidence should be packaged and disseminated relative to the Competitive-Positioning Compass provides some useful guidance (see page 234).

However, before we embark on considering communication strategy for each TALC phase, there remains one more key distinguishing characteristic of high-tech marketing communications: rarely do we talk directly to our prospects and customers, although it may seem as if we do.

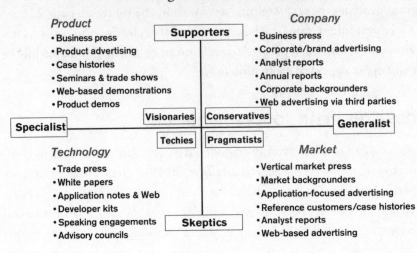

INFRASTRUCTURE MARKETING AND COMMUNICATIONS

If the Technology Adoption Life Cycle is the mother of all high-tech market models, then certainly the *Marketing Infrastructure Model* must be the mother of all high-tech marketing communications models. Regis McKenna, Silicon Valley's godfather of high-tech communications and PR, first described this model in his book *The Regis Touch.* The purpose of this model is to focus marketing communications activities on a single goal—the development of an acknowledged market leadership position within the word-of-mouth community that makes up a given target market. Once this process is under way, then the full complement of marketing communications tools and vehicles can be brought to bear to ensure marketing success.

McKenna describes the *infrastructure* of any market as the set of third parties that interact with you and your customer. Infrastructure marketing is based on the observation that customers uncertain of their choices do not rely solely on their own opinions when making buying decisions, particularly those that are seen as risky, but instead seek out the opinions of others whom they consider better informed. Accordingly, your goal is to influence the influencers.

Initially, you must establish credibility with this community so that its members feel comfortable talking about you, even recommending you. This involves conveying factual and compelling information. This does not involve bombast or hype, which inevitably is debunked, happily so, by this group. Going forward, the mission is to hasten your sales cycle by increasing the number of voices in the marketplace that can reinforce your basic marketing and sales message, and thereby decrease the number that may be contradictory. Once again, for this to work effectively, your message can't be simply hot air. The message must be based on your true position in the market.

The ultimate goal is to secure widespread acknowledgment of your position as a market leader. When this occurs, the benefits of market leadership become yours.

There is a compelling rationale for communicating effectively with an entire market infrastructure:

- *High-tech purchase decisions involve fear, uncertainty, and doubt (FUD). Minimizing this is the goal of virtually every buyer.*
- *Buyers seek the reassurance of trusted third party references.* We trust each other more than we trust advertising, public relations efforts, and other manifestations of what can be called marketing hyperbole (or *hype* for short). The network of third parties that can be referenced is called an "infrastructure." This infrastructure will vary depending on the category, the type of purchase, and the buyer profile. While techniques of communicating with each of the layers will also vary, the overall message must be consistent and credible if it is to be passed along, one layer to the next.
- *Only after a modicum of credibility has been established with the key influencers within a given infrastructure does the full range of marketing communication tools become available for effective use with the prospective customer.*

The strategy of focusing marketing budgets on infrastructure communication, as opposed solely to end user target promotion, grows out of the perceived risk of high-tech purchase decisions. In high-risk situations, where one must rely on a service provider with specialized expertise, such as heart surgery, legal pleadings, or even a haircut, buyers of such services do not respond to advertisements but instead seek the advice and counsel of friends, colleagues, or disinterested third parties. The majority of high-tech purchases still fall under this category, although our wired society is now comfortable with categories such as personal computers and peripherals, mobile phones, PDAs, and many desktop software applications. While these categories may not require any further validation, companies that sponsor offers within the category probably will.

To win a dominant market share in such an environment, one must be positioned as the market leading choice—the least high-risk decision. To be credible, this positioning must come from disinterested third parties, not from the company itself. Securing such positioning is the goal of an infrastructure communications program. Once such positioning is secured, and the buying decision is out from under the cloud of FUD, marketing messages can increasingly be directed to the ultimate end user.

**Infrastructure Communications
(Example)**

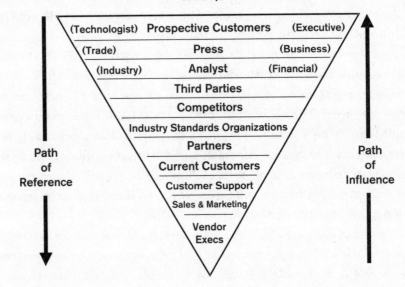

In order to approach communicating with a word-of-mouth community in a systematic way, one must model the various constituencies that make it up and how they relate to one another.[1] The model begins at the top with the prospective customer who asks, when faced with a high-tech marketing proposition, Whom can I look to for advice and counsel?

---

1. The layers in the middle of the pyramid are subject to the most change, depending on the category under consideration. The diagram illustrates a generic infrastructure.

Perhaps the easiest source of counsel is the press, the start of a *path of reference*. The trade press covers technology developments, reviews products, and analyzes applications. The business press covers markets, tracks company performance, and assesses market leadership positioning. But whom do the press ask, after they have been pitched by some high-tech vendor? One typical resource is the analyst community. Industry analysts are favored by the trade press, and financial analysts by the business press. Reputable analysts make it their business to get the inside information on what is real and what is merely hype or wishful thinking. And so, to whom do the analysts look? They interact with the myriad third parties that make up any given market segment, including distributors, hardware and software suppliers, competitors' industry associations, perhaps university thought leaders, and, especially, current customers. Finally, to whom do these constituencies look? They consider the company itself, typically through the windows of its customer support and account management.

Now consider the *path of influence*. This flow is the opposite of the path of reference. That is, if we want to influence any given layer in the infrastructure, we want to communicate first with the layers below it, the ones that the targeted layer will turn to in order to validate a marketing claim. Any time we introduce a new message into a target market—for example, the launch of a new product or the repositioning of a company or product line—we need to plan the communications to flow upward through the inverted pyramid. Thus, the infrastructure model provides the sequence of any communications initiative.

The other key point to isolating layers of the infrastructure is to acknowledge that each constituency has its own interests, its own path of communications. Typically, a few key influencers dominate most layers. The goal of a leveraged communications program is to win support of these critical few and then count on the existing word-of-mouth linkages to spread their opinions to the rest.

The infrastructure model becomes actionable when it is translated into a database of actual people, detailed further by infrastructure category. This database is the primary asset of the marketing communications process. It is the equivalent of a salesperson's customer database. Each layer needs to have an *owner*. The owner is the person in the organization who has responsibility for making the initial contacts and then sustaining a relationship with the key influencers in any given infrastructure segment. In addition, key messages and key communication vehicles can also be sorted out by layer as well. Be aware that few of these layers will wish to be owned by marketing communications professionals. Some will want to talk with technology experts; others with key executives; others with business development or product marketing responsibilities. In these cases, marketing communications should own the process of keeping and centralizing the database, but coordinate and facilitate the key contacts that will be owned by other people.

As a quick test of your current marketing communications program status, if you do not have an actively utilized infrastructure database, you are probably not in control of your marketing communications, and you are probably not utilizing the tools available to you in the most efficient manner.

▶ A JOURNALIST'S LAMENT

by Kevin Maney, technology editor, *USA Today*

Maybe you'd like to look over my shoulder while I read my actual, real-life e-mail: "The General Asset Recovery (GAR) division of Neoforma.com Inc., a leading provider of business-to-business e-commerce solutions . . ."

DELETE! I don't know what a General Asset Recovery (GAR) division is and I don't care. I don't know who Neoforma.com is. And if I had a dime for every time I read "leading provider of business-to-business e-commerce solutions," I'd have a butler and a hockey rink in my backyard.

Next: "PermitsNOW, a powerful online permitting service . . ."

DELETE! What in God's name is an online permitting service?

"You have been chosen to receive a press release from A&M Business Services Inc. Please visit [the URL below]."

DELETE! I've been chosen? What is this, a Publisher's Clearinghouse mailing? I have no reason to want your press release, much less click an extra time to get it. This is like telling a commuter, "You've been chosen to sit in gridlocked traffic!"

We'll look at one more e-mail. Oh, great. When I call up this one, the first two screens are filled with the e-mail addresses of other, competing journalists who are getting the same release at the same time. I see some of my friends there. It reminds me to e-mail them. But I don't have much interest in a mass press release that gives me no advantage over any other publication.

DELETE!

It's astounding to me how so many companies and public relations professionals have no clue about the realities of my job. I'm the senior technology writer at *USA Today*. I write one of the most visible weekly columns about technology. I'm in demand. I'm a target. But then again, so is just about every tech writer at any major newspaper or magazine.

There is a ton of technology news out there. No beat has more going on. Compared to technology, covering the auto or banking industry is like watching corn grow. Technology companies are desperate to break through the clutter. They need good press to lure customers, employees, investors, and partners. The competition is fierce.

On my end—like any reporter—I'm under almost constant deadline pressure. And it's just me sitting there. I don't have a staff to delegate to. I don't have an administrative assistant to screen the deluge coming in. Nobody in print journalism does. So what happens when you add up all this? Basically, in most cases, I am not happy and you, the technology executive who wants some press, are not happy. I get two hundred to three hundred e-mails a day, at least. Frankly, I've never counted. I probably delete 80 percent of them based just on the subject header. I probably really read 2 percent of incoming e-mail from companies I don't know or people I don't recognize. (I read and respond to all e-mail from people with whom I have a relationship. More on that in a minute.) I also get a good forty unsolicited PR phone calls from strangers a day. If the caller gets me live, I probably can't wait to get rid of him or her. If he or she leaves voice mail, I won't return the call. I can't. There aren't enough hours in the day.

I'm not even mentioning the tubs of snail mail that come in. Most of it goes in the trash without getting opened. Then there's overnight mail. And faxes. Believe it or not, if you asked my colleagues, they'd say that I'm more courteous on the phone and more conscientious about looking at my mail than others in my position. No kidding.

Now that you know the situation, I believe I can help you be less frustrated, spend less money on PR, and get better results. This is entirely self-serving. If you do these things, you'll also alleviate some of my pain and help me produce better columns and stories. Isn't that the basis of a great supplier-customer relationship? Which leads directly into point number one:

I'm a valuable business customer.

I'm not sure how most companies view me, but I'm sure it's usually not as a customer. But that's exactly what I am. You're selling information. I'm buying. Sure, there's no money directly involved. But if a satisfying transaction is completed, we both win. You sell me some interesting news or background or resource; I buy it, use it, add it to other things, and produce something that my newspaper then packages and sells to consumers. You get publicity. I get happy readers.

But if I'm a business customer, treat me like one. Don't fling random information my way. Don't waste my time. Don't make me think of you the way I think of telemarketers who call at dinnertime. Figure out what I want and need. Win my trust. Give me good value for the time I spend on you (because time is my precious resource). Be a solution, not a problem. Which leads to the other points, starting with:

Relationships count.

Absolutely no question—the people who have the most success getting their messages to me are those with whom I have a relationship. Theirs are the e-mails I read and the calls I take. It's not because I like them, though that certainly helps. It's because the relationship brings value to me. Those people tailor messages to me and attempt to bring me quality information.

On the other end, this suggests some definite no-nos. Having transitory public relations people doesn't help. Relying solely on an outside PR agency is rarely a good thing. It puts a layer between me and your company and often gets in the way of the relationship that would most benefit both of us. A few PR agencies—very few—are good at creating their own relationships with journalists and then using that to shepherd a relationship between journalists and the agencies' clients. Do some research and find out which agencies fit that description.

Finally, don't confuse a gimmick with a relationship. You wouldn't believe how many things I get that fall into the category of "stupid PR tricks." I've been sent stuffed animals, T-shirts, hot sauce, a miniature blimp, a shovel, and a full-size Austin Powers cardboard cutout that said, "Oh behave!" when someone walked by. All were tied to a cute pitch. Invariably, the press materials get tossed even if the item gets saved for my kids. Oh, and if you send food, which happens weekly, everyone in the newsroom eats it. No one remembers for a second who sent it.

Know what I do.

Lots of calls and e-mails are way off target. If someone took the time to read my work, they'd at least have a general idea of what might appeal to me and what might not. If I've never written a review of a website, why pitch me an idea for a review of your website? And if you show me that you've been reading me, at least I might be flattered enough to listen to you. After all, we journalists are human, too.

But be smart about this—look for trends, not specifics. See that I write about technology breakthroughs and would want to know about other breakthroughs. Don't see that I wrote about quantum computing and assume I'm going to do a lot more on quantum computing.

And be humble enough to play a supporting role. You might read my work and realize that I'd probably never write a whole piece about your company. But I might write a broader story in which your company could be a paragraph or example, or your CEO could be quoted as an expert. That kind of publicity never hurts.

Know whom I trust.

This is a sneaky one. I'm not a programmer, an engineer, or a scientist. Few technology journalists have that kind of training. It's unlikely that I'm going to evaluate some new technology that nobody's heard of and, all on my own, conclude I should write about it. I rely on a web of people to sift and bubble up ideas for me. It's totally ad hoc. I'd bet most of those people don't even know that's what they're doing.

For instance, I have good relationships with some venture capitalists. They see all kinds of business plans. We talk. They tell me about ideas or technologies that intrigue them. I take note and consider it something I might want to write about.

I read a handful of technology newsletters that tend to give me trustworthy early warning signals. I go to a few conferences, especially those that do a good job of finding up-and-coming companies or entrepreneurs and giving them the stage.

You can't know specifically whom I trust—in fact, I probably wouldn't tell you. It's kind of a trade secret. But you can learn which people and institutions tend to influence journalists. Winning them over can be a worthwhile investment.

Know what I want.

I'd guess that any journalist would gladly tell you this if you asked. In my case, I want to be able to write something that's fascinating to my audience and that hasn't yet been in any general interest or business publication. In other words, I want to show up my competitors.

I want to talk to people who really know interesting stuff—the CEO, the chief technologist, the inventor. I don't want to talk to PR or marketing people. I want to be able to get what I need from your company, whether it's an interview with the CEO or simply a product photo. I want it to be hassle free.

Be patient.

Very important. You might think you have a hot story that needs to be done now, but I'll forgive your tunnel vision if you can appreciate that I've got a lot going on. Remember, this is a relationship we're building. Many, many times, I've been told about a development but couldn't or wouldn't do anything right away. But I've filed the thought and put it aside. There, it would simmer. Something related would come across my radar. I'd add it to the pot. I might see other items that fit in. Perhaps six months later, it would all coalesce and become a story.

Yes, in the end a reporter's mind works in mysterious ways. But by playing it smart and building a relationship, you can certainly increase your chances of worming your way into journalists' brains. Otherwise, you're destined to be another victim of the delete key.

◀

DELIVERING THE MESSAGE AT EACH TALC INFLECTION POINT

If the overall goal of marketing, and thus a marketing campaign, is to create demand for one's products, services, and company, the weapons at our disposal, such as advertising, public relations, merchandising, and sales promotions, must be used effectively, efficiently, and correctly. Too often, organizations utilize a rather predictable combination of techniques driven largely by budget considerations—"this is what we can afford"—or they rely on a particular technique, the result of the prevailing recommendations of their advisory partners, who, not surprisingly, weight their recommendations based on what they deliver.[2]

Remember that you are about to do battle on the field of public opinion and that you're attempting to win the hearts, minds, and wallets of those customers you truly covet. Accordingly, you are advised to consider once again a time-honored tenet of warfare: *Any force can defeat any other force—if it can define the battle.* If we get to make the rules, why would we ever lose? Sadly, the answer lies in getting it wrong from the very beginning. Not understanding our own strengths and shortcomings, or those of our competitors, plays a key role in marketing debacles. More typically, such failures are the result of not understanding what our customers want—confusing their compelling reason to buy with our compelling reason to sell, for example. Or even if we understand the former, we fail to provide the means to deliver satisfactorily. We overpromise and underdeliver.

To consider marketing communications in the context of the TALC, we start with the *positioning* adopted during the development and validation of the overall market development strategy. To build compelling and persuasive communication programs, positioning must answer the questions in the figure on page 244.

If we are to succeed in winning over each customer group within the TALC—technology enthusiasts, visionaries, pragmatists, and conservatives—we must transition our positioning and the resulting messages to appeal to each of their predispositions, as noted in the previous diagrams.

---

2. This is not intended as a criticism per se of advertising or public relations agencies in particular. These firms can provide significant, actionable insights into the behaviors and attitudes of various constituencies within a market infrastructure. Ad agencies, notably, *want* to do advertising and will typically emphasize it as the overwhelming technique of choice. To a corporate identity or branding firm, there are few marketing problems that can't be redressed through a new logo or package design. Caveat emptor. In fairness, it should also be pointed out that business and management consulting companies that attempt to dismiss or co-opt these rather creative processes with their own, overly analytical, "boil-the-ocean" approach provide scant help when clients ask, "How do we take all this to the market?"

From Positioning to Communication

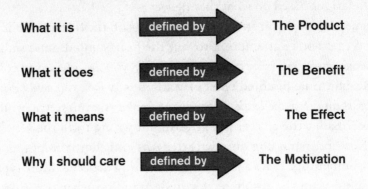

What it is	defined by →	**The Product**
What it does	defined by →	**The Benefit**
What it means	defined by →	**The Effect**
Why I should care	defined by →	**The Motivation**

Since strategy, and therefore positioning, changes for each market phase, our ability to *define the battle* will hinge on our ability to (a) *define* the early market, (b) *build* the market in the bowling alley, (c) *dominate* the market in the tornado, and (d) *extend* the market on Main Street. Fundamentally, this means moving from a product-centric value system to one that is market-centric. The value system is the set of elements that are prized by each customer set. They are ultimately what motivate the customer to select us rather than competing alternatives.

Let's now examine how several of the techniques that account for significant marketing communications expenditures fit into each stage.

WINNING EARLY MARKET ACCEPTANCE

As noted in chapter 3, promising new technologies and products run the risk of an early demise because technology enthusiasts fail to endorse the new effort at the outset. More typically, though, early market efforts fail during the time between adoption by technology enthusiasts who initially may be enthused by what they see and visionaries who fail to rally behind your cause due to their inability to understand or support the new paradigm. This lack of enthusiasm (and consequent lack of adoption) may be because the approach and resulting benefits are unclear, confusing, contradictory, or simply too risky relative to other new paradigm alternatives or simply doing nothing.

Thus, the challenge in the early market is to use marketing communications to *define* a potential market opportunity by what we referred to in chapter 13 as *naming and framing* the innovation. In other words, we need to identify what this new thing is and the numerous advantages it conveys to the early adopter.

Our chief competition is the inertia in the marketplace, anchored by the status quo and/or existing paradigm now in operation. Thus, we must create a crisis—a real or predicted state that exists (or will exist) as a result of the existing paradigm—a state that no self-respecting technology enthusiast or visionary would be content with for long. However, attempting to do this through directly sponsored marketing communications like advertising will largely be viewed as self-serving. Therefore, we have to get someone else to do it, or do it ourselves in the context of something perhaps more noble.

Creating a crisis means creating an issue around an unmet need or an unexploited advantage that is uniquely addressable by your new thing. Unfortunately, you have little credibility to point this out. Therefore, you have to induce, incite, or invite others to do it for you. This is the province primarily of public relations (really, market relations). It is typically *not* the province of advertising and merchandising, save for those products that are aimed directly at end user consumers and/or pose the least risk in adoption primarily due to their low acquisition costs.

While it has been fashionable over the past few years to "build brand early," branding in the early market stage has little to contribute to ultimate success for most categories. A brand is not what is sought by techies and visionaries. What such people are seeking are discontinuous alternatives that may or may not be ultimately selected to achieve the goal of getting ahead of the herd. As a result, it's not about what you say that matters as much as it is about what other visionaries say. Your job is to foment this discussion, make it seem very important, perhaps stimulate a debate, and ultimately influence the outcome in your favor. The goal of early market positioning is to create the perception that you and your company represent a thought leader for the new paradigm—both evangelist and disciple. The evidence to support this comes in the form of elements of the market infrastructure, notably the analyst community, along with some visionary and loudmouthed customers, who are eager to support your views and sing your praises. Your crisis, successfully created, can then be addressed with your own technology and product prowess. Need a demonstration? Go rent the movie *Wag the Dog*.

CROSSING THE CHASM

The goal of chasm crossing and the bowling alley strategy that extends this activity is to gain adoption of a discontinuous innovation by mainstream customers in advance of widespread market acceptance. To achieve this requires focusing on segments that have compelling needs that are not currently met by the existing paradigm (typically as a result of the shortcomings of the status quo). Key to success is ensuring that a complete whole product solution is fielded such that a buyer achieves favorable ROI.

Competition, previously the status quo in the early market, now extends beyond the players representing the existing paradigm, which consists of mature horizontal or vertical applications, to those that represent new, emerging paradigm alternatives, typically horizontal in nature.[3] We must cope once again with market and customer skepticism and thus move from the familiar ground of product-oriented communications supported by visionary enthusiasm and adoption to the less familiar ground of application and/or market-oriented issues, where support from pragmatists will be hard won.

To achieve our positioning goal, that of the acknowledgment that our product and application are the most complete and therefore the most relevant and appropriate for the needs of a given segment, will require communication efforts that are directly targeted to the specific segment targeted. While we can extend our communication efforts to, for example, the analyst community, it is time to start targeting and appealing to the specific customers we want to sell to—and to reach them quite literally. In addition to refining our PR messages to reach opinion leaders and influencers who follow closely the segment(s) targeted, we can now extend our reach through paid media—advertising specifically, which is targeted to end users and economic buyers through both message and media plan.

---

3. *Vertical* and *horizontal* refer to the relative breadth and specificity of the product application.

Using the Competitive-Positioning Compass and selecting the right evidence (see the previous diagrams) as a guide, messaging must also be reformatted and represented as exemplified in the following:

Product-Centric to Market-Centric Communication

Newest technology	→	Second-generation application
Elegant architecture	→	Emerging standard
Best product	→	Growing installed base
Easiest to use	→	Most third-party support
Attractive pricing	→	Cost of ownership
Unique functionality	→	Quality of support
The next big thing	→	Relevant alternative

Also recall from chapter 13 that your message does not have to be about providing superior benefits, typically embodied in product-centric messages, to those of all other competitors. The high ground you seek is occupied by convincing your target that you can provide a superior alternative to that which is now in use, based on the best *combination* of both benefit and differentiation. The benefit is an expression of your product capabilities and is derived from your understanding of the target segment's compelling reason to buy. Your differentiation is based on your knowledge of the target segment's particular characteristics and situation and correspondingly your ability to translate this knowledge into segment-specific value and utility.

There are myriad ways to execute this type of communication, both in form and in substance. Whatever you choose must be targeted precisely at the segment you're trying to reach—and no other segment! Targeting other segments, as highly desirable as this may seem, actually will defocus your message, particularly when rendered into advertising. There are simply too many supposed benefits and points of differentiation that managers acting individually and as a group can conjure up. Rest assured, they will all find their way into an ad, a website, and so on, turning the equivalent of the most poignant prose into copy you would find in a telephone directory. It will also be just as interesting to read. This recurring, almost pathological desire to be all things to everyone by regurgitating every blessed feature or function of the product into a single-page ad explains one of the reasons why most high-tech advertising is, well, crap.

▶ TO GET GREAT ADVERTISING, BE A GREAT CLIENT
by Peter Angelos, executive creative director, North America, DMB&B Worldwide

"What makes a great client?"

This is an easy one. For I once asked a client of mine, a great client and a great guy, this very question. And the answer, anecdotal as it may be, should resonate as piquantly with you as it did with me.

His name is Ray Cole and he was the head of marketing for Sunkist Growers (a citrus fruit growing cooperative). The work we did for him was then considered the best and the brightest of Foote, Cone & Belding's canon for many years. It succeeded in establishing Sunkist as *the* (please note the definite article) premium brand of fresh fruit. It helped give the growers within the Sunkist cooperative tremendous marketing advantages with both consumers and retailers. It also created a fresh, buoyant image for the brand, which allowed Sunkist to ask for, and receive, premium prices for their premium products and to license their good name to other kindred products around the world.

And, for what it's worth, the campaign won, I think, every single award the advertising industry offers. In print, television, and outdoor.

So, there I was one day at the office, after presenting some work we were especially proud of, when I said, "Ray, you're our best client, by far. Why? Is it because you're a champion of the work?"

He said no.

I wondered if it was because he had the guts to support—and stick to—a strategic positioning that was single-minded and focused.

No, again.

Well, was it due to the fact that he was a genuinely good guy who was fun to hang with?

Nope.

It was simpler than that. He said, and I'm paraphrasing here, that all he ever did was make sure that Sunkist was the one account at FCB that everyone wanted to work on.

Now, I could have conjured chickens and eggs, cause and effects, and asked for more specificity. But I didn't. Because I knew that he was right. It was that simple.

People were dying to work on his business. Creatives, account people, planners, producers. It was, as I remember, the smallest account at the agency, billing less than 5 million bucks. No one cared. Was it because it was their best shot at doing great work? Because it was a world-class brand? Because it was so damn fun and the product so damn likable?

Didn't matter. Ray had created an ecosystem wherein client and agency alike could have the most fun, doing the most imaginative work; where no one held back because no one was afraid to fail.

So. If you're the client, do this one thing and the best people will beat a path to your conference room door. If you work at the agency, you probably already know who the Ray Cole is at your place. Motivate every cell in your torso to work on that piece of business. From this simple and sensible design, you will be rewarded.

◄

INTO THE GATHERING STORM

Now things really start to get interesting. Tornado markets require the marketing communication equivalent of all-out war. There are few rules to speak of, and there are enormous penalties to those who can't or won't fight for their fair share. Mixing—indeed, mangling—the metaphors, there are tremendous penalties for those who refuse to ante up in order to play in what now has become a very-high-stakes game.

The target customer is the infrastructure buyer. The compelling reason to buy is now obvious. From whom the buyer will buy, however, is not. Thus the battle is joined. Recall that the goal of tornado strategy is to capture as many customers for life as possible during what will be a relatively brief flurry of activity as one infrastructure is swapped for another. The product/application value proposition and message that were carefully crafted and focused on specific target segments during the bowling alley must now be retired in favor of those that promise a rapid, risk-minimized transition to the new way now sweeping across the market. It is your goal to position yourself as the best among your "new-wave" competitors.

Does this mean that we are back in the realm of product-centric messages? Yes and no. Yes, from the standpoint that during tornadoes, competitive pressures will be such that all vendors wishing to play will be constantly upgrading their own feature/functionality sets while simultaneously establishing new, lower price/performance thresholds. To be sure, this is legitimate grist for the communications mill. But rest assured, such positions will be temporary for all vendors. Therefore, product-centric messages by themselves will not withstand the fury of the tornado.

Instead, we must consider where we are headed within the primate pecking order. Do we have a legitimate shot at establishing our gorilla credentials? Or will we likely be awarded the Miss Congeniality crown, given to those runners-up (read chimps) that tried hard, looked smart, and tried to be everyone's friend? Or are we late to the party and now looking at the last of the canapés (read monkey)? In short, where are we placed in market-centric terms?

If you're the gorilla, you are best served by figuratively beating your chest through mass media techniques, notably advertising. Messaging here is not a sophisticate's game; rather, it is one of devising an effective, or at least not inappropriate, message and delivering it over and over and over again. Marketing communication budgets typically double, triple, even quadruple during tornadoes, because they must. When everyone else is shouting, the cost for your share of mind among prospects and customers, typically measured in terms of your share of voice, climbs dramatically.[4] The gorilla has a natural advantage here as its size and the market's predisposition to it effectively make the gorilla's communication budget work more efficiently. Gorillas' awareness figures are higher, so they don't have to buy it like the monkey does. Gorillas do not represent any technical or market risk because they are becoming de facto

---

4. Share of voice typically measures a company's advertising media budget as a percentage of the total budget spent by all competitors in a given product category.

standards, so they don't have to justify their approach or existence like the chimp does.

Gorillas, like smart poker players, also know that the time to increase the betting is when you have more chips than your opponents. Dramatically increasing one's communications budget during a tornado when you're winning the competition has the effect, as Oracle's mild-mannered CEO Larry Ellison is given to say, of "taking all the oxygen out of the room."

Apple employed a similar strategy during the first PC tornado way back in the 1980s but did so as a chimp. The goal was driving weaker monkeys out of the competition in terms of both advertising pressure against the market and exacting continued loyalty from its distribution channel. In addition, Apple communicated precisely the message appropriate to its positioning goals: It concentrated on serving specific markets (e.g., education); was committed to these markets and would defend them through both word and deed (the company donated a computer to every elementary and secondary school in California); and it developed an overall product approach (the first GUI) and tone of voice that left its devotees with the feeling that they were just a bit smarter, indeed more hip, than everyone else.

Later, Dell demonstrated best practices in communication for lowly monkeys, though the market was now morphing to a king/prince/serf model based on IBM's colossal blunder involving trying to reestablish a proprietary standard in the midst of a market tornado. Dell's advertising and direct mail was just that: very direct. It depicted its rather ungainly looking products prominently in a long-running advertising campaign that promised a variety of differently configured products and peripherals obtainable over the telephone and offered at very attractive prices. If IBM was the safe buy, and Apple was for those who wanted the best, then surely Dell was the choice of the knowledgeable and smart shopper. Dell's direct-to-consumer selling model could not have been presented more efficiently or, ironically, more elegantly.

▶ THE MOST FAMOUS FINN SINCE HUCK

But let's talk about the twenty-first century. Best practices so far? Both Nokia and IBM get my vote almost without debate. Nokia has clearly outclassed its principal rivals, Motorola and Ericsson, in the cellular phone business. Most agree that neither of these companies are sophisticated marketers, and Nokia exploits their shortcomings to the hilt by wielding its own marketing prowess composed of equal parts: product design, channel influence, and compelling message. Remarkably, it presents itself as the safe buy, the hip alternative, and the smart shopper's choice—all in one. The fruits of such success rarely fail to disappoint Wall Street as well. Something MOT and ERICY have not always managed to manage.

IBM pulled off a similar coup—not against its rivals but against its own well-instilled habit to market, and specifically advertise, every product that a $90 billion company could bring out (and that's a lot). The result for half of the previous decade was a hodgepodge of messages that did nothing but confuse a marketplace that needed reassuring at the time that IBM was indeed alive and well and a player. This collective confusion stemmed in part from each business unit's desire to "position each brand," as one executive patiently explained to me, asserting further that the AS/400, IBM's aging but still popular proprietary mid-range computer, was indeed a *brand* with a definable *brand personality* supported by—wait for it—specific and unique "brand characteristics and appeals." (Somehow it is difficult to imagine a hard-bitten IS director and his purchasing agent getting all warm and fuzzy over such things.) Exacerbating the problem, IBM had over seventy different ad agencies worldwide, each undoubtedly taking direction from its own client, whoever and wherever in the world it might be, and producing its own version of this multidimensional story as well. Brands? My sweet aunt!

Fortunately, people knowledgeable about such things came to prevail in the new IBM. CEO Lou Gerstner tasked Abby Kohnstamm, his newly appointed lieutenant in charge of corporate marketing, to make some sense of it all, and add some sensibility as well. Kohnstamm fired all the agencies and consolidated the IBM account at the venerable Ogilvy & Mather. O&M in turn staffed the business at the top with seasoned, highly skilled professionals (among them Steve Hayden, now an O&M vice chairman who, I'm proud to say, honed his craft on Apple back in the early 1980s) who knew how to develop single-minded campaigns that educated and entertained rather than reiterated the obvious or the irrelevant. The resulting "Solutions for a Small Planet" campaign, which has now evolved as of this writing into IBM's "e-solutions" campaign, is laudable for its single-minded message and a tone of voice that reflects the best characteristics of the only IBM brand that matters: IBM.

◀

MANAGING MAIN STREET

The goal of Main Street strategy is to exploit fully one or both of the market development opportunities now present as a result of a newly adopted, newly deployed infrastructure. One option calls for the continued deployment of a commodity-like version to those few late adopters that can still be reached, or extending the overall market boundaries by pushing into new geographies. The second option, requiring greater marketing sophistication, extends the base product into a series of additional products and/or applications by adding incremental value(s) to satisfy the wishes of niche markets or microsegments identified within the larger market.

Main Street requires us to reexamine again our longer-term market development goals. Key to the analysis is asking which overall direction is best suited for us, for that will largely determine the communication footing that we adopt. For example, do we intend to offer the best overall value? Or will we extend a position accorded to us perhaps during the bowling alley as the Mercedes-Benz or Lexus of the category? Not for everyone, but you know who you are. Or does our category—enterprise software, for example—call for us to shift our appeal to one that is not based on any product per se, but on our overall position and status in the marketplace? Or do we play the scrappy underdog, fighting the forces of evil so to speak, who would trap customers into unnecessarily high-priced products and "marketectures" that are really no more valuable than anyone else's?

Imagine how much fun Main Street marketing communication can be, for there are so many options open to us—or so it would appear. Whatever direction you pursue, consider the following as you develop your plan.

1. The target customer is primarily the end user community, for it is now largely in control of future purchases.

2. Your place in the primate pecking order, or royal family, will influence how your message is heard and therefore how you need to communicate.

3. Many competitions will be of the product versus product or brand versus brand variety. Effective product-based communication typically boosts short-term results, while effective brand and branding efforts sustain long-term appeal for both products and companies. Branding efforts, executed in the form of new corporate identities, logos, and advertising, have little effect in the short term and will not redress problems caused by a weak market development strategy or an irrelevant value proposition.

4. On the other hand, many +1 efforts are largely valued in the eyes of the beholder and can thus be of subjective rather than objective value. Marketing communications itself can actually be the +1, engendering the response "I like this company and its products because I like what they stand for" among end users. Also, channels may regard marketing communication efforts by their vendors as the single most-valued element, creating demand and therefore the possibility for higher margins in what might otherwise be a commodity category.

5. Communicating with the market infrastructure remains important, particularly to the financial community. Absent a compelling story, you will be ignored. You should assume that reputable press coverage is earned, not bought. By the same token, the press is largely interested in themes and angles that highlight success, failure, or controversy. Assume that any coverage you receive will be woven into one of these headlines.

▶ STREET-SMART PRINCIPLES OF INVESTOR RELATIONS
by Stan DeVaughn, independent consultant

1. Go to market and create demand.

To get its story told, management must be active (and reactive)—never passive. Investors don't discover ideas. They are introduced to them. Companies believing that simply taking care of business will result in a premium

P/E ratio are deluding themselves. This is especially true of diversified, multimarket organizations. More often than not, they languish. Stocks that remain well-kept secrets on Wall Street are typically underpriced, no matter what the underlying operating performances might be. The answer? Aggressive exposure of the individual businesses of the company. Diversified financial services companies and healthcare organizations, for example, can contain individual product and services strengths that merit discreet information programs all their own. In such cases, rifle-shot attention can equate to higher overall values in remarkably short time.

2. Creating demand for your stock is fundamental to fair valuation and orderly trading.

The financial market is, like any other market, influenced by demand and supply. A stock in demand is a stock on the rise—in price as well as awareness.

3. More is better.

Your investor-relations program helps move markets and stock prices. Information builds expectation. Expectation leads to value. Twenty years ago, Intel pioneered the hosted quarterly analyst meeting for high-tech companies. The marketplace, technology, and competition were changing so fast, beginning in the early 1980s, that the annual information event the company traditionally conducted had to be scrapped in favor of a quarterly event. The price of Intel stock began a long, steady climb immediately afterward. Little things add up.

Attracting the favorable attention of the investors you want means that your message (and medium) must match investors' preferences. If your target investors want personal, regular, one-to-one contact, you must commit to it as the basis of your outreach efforts. If they insist on more frequent formal gatherings than the annual shareholders meeting, for example, be prepared to enthusiastically accommodate them.

4. There is no such thing as "the investment community."

There are multiple breeds of investors. They all behave differently. Some of them are desirable to your company at a point in time, others not. Choose those types whose expected behavior matches your corporate needs. When John Sculley was hired to run Apple in 1983, the stock had been a favorite among short-sellers and weak hands. This changed as efforts to attract and hold long-term investors took effect. Strong hands held Apple, helped stabilize the stock, and drove off the "in-and-outers."

5. Those who snooze, lose.

Management must compete as vigorously and relentlessly in telling the company story to appropriate investors as it does in telling the product story to its customers. Know precisely whose interest you want to attract and what it takes to arouse and hold that interest. The stories of savvy CEOs who court their key investors—and complacent executives who ignore theirs—are the staple of business magazines and how-to books. Shareholders are customers. They have a choice of products. They will be sold on the product that they believe best matches their particular need. It's up to the marketer to pinpoint that need—and appeal to it.

6. There is no standard IR program.

Your specific investor-relations situation and requirements are unique to your company. They constantly change. Your efforts to attract and hold investors will succeed to the extent that you match investors' interests over time with the ever-changing story of your company's prospects. Network Equipment Technologies (N.E.T.) went public in 1987, in the aftermath of the Bell system deregulation, selling products that enabled Ma Bell's biggest customers to become their own phone companies. But as computer networking evolved away from large, private backbone networks to router-based networks, N.E.T. failed to evolve its own story to incorporate the shifts under way in big computer networking. Investors migrated to stocks that told a more compelling story and had the performance to substantiate the claims. Years later, with the emergence of the Internet, companies such as Inktomi and Veritas established brand recognition as forcefully in Wall Street as they did in the product marketplace. How? By identifying their business prospects with the growth prospects of the Internet. Another company with a similar product line, Network Appliance, took longer to convince investors of its own Internet-driven prospects. It was neither as effective, nor as aggressive as Veritas at communicating the linkage between its future and the explosion of e-business.

Go forward and sell your story!

◄

One last point. On Main Street, marketing communications planning, strategy, and execution takes on its most serious set of challenges. Creating demand for commodity-like products, teasing out the benefits associated with important but rather mundane engineering efforts, reintroducing the company on a constant basis to a market that has neither the interest nor the time to learn new stories, sustaining loyalty among members of a fickle and heterogeneous channel, and, yes, managing the brand are all efforts best led and practiced by skilled professionals. Amateurs, dilettantes, and the less experienced will soon be exposed, their efforts humbled.

KEY INSIGHT ► ► ► ► ► ► ► ► ► ► ►

Beware the hypercompetitive marketing organization. During the tornado, marketers and their companies will quite likely be trying to bash the competition at every opportunity, and rightfully so. But Main Street requires a change, from being competitively focused to being customer focused. Many organizations pay lip service to this metamorphosis, but their actions give them away. For example, they continue the habit of bad-mouthing their competition, not only in sales presentations but in advertising as well. Or features added to the next version of the product become driven by what the competition is doing (or not doing) rather than what the customer wants. It's my observation that this behavior manifests itself in predictable ways, starting with (but not limited to) senior management's own preoccupations or insecurities becoming institutionalized; which leads to the repeated development and execution of flawed strategy—often described by its sufferers as "strategy du jour."

Hypercompetitive marketing is based on fear—an irrational fear of losing to one's competition so that the healthy, aggressive, and long-term objective of winning one's fair share and more, based on merit, is perverted to that of not losing. The result of such an orientation is to develop strategies and programs based solely on what the competition is doing. That is, item seven on the Market Development Strategy Checklist, *competition,* becomes item number one, and obsessively so. Organizations that labor under this syndrome effectively cede control of their own destinies, for they are now tied inexorably and ironically to the fortunes of their competitors. This pathology is expressed in the idea "for us to win, all others must lose." Organizations under this sway will sadly pursue this unrealistic goal, much to their own lasting detriment.

17

Field Engagement Strategy

In well-ordered states, storekeepers and salesmen are commonly those who are weakest in bodily strength and, therefore, of little use for any other purpose.

—PLATO

This chapter details how positioning strategy is executed and realized via marketing communications. The intent of the communications program is to create demand for a vendor's products or services among the target market. Such programs necessarily are considered in the aggregate; that is, planning is not done on an individual customer level, though the effects of such programs should be observable in both the aggregate market and individual customer level. This chapter reviews and details a similar process for planning and executing the actual selling process. Note: This chapter is not a primer on sales methods. Rather, the goal is to enable managers to align sales strategy with market development strategy and thus be able to design a *field engagement model* that is consistent, focused, and efficient.

Plato obviously never made his living selling, to say nothing of selling enterprise-class software carrying a quota in the millions. This is not an occupation for the faint of heart, the weak-minded, or the weak-willed, or those with modest physical stamina. Selling high-tech products and services is hard work, stressful to both mind and body. Regrettably, many high-tech organizations complicate the process even further by failing to comprehend that the sales process in high-tech is less about "selling" something, and far more a consultative engagement where complex situations must be rapidly assessed, assumptions made, scenarios posed, questions asked, and answers given, possibly all for naught. Company fortunes, however, rely on a favorable outcome—the successful transaction: a result that will benefit both parties in both the short and long term. Getting it right means getting the sale.

Therefore, the strategic implications of planning this element of a go-to-market program must be to ensure that it is aligned with the overall market development strategy. Tactically, there must also be alignment between the target customer's buying process and the vendor's selling process; that is, make it easy for the customer to buy. To do this, we need to model the former in order to understand and therefore design the latter. Not surprisingly, our TALC model provides insights into this process.

Most high-tech markets (and so-called industrial markets in general) operate under a *considered purchase* model—which should be obvious given the stakes involved. To harness the ideas discussed in previous chapters, this chapter is written from the viewpoint of the *complex sale,* which typifies many high-tech industries. Successful outcomes, particularly in the early, bowling alley, and tornado markets, are most often a function of a consensus-driven decision-making process that requires direct and often multiple interactions between buyers and sellers. While we can envision this process as a funnel with a series of iterative steps—prospecting, qualification, needs analysis, recommendation and proposal, selection, and negotiation leading to a sale—we can further refine the model by determining where in the process the prospect desires or needs an intervention (actual or virtual) and thereby ascertain the goal of such meetings for both the prospect *and* the vendor. We can then map out each intervention in terms of what information is relevant, and how it must be delivered and processed, in order to get to an efficient and satisfactory result—the *close.*

Importantly, the actual selling process steps may be serial or parallel in sequence. Selling *techniques* may vary significantly from category to category, and our goal here is not to compare and contrast the merits of various selling methodologies, which are well documented and extolled by numerous and noteworthy sales training organizations. Let's be clear:

The goal of any sales process is to *make the sale!* Managers need to understand how to *manage* this process relative to each phase of the life cycle. The following model illustrates this process based on six key goals of both vendor and buyer, as follows:

Life Cycle Sales Engagement Strategy

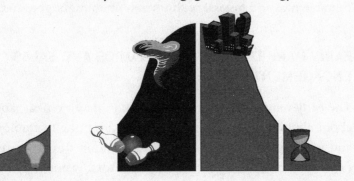

Customer Goal:	Competitive Advantage	Solve Problem	Adopt New Paradigm	Extend Paradigm
Customer Need:	Potential of Technology	Complete Solution	Make Safe Choice	Better Value
Vendor Goal:	Validate Technology	Segment Share	Market Share	Profitability
Strategy:	Demo the Technology	Show ROI	Gorilla Power!	Segment Focus
Skills:	Technology Proficiency	Customer Intimacy	Closing Deals	Relationship Management
Style:	Evangelism	Consultative	Authoritative	Transactional

We posit that during each phase of the life cycle buyers have two overriding objectives:

· Achieving a specific goal promised by a particular technology, product, or system
· Judging how competing alternatives best serve this goal

We posit further that sellers, in order to satisfy these buyer objectives, must wield certain proficiencies, or *bona fides,* in the form of:

· A relevant sales *strategy* to win the sale
· Demonstrable *skills* necessary to execute this strategy
· A complementary *style* of sales execution

Thus, designing a field engagement strategy requires a keen understanding of the overall market development strategy, parsed to perhaps its most granular level—that is, how we need to approach or engage an individual prospect. The experience and learning from this exercise translates to greater relevance, potential, and appeal to the larger market. Understanding each phase within the TALC model also points the way to fundamental and necessary shifts in how a vendor goes to market.

EARLY MARKET ADOPTION DYNAMICS AND SALES ENGAGEMENT STRATEGY

The early market is stage one of market development, and the game is about aligning with first movers—early adopting technology enthusiasts and visionaries—willing to make big bets on unproven technologies in order to steal a march on their competitors. Visionaries are not immune to the challenges of their respective markets. The difference versus the mainstream is in the timing of their response to such challenges. Accordingly, they must understand how the potential of new, discontinuous technologies can aid in their quest.

Accordingly, a vendor's key objective during this phase is to identify the senior executives (and their technology enthusiasts and acolytes) who, perhaps under extreme competitive pressures, desire to do something on a grand scale in order to change the competitive landscape, and thus improve their chances of distancing themselves from the more cautious herd. To be considered, vendors must have the ability to demonstrate their discontinuous approach—demo the technology—so the buyers can understand clearly the potential of such technology to help them achieve their lofty goals. Doing this requires a skillful approach that ensures the technology will work as promised (at least most of the time) and evangelizes the product both to the customer and, by proxy, to the visionary community—typically comprising the technical analysts and press that follow such developments.

The desired vendor approach and goal falls under the rubric of "It works! We have found the promised land." But will the customer feel the same? The customer's goal is to understand clearly the potential of this technology to further his or her aims. The prospective buyer will compare your new approach to other technologies, approaches, and opportunities that promise similar advances. As such, you may be competing against other similar innovations, or against dissimilar discontinuous innovations. Thus, the sales team is really a high-level project team. (Remember, think *project*, not product.) The engagement model should consist of identifying the visionary customer who will invest financial, human, and other resources to make it work, and the service partner (as appropriate) who will help tame the discontinuous beast and make it presentable for repetitive use.

A common mistake for many vendors is grandiose expectations. "It works," goes the thinking, therefore, everyone is a customer. While this assumption may be standard operating procedure among venture-funded start-ups, such ambitions usually result in poor forecasts and disappointment, particularly evidenced in large organizations with long-standing experience selling to the mainstream. Instead, it is far more desirable and practical for a management team to act in support of a few, evangelistic salespeople who understand and are conversant with the dynamics of selling to the mercurial visionary, in order to make sure that these early adopters buy and stay sold. After closing a number of these deals, the company begins to develop an idea of what target market may be attractive to pursue as a beachhead in the bowling alley, and what resources, process, and outcomes can be expected to lead to success in the next phase.

▶ SURVIVING THE EIGHT TRAPS OF EARLY MARKET SELLING

As I write this, many customers for high-technology products and services are considerably more than just a bit cranky. During the past five years, they have been gorging themselves at our table—elegantly laden with all manner of things high tech, much of it discontinuous, some of it not. It now seems that many have had their fill, led by the world's telecommunication giants who have spent billions building a new communications infrastructure to exploit the oft-hyped concept of *convergence,* only to find that vast numbers of their own subscribers have chosen to miss this particular dance, and instead are sitting it out waiting for something truly exciting to happen. Not surprisingly, both start-ups and the high-tech industry's behemoths are reacquainting themselves with how to sell the merits of a new technology value proposition. Since with any discontinuous innovation we must literally begin at the beginning, I have previously stated that the early market strategy is to go out and get a customer based on the market development strategy of doing a deal. Yet, in practice, we watch companies both large and small fall into a number of predictable behaviors—traps—that frustrate their efforts and, in some cases, cause the premature death of a promising idea. My partner in The Chasm Group, Philip Lay, has documented eight dangers that lie in wait for the unsuspecting.

1. Ignoring the key goals of early market sales.

Companies tend to act as if this is a time to sell to as many customers as possible, in order to build a reference list that will impress later adopters. Unfortunately, by treating all comers as early adopters, they often end up with the worst possible compromise: They get involved in extended sales cycles with suddenly hesitant customers who end up requesting custom enhancements in return for small pilot contracts that take ages to close. In those cases where companies do attract a bona fide visionary customer, they are often unsure how to manage the opportunity. Thus they jump through technical hoops to satisfy the customer's aggressive requirements, but fail to get compensated for the value they deliver.

2. Employing ineffective qualification (i.e., segmentation) criteria.

Many companies fail to recognize that early market selling does require a segmentation strategy of sorts, though quite a counterintuitive one. As a result, they spend precious energy selling to the wrong target customers. For example, in the bowling alley you segment for pragmatist managers in self-referencing groups; whereas in the tornado you segment for anyone ready to make a quick purchase decision for maximum volume; and on Main Street you segment for end users in selected niche markets whose needs and preferences you can serve effectively. In contrast, during the early market stage, when all constituencies except for the small number of techies and visionary executives automatically disqualify themselves from buying the "new, new thing," vendors must segment *relentlessly* for visionary executives in visible organizations.

3. Asking the wrong people in your organization to find and close the first few deals.

In most cases, assigning your entire sales force, large or small, to the task of finding and closing big deals with visionaries is asking for trouble. In order to engage with executives in such organizations, your *best* resources must be actively engaged. After all, these are the defining projects that will establish your company in the new category. You need to field a team that can interact at the highest levels with the three key partners in many project-led sales: the visionary customer, the technology company, and the services organization or firm.

4. Not knowing where to find likely visionary buyers.

One of the main problems associated with selling to early adopters is that there's no way of telling from their business card or job title what their adoption behavior is relative to discontinuous innovations. Fortunately, however, visionaries tend to leave a trail. While there aren't many of them, they usually have a track record of sorts. Visionary individuals quickly make a name for themselves and may often move from one company to another. One of the best ways of identifying them is to utilize the combined personal networks of your own company, management team, board, and investors. You can also follow visionary exploits in publications that detail their successful and unsuccessful projects. Using common brainstorming techniques, you can typically draw up a list of twenty or more suspects, and this is as good a place as any to start.

5. Failing to align with the visionary's goals and requirements.

From the time you first hit it off with a true visionary buyer, you must do everything possible to fit in with their vision simply because they always have a project in mind—probably before you came along. Strangely enough, the worst possible mistake is to act like a typical product vendor, because the one thing that will scare a visionary off is a vendor eager to do a deal at all costs. For example, agreeing to do complex custom product enhancements at the drop of a hat smacks of desperation, and it tends to make visionaries feel that you may not be able to deliver what they need in the time frame they need it. Remember, far from being price-sensitive, visionaries are *results sensitive*. This is because, if you think about it, their willingness to go where no one has gone before makes them vulnerable should they fail.

6. Mistaking pragmatists for visionaries.

Pragmatists, conservatives, and even skeptics read the same books on core competencies and competitive advantage as do visionaries, and they can be equally proficient in the lingo of strategy. Apart from any other consideration, talking the talk sounds much better than admitting that the real reason they came to your seminar is, well, fear that they may be missing out on something important. There's nothing wrong with being a pragmatist. It's just that if we don't listen carefully, we can waste precious time and money courting them, only to have a big deal forecast to close within three months turn into a small pilot that doesn't close for a year (if ever), with very little resource commitment by the customer. So how can you tell immediately that you are dealing with a pragmatist rather than a visionary? Look for these clues: (1) The visionary always has a project in mind that he or she is dying to tell you about, whereas the pragmatist and the conservative may be there only to keep tabs on the new stuff, perhaps to convince themselves that they don't need to do anything about it for the time being; and (2) Your prospective customer asks, "So, who else is doing this?" If the customer is a visionary, his or her expression is one of anticipating perhaps being the first in the industry to invest in this new stuff, whereas a pragmatist will *always* betray his or her nature by the concerned look on his or her face. The best way to deal with pragmatists is to let them know that you understand their lack of readiness to buy at this time, and that you will keep them informed about your progress. This reverse psychology provides them with valuable assurance, and may even intrigue them enough to result in a pilot purchase.

7. Structuring each deal as a product sale rather than a complete project.

Most software companies are designed from the start to be product businesses, even if they know they will have to provide for plenty of customization to their products by engineering and/or professional services. Often, the business model is set as a license-fee business, with service fees tacked on as a secondary, tactical sideline. This generally makes it difficult to identify and close true early market opportunities effectively and profitably. The reason is that this model causes the vendor to focus on selling a product license, which flies directly in the face of the customer's goals. The clearest sign that vendors are approaching the early market sales opportunities incorrectly is that the product becomes their key point of reference; for every question asked by the customer, they point to benefits the product provides, to show how the product can solve the customer's problem, whatever it may be. But most visionary customers see new technologies as concepts in search of proof, rather than as finished products. Furthermore, they recognize that they are the only customers willing to commit time, resources, and money to incorporating the new technology into their project—assuming it is a key catalyst to make the project viable. However, the more the vendor sets out to prove that the product does everything the customer needs, the more they get into trouble, via repeated technology demonstrations (the oft-used demo). Demos never do everything the customer wants. Repeated showings serve to reinforce such shortcomings, thereby lengthening, in most cases, the time needed to close a sale.

Instead, vendors need to think like services companies, evaluating every valid opportunity as a *project,* rather than a product sale. Engineering and implementation resources should be assigned a priori to these projects, the best and most senior talent allocated to comanaging the project and ensuring follow-through. Contracts should be structured on a risk-reward basis, and every piece of value-adding work should be charged for (large companies understand that you are not a registered charity). By and large, the deal structure should emulate the structure of large technology integration projects: The customer should commit to (a) a significant cash payment up front to fund start-up resources, then (b) milestone payments for each key project phase, and (c) a final payment for project completion and full rollout. Customers need to know that the vendor is committed to their success, so pricing and fees must reflect this emphasis. Remember, they are results sensitive, so whenever they are not charged for work that they consider critical, they will become concerned about on-time delivery of a working solution. There is only one exception to this pricing guideline: work performed to make good on basic, existing functionality should be funded by the technology vendor as a basic part of the contractual obligation—and as part of good business practice.

8. Failing to see or know when and/or how to move to the next stage.

Unfortunately, a year or two into the early market stage, there are rarely obvious indications to let you know for sure that it's time to change strategies and negotiate the delicate but vital leap across the chasm. In fact, there are only two reliable guides to indicate that you have reached the end of this big-project stage: (1) It's hard to find more visionaries—those who were attracted to your technology (and that of your early market competitors) have already made their commitments; and (2) pragmatists are still wary of making any more than a token toe-in-the-water commitment to a pilot project. Now, if you've been reasonably successful during this stage, you probably have a number of live projects at various stages of completion, and a number of pilots in place for the pragmatists with whom you managed to eke out a deal. Yet it's still not easy to know that it's time to cross the chasm. What's left to do is to review each significant project in detail, to see what competitive advantage benefits your visionary customers have realized. Selling to pragmatists in the bowling alley requires that you transform this discourse about pursuing competitive advantage into one about eliminating severe competitive disadvantage. No matter how clearly your first pragmatist customers intellectualize the positive benefits of the technology, remember that they are not sufficiently motivated to take the plunge emotionally unless they truly believe that they are suffering a "severed artery" type of emergency. This allows you to start plotting a target beachhead strategy. If herd behavior starts to occur in the same market segment, this is an indication that it is safe to proceed.

◀

BOWLING ALLEY ADOPTION DYNAMICS AND SALES ENGAGEMENT STRATEGY

"And now for something completely different" might be the best and most actionable phrase for considering how to sell to the first pragmatists of the mainstream. No surprises here. Moving across the chasm changes everything. No longer do we encounter wild-eyed visionaries with "competitive advantage" tattooed on various body parts. Instead, the vendor's goal must be to seek out and find those forlorn souls who are trying to solve vexing and chronic business problems that the status quo has either contributed to or is no longer a viable alternative in solving. Vendors must show that their alternative approach—unproven and risky in the eyes of such customers—can actually fix the problem and ensure that it stays fixed. Accordingly, vendors must marshal all their efforts to demonstrate a *complete, whole product solution* to the problem, and provide compelling evidence in the form of actual or pro forma return on investment (ROI) data for consideration. "But we don't have this evidence," you cry, "our early customers did not require it." Actually, they did. They just went to the trouble of working it out themselves based on their own situations, or they intuited it based on how they hoped to attain their own desired results. The difference in crossing the chasm and the bowling alley is that you must do the heavy lifting.

Trying to fix a problem, however painful, with an untried approach is anathema to pragmatists. Your 80 percent solution, acceptable to the visionary, is a nonstarter for the pragmatist. Such a solution is no solution at all. Thus, bowling alley sales strategy (and its first implementation, that of crossing the chasm) requires a 100 percent complete whole product solution. This includes all the complementary products and services necessary to address to solve the problem, priced on the basis of the amount of pain you are helping to relieve; asserted in the context of ROI—worked out on the customer's spreadsheet based on their inputs; or proved through proxy based on a third-party assessment of similar situations. Here, systems integrators and other technical consulting organizations can be your biggest ally. Many of these firms can and do work out the economics of applying discontinuous innovations to business problems as part of their client research or business development activities, and they do so for various industries under various scenarios. Employing these insights demonstrates the customer intimacy that pragmatists are looking for. (Recall the mantra of pragmatists everywhere: "Our business is different.") Such activities should *not* be considered a substitute or palliative for a vendor's own lack of customer knowledge. Rather, when employed correctly they serve to underscore a vendor's segment driven approach—understanding the problem of the segment and serving up the most compelling arguments that the vendor's approach can and will work, with predictable results.

A recommended sales engagement model employs a team comprising a sales representative, a business analyst/consultant who is a domain expert, and a technical sales rep or sales engineer. This triad, employed and proven during the past thirty years as the most effective methodology for selling high-tech products and services to enterprise customers, is still the most basic vehicle for achieving rapid results with early pragmatist customers, and thus producing the goal of dominance in targeted market segments.

If you have previously ramped up your sales force in expectation of rapid growth to volume sales, you should not expect to have a surfeit of crusaders in your organization, so warns Philip Lay. "Most sales and field support people are trained to sell broad offers opportunistically into horizontal markets," he notes. "Furthermore, they are accustomed to selling their product first, and second, listening to customers for a fit. It is unwise therefore to expect religion overnight about bowling alley sales strategies, and thus demand that your entire sales force adopt a segment approach all at once." The bowling alley is definitely not the favored domain of the salesperson or technical sales rep who, when asked a question, immediately whips out his or her laptop and begins showing the clever demo version of the product that marketing and engineering have cobbled together. Pragmatist customers are interested in how the product does what it does, to be sure, but only in the context of whether the overall whole product solution will meet their needs. The selling style therefore should be highly consultative based on an understanding of the customer's needs—overt and latent—and validated with the customer. Then the inevitable (and in most cases, rather pedestrian) demos can proceed.

We find this "sell the demo" behavior in an overwhelming number of our practice engagements. The origins seem to derive from behaviors held over from selling to technology enthusiasts and visionaries who prize such things, and from a persistent view that the customer is buying technology, "so we've got to show it to them" in all its gory detail.

We have found that the most effective approach is to task smaller teams to lead the charge. Once they have closed deals with the first few target customers, you can then entice others in the sales force to join in. At this point, you will also be in a better position to understand how the sales cycle is evolving in terms of key events and interventions and the average time required to close each deal. This in turn provides the management team with indications of how to forecast, set quotas, and structure compensation plans.

TORNADO ADOPTION DYNAMICS AND SALES ENGAGEMENT STRATEGY

Should the tornado strike, you will be forced to reverse almost every strategy and program you may have implemented successfully during the bowling alley. By now, you should be saying, "I know, I know. Enough already." Gentle reader, I reiterate that the success factors for tornado strategy are almost completely opposite those of the bowling alley. Yet for some sales forces the tornado represents a return to normalcy of sorts, since many companies have neither the patience nor the skills necessary to play the bowling alley game. Not surprisingly, these companies welcome a tornado should it develop (as do we all). Here's how it plays out.

In the tornado, the *customer goal* is to adopt the obvious. These same vendors see this quite willingly as the validation of the new technology paradigm that they may have been crowing about since the early market. Ah, but it's not about the technology anymore! It's not about *if* they're going to buy. Rather, it's about *from whom* they're going to buy. Absent meaningful segment or market share—won during the bowling alley phase—so as to launch their bid for gorilla status, such companies find themselves in a battle they hadn't quite bargained for. And they usually get smoked. Here's what you need to do to avoid such a fate.

First, recall the rules of tornado engagement:

1. Focus on the infrastructure buyer as the primary sponsor; the economic buyer is secondary.
2. Seek to generalize and commoditize your whole product offering.
3. Maximize your channels and modes of distribution.
4. Drive your pricing (and costs) downward to attract a maximum number of customers.
5. Attack your competition on all fronts and do so relentlessly.
6. Position your products horizontally as infrastructure or a platform, if possible, rather than as a point product. (Naturally, such positioning alternatives are subject to the nature of the category. If the applicaton or product is *not* a "platform," do not try to market it as such.)
7. Drive expansion to as many geographies as possible.

Such rules of engagement are designed to do one thing and one thing only: win the tornado market (i.e., the vendor goal). The prize is breathtaking in its implications—gorilla status, probably for the life of the category. Customers seek to understand this developing hierarchy, for they will use it to justify further purchases based on the emerging infrastructure and the resulting de facto standard, all led by the gorilla. Winning the market thus serves customers' needs, which is to *make the safe choice—a choice born not of technology prowess or superiority, but of market and value chain hegemony.*

A vendor's sales engagement strategy now must mesh precisely with the market development strategy. Since the marketing strategy is based on asserting and proclaiming your position in the gorilla/chimp (or king/prince) hierarchy, the sales strategy must also. If you are the gorilla, this is relatively straightforward. Sales strategy and the sales pitch should emphasize market dominance, as evidenced by numbers and types of customers, numbers of partners, service and support capabilities, and financial strength. The sales strategy should also encompass selling the company to partners and allies for the purposes of recruiting as many acolytes to the cause as possible. This is the province of the business development function. Importantly, business development executives and managers should be compensated using both short-term (i.e., quota-driven) metrics, as well as long-term revenue and market valuation metrics, including return on assets, to prevent business development activities from becoming a *substitute* for winning as many customers as possible.

Product arguments should emphasize *why* the product is the preferred alternative, supported by relevant case histories; the *vision* for the product going forward; and other facts that support why the product is emerging as de facto standard. Competitors will attempt to paint the gorilla as both arrogant and behind the curve technologically. The gorilla should not respond to the first challenge as it naturally comes with the territory; and it should respond to the second by pointing to its next release and/or product road map.

In sum, the gorilla's objective is to be declared the outright winner of a tornado competition as early as feasible, by as many measures as possible. The skills and style of organizations in the tornado must reflect this quest. It is not a sprint, but neither is it a marathon. Regardless of your position in the hierarchy, winning your fair share (and then some) of this competition is the most important thing you will do. It is immensely rewarding, but it will require an abiding and focused commitment.

Chimps face a different dilemma: getting out of the shadow created by the gorilla. Our experience is that most vendors are rather clumsy at doing this. Typically, chimp vendors will continue to emphasize their technological superiority versus the gorilla. Unfortunately for the chimp, the market will increasingly see such arguments as moot, even if true.

Since more customers have chosen the gorilla rather than the chimp, the chimp, through its marketing and sales posture, will seem to imply that most customers are wrong. This is self-delusional.

In chapter 13, I outlined what should be the chimp's competitive posture:

- Maximize market share by winning as many sales as possible (without resorting to rampant or ruinous price discounting).
- Target specific customer segments that are either not served (or not well served) by the gorilla, and build complete value chain solutions around these segments.

The chimp's overall sales effort should actually carry over from that of the bowling alley *once it becomes clear* that the chimp will indeed be a chimp. Recall that the goal is to achieve the number two position, conceding the gorilla its place but building barriers to prevent other chimps from improving their positions at your expense. This suggests that at the outset of the tornado, most contending vendors—those with legitimate and realistic chances to be gorillas—should adopt a tornado sales engagement footing. But once market dynamics begin to play themselves out, favoring one vendor over all others, chimps should rapidly adopt a "gorilla in the niche" posture. This reversal of sorts, while hardly popular among management teams who may have trouble accepting the obvious, actually ensures that the chimp lives to play the game again—and from a position of relative strength.

The chimp's gorilla in the niche sales engagement strategy is postulated on certain market subsegments having unique requirements that simply can't be served by a generalized de facto platform offered by the gorilla. The chimp's goal thus is to propagate its success through relentlessly focusing on these market segments, using the skills of customer intimacy to close deals rapidly, tempering the called-for authoritative style with a consultative approach.

Monkeys, on the other hand, must design an opportunistic engagement strategy that is never predicated on grandiose visions. While this may sound defeatist, the typical monkey lacks most of the necessary resources—marketing and R&D budgets—not to mention the key gorilla advantage of market clout, to compete for market share in the tornado. Monkeys need to take the money and run. Or do they?

Monkeys can benefit enormously from a tornado by virtue of the enormous spending the tornado generates. Customers demand alternatives, and distribution channels look to position themselves not only by innovation or relevant differences but also by price. Typically, the chimp fulfills the former role while the monkey provides the latter. What has become increasingly apparent to me over the past five years is how many monkeys (and serfs, for that matter) actually defined their market development strategy by virtue of their sales engagement strategy. Lacking the resources to field a viable market development strategy by the existing rules, some monkeys pursued a strategy of changing the rules, using their sales strategy as the lever. What made *some* of them successful? The Internet.

The Internet provides economies needed to compete on operational excellence, the best and only strategy available to the monkey. Consider the profile of most monkeys and serfs:

1. They require minimal R&D budgets because they are pursuing a me-too product development strategy, with manufacturing performed by educated but relatively low-paid workers.
2. They require minimal market development budgets as well because gorillas and chimps drive *category* development through their own demand generation programs. Monkeys are thus free to invest their limited budgets in *brand* development efforts and/or the modest new product launch.

Thus, on virtually every measure, monkeys and serfs are simply slipstreaming their larger market cousins.

Michael Dell showed how the serf can rise to fame by employing a completely new distribution strategy and sales engagement strategy—one that proved to be not only significantly more efficient, but significantly more desirable as well. Amazon has also shown that serfs who can ride a wave—that of the New Economy (now significantly older and less attractive)—can wrest a significant segment of the market from older entrenched competitors who fail to recognize or capitalize on a fundamental phase shift within their industry. This is not to suggest that such new distribution strategies can compensate for fundamentally defective market and product strategies, as witnessed by the dot-com meltdown of 2000. It does suggest, however, that monkeys/serfs, operating under an enlightened management vision (or freed from its grip) can and do prosper by making their sales strategy their market strategy. By taking this approach to some niche markets, some monkeys can evolve into chimps, while some serfs achieve landowner status. Most, however, will not. Take the money and run.

KEY INSIGHT ▶ ▶ ▶ ▶ ▶ ▶ ▶ ▷ ▷ ▷

Beware the hypercompetitive sales organizations that culturally or by dictate exhibit a win-at-all-costs mode of selling. They will have great difficulty developing the proper engagement model based on Technology Adoption Life Cycle imperatives. Similar to the hypercompetitive marketing organization, which is focused only on what the competition says and does, *hypercompetitive* sales behavior is characterized by trying to win every sale regardless of the consequences. Short-term resource prioritization becomes a function of whatever current big deals are in the pipeline. Eventually, this preoccupation evolves into long-term behaviors as organizations become like hunters on safari, gunning for big game only. This, of course, is self-defeating. Instead, organizations must discriminate between *strategic* and *opportunistic* revenues—between winning sales that perpetuate the vendor's segment or market share goals and winning those that are worth nothing more beyond making someone's quota. (In other words, such deals do nothing to build segment or market share and thus do not add to the vendor's overall market or customer influence.) While both deals add to the top line, the former is the entire objective of the market development strategy and the organization as a whole, while the latter is more self-directed. Unfortunately, when such self-directing activities become the norm, marketing activities themselves are compromised. The hypercompetitive sales force, insisting that all deals are good deals and thus are winnable, increasingly complain that failures are a result of poor marketing, and the marketing department's inability to prepare the sales force to do battle. More likely, the sales force will lose because the engagement strategy is not suited to TALC realities; or, worse yet, they are playing into the hands of their competitors by competing on the competitor's terms.

MAIN STREET ADOPTION DYNAMICS AND SALES ENGAGEMENT STRATEGY

The end of the tornado spells a return to market stasis. The market development strategy must shift once again, and so must the way you go to market. The resulting Main Street engagement strategy will be the one that will persist, probably through the life of the category. The overriding goal of the customer is building off the paradigm and/or infrastructure now in place as a result of a tornado. This drives the quest for a better deal—that is, lower prices—or in more features and benefits for the same price. It is now time to choose the customers you really want to serve, over and over and over again.

Such a customer is, of course, the profitable customer. For the vendor who can constantly improve their operational efficiencies, it is the customer seeking better prices, terms, and conditions. For the vendor with the knack for really understanding the makeup and dynamics of their customer base, it is those segments and subsegments that look for *and* will pay for additional functionality without the risk of discontinuity. It follows that a vendor's engagement strategy now must focus on the overriding goal of achieving such profitability possibly at the intersection of *customer intimacy*—knowing what each customer wants—and *operational efficiency,* considered here as the ability to serve each customer well, and profitably (i.e., without charging them for it).

Your +1 marketing efforts require segmentation, the overriding strategy of Main Street market development and sales engagement strategies. Segments may come as a result of microniches that evolve with the originating niche. Or niches may develop out of groups of new customers not previously recognized. Occasionally, such niches evolve into considerable segments of their own. In any event, selling strategies must evolve accordingly. *Relationship management* is the aligning idea. Each of these segments wants to be sold to in the manner they feel most relevant. Unfortunately, the selling process that has been developed, extended, and institutionalized during the tornado may no longer be adequate. For many organizations selling directly to the end customer, the concept of *account control* becomes synonymous with relationship management. Once again, this is self-delusional.

Account control is increasingly, in my opinion, either completely irrelevant at worst or easily defeated as a strategy at best. We live in a world where information is both prevalent and free. While few would debate that personal relationships between buyer and seller remain important, they are not impermeable. That is, buyers can and will seek information on an as needed or constant basis. While golf junkets with the customer may be fun, they are hardly sustainable barriers to customer exit. Real account control is determined on the basis of whether a customer is committed to a particular proprietary system or platform architecture. (Note: "Proprietary" is used here to indicate vendor origins rather than imply that such architecture is "closed.") SAP and Oracle have account control. Accenture does not. What's more, the beloved golf outings may be with the wrong people! Recall that on Main Street, the end user is our paramount focus. Executive management teams, who perhaps most appreciate a round at Pebble Beach, may no longer be the real customers! Instead, the people who actually use your product—the people you neglected to invite—now hold sway over your next purchase order. Thus it's these folks whose relationship you now need to manage.

But how can you do this profitably, when such customers may number into the hundreds of thousands, even millions?

The answer lies in managing relationships on a *transactional* basis. This is not the paradox that it would seem. On Main Street, end users have far more freedom and power to exercise how they will purchase things. By this stage in the TALC the two major sources of complexity—*adoption and solution*—have now mostly been wrung out. It follows that *marketing complexity*—how difficult something is to buy—should, well, not be difficult at all. We see many organizations miss this transition due to a continuing devotion to one type of distribution channel and selling methodology that may have once conveyed advantages but has now become a disadvantage, even a distinct liability. Such organizations now find themselves effectively controlled by their own devotion to a strategy that is no longer relevant.

Today, one no longer need be captive to one style of selling; being transactional no longer need come between maintaining relationships with customers. Somewhat ironically, the means to reconcile this are discontinuous innovations: the Internet and customer relationship management (CRM) software. Both innovations allow vendors to engage their customers accordingly, based on the level of solution and marketing complexity diagrammed in chapter 12. When solution complexity is reduced sufficiently, buyers can become relatively self-sufficient in buying. In fact, they typically will seek out, even relish, the simplest form of acquiring these products. Think Amazon; but better yet, consider any of the thousands of websites where real commerce can and does take place every day for seemingly complicated products. Today's websites convey more than just the information needed to understand the product or service under consideration. They actually provide the platform from which ongoing transactions can take place—predictably, safely, and repeatedly—every transaction customized on the basis of what is known about the buyer. Consider Amazon once again. Every purchase I make provides information to Amazon, which in turn increasingly provides a number of offers based on a running history of my purchases and purchase behavior. This electronic form of *personal shopper* is everything I need. Were it a real person, I would consider such assistance intrusive, unnecessary, and, most likely, expensive. Style without substance, you might call it. And it works.

Epilogue

Using This Book

See first that the design is wise and just; that ascertained, pursue it resolutely.

—William Shakespeare

While the science of high-technology innovations continues to mystify us, and happily so, the art and discipline of bringing the fruits of much labor to market continues to be vexing. As such, I believe that high-tech practitioners in whatever guise must subscribe to the notion of *lifelong learning*. Knowing we will get it wrong occasionally can be a liberating concept, freeing us from fear and risk avoidance and pointing us in the direction where we will get it right. We offer no guarantees, of course. As this industry evolves, we continue to be in the position of making it up as we go along, based on observation, trial and error, past experiences, and the experiences of our fellow travelers. We at The Chasm Group continue to beg and borrow from our colleagues in both industry and academia, applying their thinking and experiences to our thinking, and we offer no excuses or apologies for doing so.

Permit me to summarize what I have learned over the past two decades:

- Making strategy decisions in high-technology markets is a high-stakes, low-data game. Successful pattern recognition of market dynamics is hugely important. To quote John Maynard Keynes, "I'd rather be vaguely right than precisely wrong."

- A company's competitive advantages in sum can be sustainable over time. The parts that make up these advantages, taken singularly, are not sustainable.
- If strategies are to be implemented successfully, they must be understood and committed to by many different organizations. As such, marketing and/or strategy groups may lead this exercise, but they are not solely responsible for the outcome.
- The need for rapid and decisive responses to a shifting and ambiguous marketplace—and the need to gain teamwide commitment to these responses on a sustainable basis—requires rapid and repeatable strategy creation alternatives.
- To win, the strategy must be *executed* based on the key assumptions underpinning the strategy. Poor execution kills brilliant strategy. Brilliant execution can make up for mediocre or uninspired strategy.
- Finally, never let a strategy get in the way of a big idea. But you must recognize what is truly big, and what masquerades or is sold as such.

In closing, it is my sincere hope that having come to the end of this book, you will *not* set it alongside all the other business books you have bought, skimmed through, even read; instead, I hope you will continue to peruse, muse upon, and use the ideas, models, and suggestions found within, over and over and over again. If we have saved you from making one mistake, we are pleased, even flattered. If, on the other hand, you're not making any mistakes at all, you're either not in high tech or not stretching your abilities and ambitions. We wish you every success in the latter.

Appendix

The following exercises, tools, and descriptions can be used to aid your understanding of the concepts and recommendations found in each of the previous chapters. They may also be used independently as part of a market analysis and/or strategy development exercise.

1.0 TECHNOLOGY ADOPTION PROFILE SELF-CHECK

Consider the following scenario.

Imagine you are working in an office environment, and the company you work for has just acquired a new multimedia voice mail and video-conferencing system that integrates with everyone's desktop personal computer.

Now consider the following hypothetical responses to the scenario and rate each one between 1 and 5 as to how closely it would resemble your own response (1 = very *unlike*, 5 = very *like*).

a._____ "I'd like to wait until at least one or two pilot groups have tested the system and got the bugs out before I try it. In particular, I'd like to be sure that it really does help improve people's productivity. But if that is the case, then I'll be happy to use it."

b._____ "I am likely to be in the first group. People around here usually count on me when it comes to testing out technology products. To tell you the truth, I like trying out new stuff and seeing how it can be made to work. Technology products don't scare me—I think they are kind of fun."

c._____ "I am leery of this sort of thing and would definitely like to wait until over half the company was up and running. Even then, I won't really look forward to this kind of gadgetry, but I'll go along if I have to."

d._____ "I would like to get an early look at it and see if there is some way it might be used to advantage. If I thought it could make a real impact in an area of importance, I would probably take the lead in piloting its use."

e._____ "I don't ever want such a thing cluttering up my desk or adding more overhead to my personal computer. It's a big enough pain as it is. These high-tech products just get in people's way, and I do not intend to use any such system. In fact, I would like to question why we ever bought it in the first place."

2.0 CHASM SELF-PLACEMENT WORKSHEET

Locate the *product category* in which your product participates relative to the chasm model.

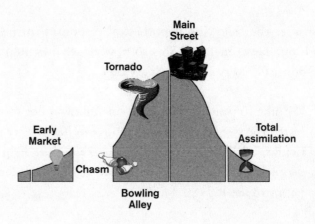

1. **The early market.** Customers are visionaries under the influence of technology enthusiasts. Each new sale is greeted with enthusiasm. The product is still immature. Whole products must be custom built for each customer, including a significant amount of special work unique to that customer's requirements.
2. **The chasm.** Early market commitments now absorb all discretionary resources such that you cannot offer any more specials to visionaries. Pragmatists, however, do not see the references or the evidence of a whole product that would make you a safe buy. Sales cycles are extended, and most that do close are for pilot projects.
3. **The bowling alley.** The product is endorsed by pragmatist customers within the confines of one or more niche markets. Sales cycles within these confines are predictable with good margins. Outside these con-

fines, there are only opportunistic sales, often at significant discounts.

4. **Inside the tornado.** The mainstream marketplace has taken off. Virtually any vendor who can supply this category of product can sell it. A fierce market share war has developed and price discounting is vicious. A market leader has emerged, establishing the de facto standards, and this company gets much better margins than the competition.

5. **On Main Street.** The hypergrowth era is over. Market growth slows down as the market saturates. To expand further, some competitors are now modifying their standard offerings to appeal to niche markets. Other competitors compete on price alone. The market leader still gets a margin premium but is under pressure to reduce price.

6. **Total assimilation.** The technology has now been absorbed into other products or applications; or it is passing out of the market, being displaced by a new category.

3.0 THE ART OF MARKET SEGMENTATION

In order to cross the chasm and further develop a market into and through the bowling alley phase, you must start with identifying your target customer segment(s). The key discipline to do this involves market segmentation: various methodologies to identify and characterize customers using a number of dimensions or factors including:

- Who they are
- Where they're located
- What their environment, function, or industry might be
- Other attributes or characteristics that provide insights that may be acted upon as a result

Organizations often can use a classic vertical segmentation model (shown on the next page) that details three primary variables: geography, industry, and profession. These variables define segments that we have described previously. First, such segments are likely to share or at least relate to unique problems based on their specific interests or situations. Next, the segments sharing these common characteristics are likely to consult with or reference each other when making high-tech (and high-risk) buying decisions.

Vertical Market Segmentation Model

Vertical Industry: Banking, Insurance, Real Estate, Construction
Profession: Finance, Sales, Manufacturing
Geography: Europe, South America, North America

The first of these elements allows organizations to develop a whole product solution that is of maximum value to the segment by its uniqueness, and thus it is highly differentiated from other products designed for a general or horizontal market.

The second element creates word-of-mouth communication channels that can spread favorable (and unfavorable) perceptions (e.g., market leading, best application, etc.) even without traditional marketing communications campaigns.

Both elements comprise the means for companies of virtually every size to target a segment and establish a leadership position within it, provided the target is appropriate, the organization can deliver a uniquely advantaged solution, word of such an accomplishment can spread, and the company can scale its business and processes to meet the needs of the segment(s) so targeted.

This vertical segmentation model is also typically highly quantifiable. Various indices, including standard industry classification (SIC) codes, reflect such attributes. Detailing *total available market* sizing is relatively straightforward.

But . . .

Strategy development using this segmentation model as an underpinning can often be thwarted or undone in real-world practice. The following diagram illustrates the dilemma:

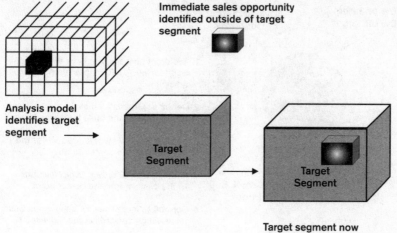

Analysis model identifies target segment →

Immediate sales opportunity identified outside of target segment

Target Segment →

Target Segment

Target segment now expanded to accommodate new opportunity

The market development strategy defines the target segment delineated with specific boundaries. The sales force finds an opportunity just outside the target segment cube. As the end of the quarter is approaching, management decides to redefine the boundary to include this new prospect. Typically, this practice is continued at the end of every subsequent quarter. Segment discipline, so crucial to chasm crossing and bowling alley market development, is now effectively forsaken.

But . . .

The problem is not with the sales force. It is pursuing its assignment: to bring in revenue. And management is undoubtedly rewarding it for its efforts. Rather, the problem is with that part of the segmentation model that defines segments by their boundaries—that is, where prospects are either completely in the segment or completely out.

To surmount this challenge, we need to think about customer segments in a different way, analogous perhaps to observing a school of fish or a swarm of bees. In other words, a community that has an identifiable center point—for example, the queen bee—but where the boundaries of the segment are somewhat indeterminate or may be constantly changing. Now the mission is to identify specifically the center point and the attributes that it reflects. Consider the following model:

Defining Segments by Center Point

20% on target
80% off target

"Ideal" Target
Customer

50% on target
50% off target

80% on target
20% off target

1. Avoid defining segments by their boundaries—leads to loss of segment discipline.

2. Define segments by their center points—the ideal target customer.

3. Commit to 100% whole product for the customer at the center point.

4. Address all marketing communications to the customer at the center point.

5. Commit to incentives for sales force that increasingly reward segment discipline.

The ideal customer at the center point of a hypothesized segment is the customer representing perfectly the kind of customer we will commit to serving through our whole product development efforts.

FROM THEORY TO PRACTICE

This idealized customer in fact may not be real. Rather, it is both a *starting point* for identifying other customer prospects who could be said to be less than ideal but nonetheless represent legitimate targets and an *aiming point* for all marketing and sales activities. Marketing communications in particular, to be effective, should target precisely a specific target group. This discipline is finely honed in consumer marketing but sadly is absent from many high-tech communication programs, notably advertising. High-tech marketers seem to operate under the mistaken notion that to broaden your target opportunities, you must develop communication efforts that are likewise as broad. The resulting communication, poorly targeted, follows a "we are all things to all people" orientation or delivers no real message at all, being instead a recitation of features or clichés about being "best of breed" or other such blather.

Experienced consumer marketers, on the other hand, know that prospects, if given the slightest provocation, tend to self-select themselves *into* a segment rather than out, when they can identify with the talked-about segment's condition or travails. This explains partially why celebrities may be used to pitch products that are commodity-like or are otherwise in so-called *low-interest* categories. We identify with the celebrity and therefore with the product he or she is associated with. Similarly, so-called slice-of-life advertising is often employed for packaged goods. Television advertising depicts Mom's never-ending battle against carpet stains or Dad's bumbling attempts to tackle some do-it-yourself household project in a thirty-second tableau, and we see (regretfully in many cases) some part of our self or our own experience.

A corollary to this focus translates into a segment discipline that also can be deployed in the field as effectively.

If a sales prospect maps directly to the ideal customer, the market development strategy calls for a whatever-it-takes commitment from all parts of the organization to win this segment and make sure that it is completely successful satisfying that customer's buying motivations. If this customer segment can't be won over by the strategy, then the strategy itself must be reconsidered.

If the prospect is less than ideal but nonetheless in the target zone—that is, more in than out—your efforts should be rewarded as well, because much of your center-point focus in whole product development and communications will be applicable. You should not make a 100 per-cent commitment here, particularly as it pertains to whole product development, because you run the risk of increasingly developing specials or one-offs for every new customer won, however monetarily attractive they may be. Remember, the key issue is keeping the entire organization on point and, importantly, not devoting engineering or manufacturing resources to systems integration efforts. A standard compensation plan is probably warranted for winning such customers.

When the prospects that are more out than in, or may be out altogether, are pursued, we call it *opportunistic revenue*. And no one who has ever sold for a living is prepared to walk away easily from such deals. They are part of every organization's overall sales goals, and practically speaking, part of every salesperson's individual sales plan. Some part of every organization's budget will support such efforts. But the key is to keep that portion relatively low, focusing instead on target goals. The answer to the field in this case must be akin to "Good luck, but you're on your own for the most part, and no part of any other organization is prepared or willing to rush to your aid." To discourage prospecting outside the target, I often recommend that compensation plans again be modified to discourage such behavior, or at least to not provide any special incentive for it.

But what if one of these deals is, well, a really *big deal*? (Or what a former colleague called "superstrategic," which I later came to realize *was not* that at all for the rest of the organization, but *was* to his personal compensation.) Such an opportunity probably merits special attention. However, the undoubted shift in resource allocation as a result of taking the deal on directly threatens the organization's commitment to focus and can be ruinous to such efforts as well as overall morale if allowed to proliferate. Instead, the "superstrategic" thing to do is recruit third parties to do whatever is necessary to make the product or application work for this big customer. Naturally, these parties are going to want to be paid for their efforts. The vendor, on the other hand, can book a high-volume/high-revenue deal without compromising its true strategic objectives.

In any event, your success will ultimately be a result of your commitment to the target. It must be more than lip service. There must be tangible incentives to all in order to navigate the chasm and the bowling alley. The more solid the whole product, the more compelling and persuasive the marketing communications, the more the field sales force or channel will voluntarily sell within the segment. Of course, a little sugar can make the medicine go down.

DESCRIBING THE IDEAL TARGET CUSTOMER

The Chasm Group uses a one-page description of a customer scenario to help organizations brainstorm the possible variety of segments they could target (see the worksheet section that follows for a scenario template). Developing various scenarios allows you to focus on a business problem as seen through the eyes of an *end user,* but always with an *economic buyer's* interests and motivations at heart.

The end user is defined using a variety of descriptors including profession, geography, industry, key responsibilities, and any other factors that seem relevant and actionable. The process itself is modeled after the classic "before" and "after" situation. That is, the "before" describes the key frustration of the end user that adversely affects its ability to carry out its key responsibility, task, or function satisfactorily. The "before" should also describe how the end user has attempted to ameliorate or mitigate its condition, all without success as a result of *confounding* or *interfering factors*. Finally, the consequences of the end user's frustration and/or failure should be noted *but from the perspective of the economic buyer*. The end result forms the motivation for considering alternative paradigms, specifically yours.

The "After" section describes this alternative approach, with a particular focus on the enabling factors that make the new approach plausible, preferable, and ultimately successful. Finally, you should highlight the economic consequences—the ROI argument—for this new way. Thus, each scenario becomes a possible ideal target customer segment.

Now, how do you decide which scenario describes the ideal target, and the relative attractiveness of each that follows it?

Use the following to rank your scenarios accordingly:

Scoring Scenarios

Factors	Weighting (Optional)	
1. Accessible, Well-Funded Target Customer	20	Market Creation Variables
2. Painfully Compelling Reason to Buy	30	
3. Feasible Whole Product	10	
4. Known Partners & Allies	5	Market Attractiveness Variables
5. Effective Whole Product Distribution	5	
6. Attractive Whole Product Pricing	5	
7. Opportunity Not Preempted by Competition	10	Market Penetration Variables
8. Consistency with Current Positioning	5	
9. Good Follow-on Segment Potential	10	

This list provides insight as to what scenarios are attractive for serving as a beachhead segment. The weightings are designed to show numerically the relative importance of each factor, particularly in the case of beachhead selection (though the meticulous assignment of numerical weights can become somewhat cumbersome in practice). The process is designed to quickly identify potential segment candidates that may emerge from a current familiarity with the marketplace—specifically, market segments that are currently under stress. Or such a process can be used to stimulate, capture, and collate the results of brainstorming. The process ends by evaluating the scored scenarios and discarding the low-scoring ones. The predisposition to the first three factors in the scoring is consistent with the idea that in fact, they can't be *invented* if not strongly present in the situation itself. The other factors, for the most part, may or may not be obvious or can be negotiated and overcome as a function of investment.

A FOUR-STEP PROCESS FOR SEGMENTATION

Developing scenarios and ranking them is part of a four-step process for reaching a consensus on a particular beachhead segment and/or additional segments as part of a bowling alley strategy. The complete process can be modeled as follows:

The Segmentation Process

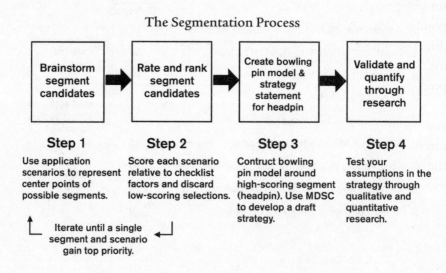

Brainstorm segment candidates	Rate and rank segment candidates	Create bowling pin model & strategy statement for headpin	Validate and quantify through research
Step 1	**Step 2**	**Step 3**	**Step 4**
Use application scenarios to represent center points of possible segments.	Score each scenario relative to checklist factors and discard low-scoring selections.	Contruct bowling pin model around high-scoring segment (headpin). Use MDSC to develop a draft strategy.	Test your assumptions in the strategy through qualitative and quantitative research.

Iterate until a single segment and scenario gain top priority.

Step 1 involves developing as complete a list of potential target segments as possible. This process ends when you can no longer imagine another application for the product that does not essentially repeat one of the scenarios already developed.

Step 2 seeks to narrow the search to the most promising alternatives based on rating and ranking them relative to the Market Development Strategy Checklist. All scenarios should first be evaluated on how well they score on the first three elements of the list. Participants in this exercise should first work individually, then work toward a consensus score with other group members as appropriate. Seek to assemble the top one-third of all candidate scenarios based on their rankings on the first three MDSC elements, discarding the remaining scenarios, then rate and rank again the top-tier scenarios based on the remaining six elements in the checklist.

Step 3 is to select from the remaining target candidates the one candidate that creates the best bowling pin potential going forward. This selection should be both an attractive candidate on its own merits and provide for the best follow-on market potential based on leveraging a whole product solution and customer references. As the remaining candidates are arrayed, each candidate representing a potential segment, and a strategy for winning the first or lead segment, should be outlined using the nine-point MDSC, noting the key assumptions that made the selection attractive during the rating and ranking step. Thus, far from being novel or surprising, the strategy now becomes a natural extension of the segmentation process.

Finally, step 4 should be used to validate current thinking and assumptions. This research either can precede go-to-market planning or can be done in parallel depending on your time constraints. But, whatever the case, *it should be done!* The point of subjecting the strategy to scrutiny is to test the very assumptions that you have made in its development *prior* to actually launching a new market development initiative. Since the entire process is iterative, our practical experience suggests that by this stage the team is now at least on the right track. But poorly formed hypotheses are still possible, which is why you want to subject the strategy to the scrutiny of the very constituencies you will be asking to take action of some kind, and there is simply no worthy rationale for avoiding such research in an attempt to cut corners. It is far better to have the strategy fail in test, rather than fail in the market.

PROCESS SUMMARY

1. Develop segment candidates for your product.

   - Consider applications for industries, functions, or organizations now under stress
   - Focus on departments or individuals affected by such stress
   - Pick a specific geography with which to begin

2. Pick good opportunities and translate them to scenario form.

   - The end user function in the stressed environment
   - The economic buyer, the person in charge and thus affected by poor outcomes
   - Describe a day in the life of the end user, but specify the consequences and rewards for the economic buyer

3. Score the scenarios in terms of key chasm-crossing and/or bowling alley criteria.

   - Accessible, well-funded economic buyer
   - Extremely compelling reason to buy (for economic buyer)
   - Feasible whole product solution
   - Absence of entrenched competition
   - Good follow-on potential

The scenario process may also be used for Main Street market segmentation; however, the focus of the scenario process should then be to identify target customer segments of end users who may be underserved, marginal customers, or customers seeking additional benefits that now reflect either the uniqueness of their circumstances or the overall development of the market as a whole.

THE APPLICATION SCENARIO PROCESS

Identifying the Beachhead Market Segment for a Chasm-Crossing Strategy

This document is intended to be used with the Scenario Worksheet and the Scenario Analysis Worksheet to facilitate the brainstorming and qualification process that governs identifying the beachhead target market segment in a chasm-crossing market development strategy.

The fundamental concept behind the application scenario process is that vertical niche market segments of the sort targeted when crossing the chasm are best described by customer application scenarios, and that by generating as many scenarios as it can recall or imagine, a group will express and develop its market segmentation ideas quickly and efficiently. To that end, the Scenario Worksheet represents a one-page format for putting any segment candidate into play, and the Scenario Analysis Worksheet represents a commentary on that same scenario.

The basic idea is a before/after scenario. In the "Before" section, the goal is to capture a particularly frustrating moment in a day in the life of a potential end user for the new product; and in the "After" section, to remove or resolve that frustration by applying the new product to the problem. In both cases, we are particularly interested in the *economic* implications of achieving this change: How does the economic buyer lose money *before,* and how does he/she make money *after*?

Worksheets

Scenario Title:	Give each scenario a short descriptive title for ease of reference.
Profile:	The scenario should focus on the end user of the product. The profile section gives background on this end user.
Supervisor Title:	The economic buyer in most scenarios is someone to whom the end user reports. It is critical in chasm crossing to sell to the economic buyer, hence the need to identify him or her by job title.
Primary Value Added:	The focus of the scenario should relate directly to the primary value that the person in this job is expected to add to the organization, their primary job purpose.
Scene or Situation:	Set the context for the scenario.
Desired Outcome:	What is the end user trying to accomplish? This should relate directly to their primary value added.
Economic Buyer:	This is the person whose budget ultimately funds the purchase of the product. It is typically someone to whom the end user reports. It is typically not the chief information officer (CIO) unless the end user is someone who reports into the IT organization.
Compelling Reason to Buy:	In the case of the economic buyer, frame this in terms of economic consequences and rewards.
End User:	This is the person whose productivity or overall condition should be improved by the application.
Compelling Reason to Buy:	This person's reason to buy is typically tied to performance improvement and increased effectiveness.

Technical Buyer: This is the person who evaluates and selects the product, then installs and supports it, often including training of the end user.

Compelling Reason to Buy: This person's reason to buy typically focuses on the impact the product has on the overall systems environment. With chasm-crossing products, this is sometimes a negative rather than a positive, hence the importance of not making the technical buyer your primary sales target.

Whole Product Challenges: The whole product is the minimum set of products and services necessary to fulfill the target customer's compelling reason to buy. In crossing the chasm, the target customer is the economic buyer. Looking at that customer's reason to buy, what components of the total solution to his or her problem might prove most challenging to put in place?

SCENARIO WORKSHEET

(To be used in conjunction with determining an ideal customer. See Appendix section 3.0, "The Art of Market Segmentation.")

Scenario Title: _____ **Author:** _____

Profile

Name: _____ Occupation: _____ Age: _____

Employer: _____ Location: _____ Supervisor title: _____

Primary value added: _____

Before

Scene or situation: _____

_____

_____

Desired outcome: _____

_____

_____

Attempted approach: _____

_____

_____

Interfering factors: _____

_____

_____

Economic consequences: _____

_____

_____

After (assume same scene, same desired outcome)

New approach: _____

_____

_____

Enabling factors: _____

_____

_____

Economic rewards: _____

_____

_____

SCENARIO ANALYSIS WORKSHEET

(To be used in conjunction with target customer identification.)

Name: _____ Product: _____

Application: _____

Description: _____

Segment Focus (Vertical, Professional, Geographical, or Other): _____

_____

_____

Economic Buyer: _____

Compelling Reason to Buy: _____

_____

_____

_____

Primary End User: _____

Compelling Reason to Buy: _____

_____

_____

_____

Technical Buyer: _____

Compelling Reason to Buy: _____

_____

_____

_____

_____

Whole Product Challenges: _____

_____

_____

_____

SCENARIO RATING PROCEDURE

(Use to score segment scenarios.)

The scenario rating procedure covers the market development strategy team's efforts to score each candidate scenario in terms of nine factors that measure potential chasm-crossing market segment attractiveness. These factors break out into two sets, as follows:

1. **Critical success factors.** These are the show-stoppers—things one cannot change in the near term and which must be rated positively to make a target market segment viable. They include:

   - **Economic buyer.** For a successful chasm crossing, the target market segment should include an economic buyer who is already in place, readily identifiable, likely to want to invest in the type of improvements promised by the scenario, and, perhaps most important of all, well funded.
   - **Compelling reason to buy.** Successful chasm crossing requires customer sponsors who will pull for you against the normal pragmatist resistance to anything new. Such customers need a powerful reason to buy to take this kind of personal risk.
   - **Whole product.** The key to chasm crossing is to achieve market leadership quickly in the initial target segment. This can only be done by delivering 100 percent of the whole product requirement right from the outset. If this is not feasible, then a new target must be found.

2. **Market penetration factors.** These are factors that will affect your organization's effectiveness in penetrating its target market segment. Although they are important to your success, you can usually work around problem areas. They include:

   - **Partners and allies.** Delivering the whole product typically requires the support of segment-specific partners and allies. If the company already knows these allies and has good relationships with them, it is a big plus.
   - **Whole product pricing.** Chasm segments are easiest to develop when the whole product price is several times less than whatever the current approach to the problem entails. Additionally, the ROI must be relatively immediate, typically one year or less to breakeven.

- **Whole product distribution.** To develop the chasm segment quickly requires a distribution channel that already knows the economic buyer and the application of the target end user. If the client company lacks such a channel, then it will have to find one and make it a partner and ally. If no such channel exists, then normally a new target must be selected.
- **Competition.** If the chasm-crossing target is a beachhead, the best strategy says that you do not attack a beachhead that has a fortress on it. If the target segment already is well served by an established market leader, the client must look elsewhere.
- **Positioning.** The impact of positioning on chasm-crossing success is a function of whether the marketplace believes it has a problem worth solving and can readily accept the company as an appropriate source for the market-leading solution.
- **Bowling pin potential.** This criterion assesses the leverage that winning market leadership in the target segment provides as a basis for further market expansion into related marketplaces. This leverage will come either from whole product carryover or word-of-mouth referencing.

STANDARD RATING CALIBRATION

(5 = best, 3 = neutral, 1 = worst)

The following are intended as guidelines for teams scoring the various scenarios, so that their individual ratings can have a basic level of consistency across the team.

A. CRITICAL SCREENING FACTORS

Economic Buyer

5: There is an existing economic buyer for this scenario and he or she has the authority to make the purchase, is currently making investments to achieve comparable types of benefits, and is typically well funded.

1: There is no existing economic buyer (although perhaps one could be found), and in general this application is characteristically underfunded, if invested in at all.

3: There is either a clear economic buyer in place with the appropriate authority but who may have trouble getting sufficient funds; or we expect there may be funds available, but there is no track record to date of investing in this area, and thus it may be unclear who exactly would sponsor this purchase.

Compelling Reason to Buy

5: I must have this because (a) it gives me a major improvement on a critical success factor, or (b) it gives me dramatic productivity improvements in an area where I routinely spend a lot of resources. I would buy this even when money is tight.

1: I am not quite sure this is a good idea, particularly if one takes a pragmatic point of view. I am not saying it couldn't work—I just think it is a bit far-fetched for now. I am not interested in purchasing this at the moment.

3: This is very nice. I can see how it could be quite useful. However, if money is tight, I am probably not going to buy it this year.

Whole Product

5: Working with existing products and service providers, we can readily fulfill all the whole product requirements by the time we introduce the product into the target market.

1: There is at least one showstopper we know of, based on what we know today, that directly prevents us from providing a complete whole product.

3: Getting the whole product will be a big stretch. We know of no reason why it *can't* be done, but there are many unknowns that we have yet to investigate.

B. MARKET PENETRATION FACTORS

Partners and Allies

5: We know all the partners and allies that must actively contribute to the whole products, and we have good working relationships with them.

1: There are key whole product or distribution partners implied by this scenario whom we do not know at all or whom we know but are not friendly with.

3: We know most of the key players at least vaguely but have no strong ties to them.

Whole Product Pricing

5: The whole product price for our solution is several times less than the cost of the existing market-leading solution that is currently being bought by our target economic buyer, and we expect an ROI such that the buyer can break even on the purchase within a year.

1: The minimum whole product price exceeds the budget normally available to the target economic buyer, and the ROI will take two years or more.

3: The whole product price for our solution is a reasonable expenditure for the promised result—assuming that that result is actually achieved, with break-even ROI coming in eighteen months.

Whole Product Distribution

5: The target customer we have in mind will want to purchase the whole product from an existing distribution channel that can provide the appropriate value added and with which we already have established a successful distribution relationship.

1: The target customer needs a lot of value-added services from a distribution channel that does not exist today.

3: The target customer needs value-added services that can partially be provided from an existing distribution channel with which we have a modest amount of experience.

Competition

5: The customer is currently purchasing a significantly inferior solution to the problem we address, utilizing products that are late in their product life cycle, from vendors who are taking this market for granted.

1: A market leader is currently serving this marketplace with solutions that are early in their product life cycle, and the segment enjoys the active marketing attention of this company.

3: There is no market to date, hence no competition to speak of.

Positioning

5: The problem we solve is already recognized as approaching crisis proportions and falls within the class of problems our company is already known to address.

1: The problem we solve is not yet understood to be a problem at all. When it does become recognized, our company will appear to be an unlikely candidate to provide a viable solution.

3: There is a vague sense of a problem to be solved, eventually, and there is modest reason to believe our company should be qualified to cope with it.

Bowling Pin Potential

5: The whole product we must provide for this segment can, with minor modifications, be used to serve a number of other segments, some of which have strong communications ties with the target segment.

1: The whole product for this segment requires a segment-specific investment that cannot readily be leveraged into other segments, and the customer leaders in the target segment do not have market influence outside the segment's boundaries.

3: The whole product for this segment will be useful elsewhere, but only after significant additional investment, and the customer leaders will be credible references in a general way.

WHOLE PRODUCT WORKSHEET

Use this worksheet to brainstorm the whole product required by your target customer in order to fulfill the compelling reason to buy.

Wherever possible, convert the generic component element into an actual named product or service available in your target market today.

For each component element, determine the status, as follows:

C = Custom. This component must be created for customer's application.
T = This component is part of the whole product solution but must be tailored to fit.
S = Shrink-wrapped. This component comes ready to use.

Since C components prevent crossing the chasm, plan to convert each one to T.

Finally, for each component, determine the responsible partner—either the customer, yourself, a sister division, or a third party.

COMPONENT ELEMENTS	STATUS	RESPONSIBLE PARTNER
Required		
Solution concept		
Systems analysis		
End user application software		
Hardware & systems software		
Network connectivity		
Peripherals		
Sales and presales support		
Installation and integration		
System administration		
Training, service, and postsales support		
Other		

COMPONENT ELEMENTS	STATUS	RESPONSIBLE PARTNER
Optional		
Ongoing system modification		
Financing		
Adoption consulting		
User-programmable extensions		
Interfaces to legacy applications		
Consumables		
Middleware		
Industrial design		
Other		

Are you sure that with this whole product, your customer will fulfill the compelling reason to buy? If not, what else can you do?

Index